THE CONSTRUCTIVIST LEADER

THE CONSTRUCTIVIST LEADER

Linda Lambert,
Deborah Walker, Diane P. Zimmerman,
Joanne E. Cooper, Morgan Dale Lambert,
Mary E. Gardner, and P. J. Ford Slack

FOREWORD BY MAXINE GREENE

Teachers College, Columbia University
New York and London

Published by Teachers College Press, 1234 Amsterdam Avenue, New York, NY 10027

Library of Congress Cataloging-in-Publication Data

The constructivist leader / Linda Lambert . . . [et al.] : foreword by
  Maxine Greene.
          p.   cm.
    Includes bibliographical references (p.   ) and index.
    ISBN 0-8077-3463-2 (alk. paper).—ISBN 0-8077-3462-4 (pbk. : alk. paper)
    1. Educational leadership—United States.   2. School management and or-
ganization—United States.   3. Constructivism (Education)—United States.
4. School administrators—United States. 5. Educational change—United
States.   I. Lambert, Linda, 1939–   .
    LB2805.C634   1995
    371.2'000970—dc20   95-11213

ISBN 0–8077–3462–4 (paper)
ISBN 0–8077–3463–2 (cloth)

Printed on acid-free paper
Manufactured in the United States of America

02 01 00 99 98 97 96 95   8 7 6 5 4 3 2 1

Contents

Foreword

In the view of public schooling still widely taken for granted, images of hierarchy and management dominate the scene. The young are expected to learn what is doled out to them in texts or classrooms. They are to acknowledge and accept objective realities defined by people in authority; they are to master whatever skills are required to meet market demand. This, after all, is the way of conservatism. Traditions and social realities are not subject to interpretation, nor are they contingent on point of view. Neither the young nor their teachers are expected to say how, from their own situated perspectives, they make sense of the complex world around them. They are not asked to explain how events impinge on their lived experienced or what those events mean from their vantage point. The meanings, after all, are considered inherent in what occurs; they are "given" to the same degree that the classroom chairs are given, the bells that mark off the periods, the principal's office door. They are, simply and objectively, *there.*

The last decade, however, has been marked by remarkable challenges to all this, and the domains of educational discourse have been alight with new visions of possibility. Pondering numerous educators' changing views, we find it hard not to be reminded of Albert Camus' writing (in *The Myth of Sisyphus*) about the feeling that stage sets are collapsing. "One day," he says, "the 'why' arises and everything begins in that weariness tinged with amazement. 'Begins'—this is important." Against the background of "Goals 2000," "world class standards," predefined outcomes, and the rest, new ideas are finding articulation. There is a coming together of newly honed "progressive" approaches, qualitative research, and an awareness of multiple realities in the worlds of schooling.

For many (including the writers of *The Constructivist Leader*) these modes of sense-making bring with them what Camus calls "the definitive awakening." They cannot imagine a retreat to outmoded behaviorisms or to conceptions of truth as a correspondence with an objectively existent reality. Crucial to their contemporary orientation is the recognition that reality is socially constructed, and that a great number of once silenced people (including students, teachers, and parents) participate in that construction. In schools and district offices, where right answers were determined by administrators alone, this represents a breaking of many frames. It argues strongly, therefore, for a theory of constructivist leadership.

There is something in the nature of a breakthrough as well in the realization that reciprocal processes within complex educational communities must now take the place of imposed agreements and totalities. Handed down as they so often have been through bureaucratic structures, they have frequently affected people as the consequences of what Hannah Arendt calls "rule by nobody." The anonymity of decision-making, like the impersonality of so much of what has been handed down, is exposed and challenged in this book. As its arguments develop, all sorts of meanings radiate from such exposures and challenges. They are meanings that have been achieved (and are in the process of being achieved) by diverse thinkers and practitioners in a variety of contexts. Readers will be familiar with such notions as shared inquiry and shared decision-making, as they will with the idea of a community of learners pervaded by critical questioning. The names and work of such predecessors as John Dewey, Jean Piaget, Lev Vygotsky, Jerome Bruner, Gregory Bateson, Howard Gardner, and others will be familiar as well. The interesting thing, however, is that they now appear in a novel configuration due in part to the writers' consulting a rich variety of contemporary psychologists, anthropologists, linguists, narratologists, and practitioners in many dimensions of existing schools. The book is enlivened and strengthened by concrete examples of efforts to reconceive leadership in a school and a school district, both marked by interdependent learning communities. The ideas derived from social and human scientists lose their abstractness and take on new meanings as we find ourselves attending to dialogic conversation, and to what Linda Lambert calls "partnering" and "sustaining" conversations—each of them interacting with or infusing "inquiring" conversations geared to problem finding and problem resolution, or with conversations seeking shared intentions and opportunities for reflections on experiences that are open to common understandings.

Constructivist leadership is conceived as "the reciprocal processes that enable participants in an educational community to construct meanings that lead toward a common purpose about schooling." Dr. Lambert and her colleagues go far beyond both the management ideal and the monological norm. The very notion of reciprocity summons up not only interactions of many kinds but the kinds of imaginative activities that enable people to recognize how those with whom they are involved perceive the common world. Clifford Geertz writes about the importance of "regarding the community as the shop in which thoughts are constructed and deconstructed" and about how cognition, perception, imagination, memory must be conceived "as themselves, and directly, social affairs." It is with such an approach that Linda Lambert and her exciting co-workers go at the exploration of "constructivist leadership." Like Geertz, they hope to make it "possible for people inhabiting different worlds to have a genuine, and reciprocal impact upon one another." What is fascinating about what they say is the vision of educators, as they strive to render their practice meaningful, defining (yes, and redefining) a common purpose when it comes to schooling. Leadership then becomes an act of release as well as transformation. Persons are freed to envisage what might be and what should be, even as they are supported in their efforts to devise their projects in an always ambiguous world.

Story-telling, focused conversation, mentoring, humor, metaphor: all these may lead to new modes of discourse, to new ways of risking a breaking of the frames. Yes, difference must be affirmed as well as coherence, plurality as well as community. This book takes its readers on a remarkable journey through the landscapes of our culture, even as it moves us to see ourselves as collaborators working toward a "sea change" in public education. The book is scholarly, inclusive, and oddly energizing. It asks its readers to interpret what they find. It asks that marvelous "why" to arise with the hope that we who choose constructivist leadership can defininitely begin.

Maxine Greene
Teachers College
Columbia University

Introduction

Linda Lambert

In this text, imagine leadership as the facilitation of constructivist reciprocal processes among participants in an educational community. In the process of developing this definition, we will redefine many ideas and terms that have shrouded notions of leadership: leader, follower, relationships, community, purpose. This is not an additive process; that is, we are not simply adding another dimension to past practice. We are asking our readers to reconceptualize leadership and, in so doing, to rethink such questions as: What is the relationship between constructivism and leadership? What does it mean to lead? How are leadership, change, and purpose related? How do we prepare constructivist leaders?

While this work is built on multiple concepts, some in new combinations with one another, the *key ideas* that inform both this book and the notion of Constructivist Leadership are:

1. *The lives of children and adults are inextricably intertwined.*

This book is informed by the assumption that the lives and needs of adults and children are closely tied together. It is important that we come to understand and interpret the learning needs of children and adults as patterns that repeat themselves—the learning patterns of all humans. If something is worthy for children, it is also worthy for adults. Democracy must be experienced by both children and adults, as must trust and positive regard. Authentic work must be experienced by adults as well as children, as must authentic relationships and possibilities. These patterns of learning must repeat themselves throughout the lives of individuals if our personal and community endeavors are to make sense to us, to have coherence and meaning.

2. *Constructivism is the primary basis of learning for children, adults, and organizations.*

The patterns of learning at the heart of this work lie in constructivism, an epistomological concept underlying theories of how children, adults, and even organizations learn. Individuals bring past experiences and beliefs, as well as their cultural histories and world views, into the process of learning; all of these influence how we interact with and interpret our encounters with new ideas and events. As our personal perspectives are mediated with the world, we construct and attribute meaning to these encounters, building new knowledge in the process. This constructive, interpretative work is facilitated and deepened when it is undertaken with others and with reflection.

Our chief understandings of constructivism today arise from our work in early childhood development and science, mathematics, and writing curriculum for children. In this text we apply and extend constructivism to our work with adults and communities, identifying the reciprocal processes that enable individuals to construct meaning and knowledge. We further advance the notion that when such learning occurs among participants in communities, the construction of meaning and knowledge leads toward heightened possibilities for growth and the development of common purpose.

3. *Communities that encourage the growth of human potential are based on the principles of ecology.*

Biological systems are based on principles that can be applied to social systems as well. From this parallel understanding, a second set of essential patterns emerges: patterns of relationships. Chapter 2 discusses in detail the principles of ecology that involve the participants in systems—referred to as educational communities—in interdependent patterns of relationships, bringing together human development and purpose. We contend that the energy that drives both communities and development is constructivist learning. As participants construct meaning and knowledge together, the professional culture of the educational community becomes more coherent and focused on emerging common purposes for teaching and learning.

4. *Patterns of relationships form the primary bases for human growth and development.*

These emerging patterns of learning and patterns of relationships are central to human growth and development. The recent and significant Claremont study, *Voices from the Inside* (Poplin & Weeres, 1993), identifies relationships or the lack of them as being a key factor in school problems and disengagement. The principles of ecology place patterns of relationships at the heart of successful, self-renewing schools and districts. We have come to realize that these patterns are the connecting nodes of the educational community through which meaning and knowledge are constructed and shared. These connections form the basis for reflecting on and making sense of who we are and how we work. Relationships may well be the most important factor in our pasts, present, and future possibilities.

5. *Diversity provides complexity, depth, and multiple perspectives to relationships, thereby extending human and societal possibilities.*

Working and learning from diversity requires some essential prerequisites of understanding. Among these is that diversity is a fundamental complexity in relationships and perceptions. Jerome Bruner (1994) has reminded us that diversity grows with increased consciousness, for its roots are in multiple frames, perceptions, perspectives, and interpretations. Constructivism, by evoking multiple interpretations and perceptions, fosters diversity. When the multiplicities of our own thoughts, and those of participants working together in educational communities, are liberated, embracing diversity can be a natural understanding we meet on the road to learning and leading.

Throughout this text, the complexities and opportunities afforded by diversity inform our work. Open professional cultures encourage patterns of learning and relationships that enable individuals to create diverse insights, to generate and entertain diverse information, and to construct new ideas that spring from and add to the diversity of our communities. Diversity is vital to our professional and personal lives, and therefore to the growth and development of children and adults.

These five key concepts form themes that weave themselves throughout the following chapters.

ABOUT THE CHAPTERS

In Chapter 1 Deborah Walker and Linda Lambert trace the dynamic history of learning and leading during this century, concluding with an in-depth survey of the constructivist theory of learning. Because concurrent theories of leading were also developed throughout the century, the history leaves us with a compelling question: Can we now generate a theory of constructivist leadership?

In Chapter 2 Linda Lambert responds to this question by constructing a theory of constructivist leadership, building on a new conception of the meaning of leadership—what it is to lead and who leads. This definition incorporates constructivist human learning, community, patterns of relationships, and diversity.

In Chapter 3 Linda Lambert applies this theory of constructivist leadership to our understandings of new emerging themes in a constructivist concept of change. She tells the story of Evergreen Middle School as it struggles through 3 years of constructing school-based change.

In Chapter 4 Linda Lambert conceives a primary role of the constructivist leader as being a leader of conversations—presented as dialogic, inquiring, sustaining, and partnering. This chapter also shapes a learning agenda for leaders as they prepare themselves to lead the conversations.

In Chapter 5 Diane Zimmerman surfaces language and communication approaches that give depth and energy to the reciprocal processes of constructivism. Through practical examples and a compelling rationale, she reveals the vital role of language in the construction of meaning and knowledge.

In Chapter 6 Joanne Cooper provides rich examples of practitioners as they write reflectively about their work. Narrative and story form and reform meaning as they serve as media for constructing personal and group insights into the changing nature of our work. Here we come to understand the role of narrative in schools and its relationship to growth and development.

In Chapter 7 Morgan Lambert and Mary Gardner describe the role of the school district in creating an environment among schools and their communities that supports constructivist leadership and creates constructivist approaches to the work of schooling. The authors challenge established practices in personnel, envisioning and planning, negotiating and finance, professional development, and the roles of the board and the superintendent. They include stories and references to school districts that have started the constructivist journey.

In Chapter 8 P. J. Ford Slack reflects on the nature of community and constructivist leadership and focuses on restorying three "communities of difference"—a Native American reservation school, an African American charter school, and a teaching community in China. She challenges us to consider alternative metaphors for community.

In Chapter 9 Deborah Walker returns to suggest innovative approaches to preparing constructivist leaders. She describes programs based in constructivism and offers guiding principles, processes, and content that create constructivist learning experiences for potential and practicing administrators.

And in Chapter 10 Linda Lambert sums up the implications of our work in constructivist leadership and imagines the possibilities of creating together new root metaphors for leading, learning, community, and democracy that may frame our renewed social and cultural understandings.

Acknowledgments

The authors of this text have been fortunate to enjoy the friendship and colleagueship of many individuals throughout our personal and professional lives—people who have influenced our work, supported us in boldness, sharpened our values, and challenged our thinking. We acknowledge a few of these good friends, recognizing that these individuals are too numerous to be named in full. We trust that future publications will provide opportunities to further chronicle lives rich in relationships.

Linda Lambert acknowledges her early work in Colorado and California with Jim Olivero, from whom she learned the value of process; work in the 1970s with California's Reform in Intermediate and Secondary Education (RISE) program and the beginning of critical friendship with Morgan Lambert as they sought to understand the nature of democratic participation and the qualities that made schools work for children and adults. Del Della Dora has, for nearly two decades, sharpened those understandings of democracy and self-direction and been a close friend and colleague. Art Costa and Robert Garmston brought further understandings and strategies to human interactions based on trust, autonomy, and learning. In the early 1980s, doctoral advisor Ellen Herda ushered in a shift in perspective (and in career) when she suggested readings and held conversations in critical theory and the new sciences. Linda's friendship with Mary Gardner has given further meaning to reciprocal learning as they have inquired together into leadership and constructivism. Perhaps most of all, she thanks her mother, Lucretia Mae Todd, for teaching her how to learn.

Deborah Walker acknowledges two people in particular: Delmo Della Dora, a university partner, and Maribeth Smith, a school district partner. Del modeled for her democratic practices in both his teacher and leader roles, showing her how powerful university instruction can be when the students take an active role in decision-making and self-assessment. Maribeth Smith demonstrated for her the impact professional development activities can have when teachers are able to construct their own professional knowledge, make meaning together, participate in shared inquiry, and take responsibility for their own growth and learning.

Diane P. Zimmerman takes energy and inspiration from associations with several communities of conversation. For their unending tenacity in pursuing intellectual questions, she thanks her colleagues in the Institute of Intelligent Behavior and the larger community of learners known as the Leather Apron Club. Special thanks go to Arthur Costa and Robert Garmston for their vision in creating this community of learners. Influential in this work have been conversations with William Baker and Stanley Shalit, Daisy Arredondo and Judy Lechner-Brody, and Laura Lipton and Joseph Sabin. Intellectual pursuits require support and encouragement, and for this Diane thanks Norm Enfield and William Sommers. Finally, without the willingness of her husband, Richard Zimmerman, to "hold down the fort" while she pursued her intellectual dreams, she could not have contributed to this work.

Joanne E. Cooper's work was originally influenced by Dale Spender while Joanne was on sabbatical in England. Diane Dunlap, her doctoral advisor, and Madeleine Grumet both encouraged and validated her work at important junctures. Most recently her work has intersected with that of Margreet Poulie and Hubert Hermans of Holland.

Morgan Dale Lambert's intellectual twig was bent by very early interaction at the University of California, Berkeley, with Edwin Chace Tolman and R. Nevit Sanford, and later guidance from Theodore Parsons and James Stone. More recent influences include Del Della Dora, Art Costa, Bob Garmston, and Bruce Joyce. In retrospect, it is clear that interaction with colleagues in three California school districts (Castro Valley, Novato, and Lagunitas) helped powerfully in the construction of meaning about change and renewal. The interactive learning continues in his current work in restructuring networks. Most significant has been the deepening of understanding that has grown out of a 20-year co-mentoring relationship with Linda Lambert.

Mary E. Gardner acknowledges Roland Barth, Sarah Levine, Linda Lambert, Morgan Lambert, and Nancy Giberson, who, as critical friends through many conversations, helped her develop an understanding of leadership; Saratoga school district colleagues and community, who gave her the opportunity to practice constructivist leadership; and friends and family, especially daughters Deirdra and Kimberly, who helped her to laugh.

P. J. Ford Slack thanks the community voices that appear in her chapter. Without their voices, the words would be empty and lack music. Nadine Chase and Maxine Greene offered a musical line with stories of humor and life; Anne Auten's caring eye added structure and breadth to the tune; colleagues in educational leadership at St. Thomas have been a critical and supportive audience, as have Nina Bascia, Diane Dunlap, Sam Hollingsworth, Chet Bowers, and David Rupp. The melody and harmony came from the educational community of the Bug-O-Nay-Go-Shig School, the 1993 Principalship class, and the dynamic and insightful students of City Academy. Lotus Wang and Li Jing offered continuing words and wisdom that stretched her ear to hear a different song of community. The other authors of this book, her community in St. Paul, and Claire Dunlap's gentle teaching have all contributed to this chapter on community.

The authors of this book particularly acknowledge the careful editing of Del Della Dora, Bob Garmston, Art Costa, and all others who gave generously of their time and of themselves. Further, we acknowledge Linda Lambert for creating the idea of constructivist leadership and for inviting each of us to contribute to this work. Without her voice and vision, we would not have had the conversation. We look forward to future collaborations.

THE
CONSTRUCTIVIST
LEADER

CHAPTER 1

Learning and Leading Theory: A Century in the Making

Deborah Walker and Linda Lambert

It is a cardinal precept of the newer school of education that the
beginning of instruction shall be made with the experience
learners already have.

John Dewey
Experience and Education (1938, p. 74)

More than 50 years ago John Dewey challenged prevailing views of learning
by suggesting that education is an internal process in which the learner uses
prior knowledge and experience to shape meaning and to construct new
knowledge. The debate was not new to Dewey's time, but rather reflected a
continuing struggle to understand how students learn and how schools are
capable of fostering that learning. The purpose of this book is to advance a
theory of learning and leading and, in doing so, to enter the debate in which
Dewey was a significant voice. Using the theory of constructivism, this book
suggests new directions for the structure of schooling and new roles for those
who lead schools.

Constructivism is a theory of learning, and it is also a theory of knowing. It is an epistemological concept that draws from a variety of fields, including philosophy, psychology, and science. Fosnot (1992) points out that
constructivism "is at once a theory of 'knowing' and a theory of 'coming to
know'" (p. 167). The theory of knowing, as first articulated by Piaget, is
essentially biological in nature; that is, an organism encounters new experiences and events and seeks to *assimilate* these into existing cognitive structures or to adjust the structures to *accommodate* the new information. The
cognitive structures, or schemas, are formed and re-formed based on experiences, beliefs, values, sociocultural histories, and prior perceptions. Piaget
noted that schemas are "under construction," meaning that the cognitive
structures evolve as individuals interpret, understand, and come to know
(Piaget, 1971, p. 140, in Duffy & Jonassen, 1992).

The "what" and "why" of knowing render the process both a psychological and a philosophical one. Individuals do more than assimilate and accom-

1

modate as described in biology; they reformulate their schemas to make sense of dissonant information and experience. Growth and development are prompted by discrepancy or "disequilibrium" between what is believed to be true and what is now revealing itself in experience. The reformulation of personal schemas has coherence and purpose: It is shaped by the values that contribute to an individual's being able to make meaning. Thus individuals assign meaning to experience and at the same time construct knowledge from experience.

The processes of "coming to know" are influenced and shaped by reflection, mediation, and social interactions. Both Bruner (Bruner & Haste, 1987) and Vygotsky framed current understandings about the social construction of knowledge. Bruner (1966) described the role of language and prior experience in creating mutual representations for interpretation. Vygotsky (1962, 1978) described the "zone of proximal development" through which knowing is mediated and negotiated. In recent decades, Reuven Feuerstein's work (Feuerstein, 1990; Feuerstein, Klein, & Tannenbaum, 1991) has added significantly to our understandings of the mediated construction of the self, or self-modification. In the process of encountering new experience and applying reflective interpretation within social contexts, the individual learns and comes to know.

This psychological process is also a developmental one; it is a process in motion. Kegan (1982) advanced the idea that "meaning is, in its origins, a physical activity (grasping and seeing), a social activity (it requires another), a survival activity (in doing it, we live). Meaning understood in this way, is the primary human motion, irreducible" (pp. 18–19). Meaning, by its very nature, is developmental; that is, it propels us and causes us to evolve. It is motion.

Understandings of how individuals come to know have been translated into theories of constructivist learning and classroom practices. In this text we apply these same understandings to adults in educational communities, in their roles as learners and leaders.

THE EVOLUTION OF CONTEMPORARY EDUCATIONAL THOUGHT

As educators we struggle to define the purposes, processes, and structures of education. This is not an easy task. Education serves not only students and their families but also the social, political, and economic needs of our nation, and so it is influenced by many sources outside the educational sphere. A historical compact has enlisted us all to varying degrees into an agreement that public education prepares our children for citizenship in a democracy, but a closer look at schooling reveals that this commitment is not the dominant agenda. The prevailing winds of history, often those perceived of as threatening democracy, cast a long shadow into our schools. During this century, the schools have served a nation in populist reform, at war, in depression, in international competition, and in civil upheaval. Each of these forces has advanced different themes and concerns. For example, the 1950s were concerned with national security and the race to establish dominance in outer space. The resulting educational policy emphasized science, foreign-language instruction, and new approaches to mathematics. The women's movement, fueled by the factories of World War II, merged with other civil rights movements and exploded in the 1960s, bringing efforts to achieve educational equality and choice. In turn, the 1970s were characterized by a return to the "basics" in curriculum, the use of behavioral models of instruction and teacher supervision, and a focus on standardized measures of student achievement, all with the purpose of creating a more uniformly educated workforce for a faltering economy. *A Nation at Risk* (National Commission on Excellence in Education, 1983), issued in the mid-1980s, portrayed our educational system as weakening our stamina and abilities to fight the Cold War. By the mid-1990s, *America 2000* (United States Department of Education, 1991) had merged into Goals 2000 (1994) in a call for systemic reform, and the driving force is still the economy.

Even within education, there is wide variation as to philosophy, beliefs, and professional knowledge regarding how students learn and achieve. While educators are influenced by social, political, and economic trends, and sometimes the funding attached to these priorities, they tend to formulate their notions about education according to those theories and styles of instruction that fit their own learning patterns and experiences and their own world views. Educators can be socialized by district and school norms: for example, to be inclusive in their attitudes toward student differences and parent expectations; or to be exclusive, expecting student behavior and parent expectations to conform to institutional norms, rather than accommodating differences. Recent efforts at teacher, and now administrator, induction are aimed at creating a socialization process that enables beginning educators to understand and apply common insights regarding teaching and learning. In spite of these efforts, educators continue to subscribe to a wide range of theories and beliefs regarding the education of students and their own roles in the learning–leading process.

This chapter provides a brief retrospective survey of the evolution of educational theories of learning and leading within the context of recent history. The historical context provides a vehicle for understanding how educational theories are influenced by their times and by the dynamic between and among theories. It is important to note that even as new ideas about learning and leading develop and are tested, traditional theories continue to exert

their influence, and in some instances they remain dominant. They are based
on past practice, convention, and what is often referred to as teacher and
community lore; that is, believing educational tenets to be true because they
have been repeated so often.

As we progress through the twentieth century, we will begin to converge
with a powerful stream of influence that began with Dewey, Bruner, Piaget,
and Vygotsky and has joined with new understandings of intelligence and
the brain to form constructivist learning. As we reveal the roots of constructivism, this chapter will set the scene for the description of the next new
edge of leadership theory: Constructivist Leadership.

LEARNING AND LEADING: PARALLEL DEVELOPMENT

Educational literature abounds with the influences of learning theory
on school leadership. For example, behavioral principles, when applied to
learning, result in a system emphasizing skill development based on task
analysis and rewards for progress made. When applied to leading, behaviorist
principles result in school leaders' emphasizing external targets for teacher
growth supported by a system of rewards. This example vividly reminds us
that typically education has derived its theoretical principles from fields outside of education, such as psychology and sociology. Educational administration, as a subset of education, has also looked to business and industry for
theories of how leaders lead and how organizations develop. The influence of
the social, political, and economic forces referred to above and the evolving
theories from other disciplines have given rise to parallel themes or movements that attempt to define both learning and leading in our schools.

These parallel and mutually influential themes or movements constitute
dominant eras in learning and leading, which we will call: traditional, behavioral, grouping/tracking and contingency/situational, effectiveness and instructional leadership, community of learners and community of leaders, and
constructivist. Figure 1.1 offers a description of each of them and highlights
of the prevailing assumptions and key theorists. Such attempts at categorization must be accompanied by several caveats. Each era experienced forces
from multiple schools of thought. Each theorist's ideas are complex and
evolved over time; notably, key theorists of one era often led the transition
to the next.

The various movements in learning and leading dominated during specific eras, yet each world view continues to exert some influence on our institutions today. Learning and leading theories, as we shall see, have exercised
a dynamic influence on each other. Teachers and leaders, separate actors
through most of our history, have been cast as parallel characters, each as

authority figures possessing formal knowledge and practical know-how as well as charged with carrying out the mission of the school and the larger society.

HISTORICAL ANTECEDENTS TO CONSTRUCTIVIST THEORY

Traditional Approaches to Learning and Leading

We entered this century with thousands of years of convention behind our notions of traditionalism. It is not surprising that this impulse remains strong. In communities in which parents make contributions to the design and purposes of schools, traditional school formats tend to be adopted at both the elementary and secondary levels, characterized by a uniform curriculum, an emphasis on basic skills, strict discipline, and in some instances dress codes and student uniforms. Traditional schools provide for continuity and assure parents an education for their children that is similar to the one they themselves experienced in school. While innovative teaching may take place, program innovation is not central to the traditional school philosophy. Whole-group instruction, lecture and drill, and a focus on standardized measures of student achievement are typical of traditional schools. This approach embodies the view that learning is externally motivated and determined and that students do not possess within themselves the necessary knowledge and experience to take a more active role in constructing knowledge and shaping meaning. The teacher, depository of classical curricula, is seen as the sole source of knowledge and learning. Thus classroom structures tend to be teacher centered and hierarchical, fostering adherence to a single set of standards.

In 1927, at a major conference on leadership, Steward defined leadership as, "the ability to impress the will of the leader on those led and induce obedience, respect, loyalty, and cooperation" (quoted in Moore, 1927, p. 124, as reported in Rost, 1991, p. 47). Obedience, respect, loyalty, and cooperation were, and often still are, most highly valued for teachers as well as students. In traditional schools, lines of authority are usually clear, with the principal or headmaster functioning as the decision-maker, policy-setter, and taskmaster. Since it is assumed that the values of a traditional school are closely aligned with those of the community, teachers are expected to conform to those standards and to maintain the status quo, as directed by the principal (Mitchell & Tucker, 1992). Teacher supervision may follow one of several patterns. Teachers may be closely supervised, with the principal setting job targets and fulfilling a quality control function; or supervision may be perfunctory, based on the assumption that everyone understands the standards

(continued on p. 10)

Figure 1.1. Leading and Learning: A Framework of Parallel Development

LEARNING	THEORISTS	LEADING	THEORISTS
Traditional			
Students learn a prescribed body of knowledge through memorization, with knowledge viewed as true and unchanging. Strategies for learning focus on the teacher as the source of knowledge and students as recipients, with knowledge existing outside the learner. Emphasis is on obedience to authority. While an important learning goal is preparation for participation in a democracy, the classroom does not mirror or give students experience with democratic processes.	Jefferson Rush Mann Swett	The leader serves to maintain tradition and direct efforts of the teaching staff. Teachers have little authority over decision making related to goals, curriculum or student progress. Leadership does not reflect democratic processes and is autocratic in nature. Notions of leadership are influenced by scientific management theory, with emphasis on efficiency and quality control.	Moore Schenk Taylor Bobbitt Fayol Gulick Urwick
Behavioral			
Learning takes place when knowledge is broken down into smaller pieces and students are rewarded for successful performance. Direct teaching strategies dominate, based on the belief that student behavior can be measured, diagnosed and predicted. The aim in the classroom is to calibrate behavior to achieve set learning objectives and goals.	Mager Thorndike Popham Skinner Hunter	The role of the leader is to shape human behavior to match organizational aims. Leaders, such as principals, reward desired teacher behavior and use sanctions when teachers do not cooperate. Leadership is viewed as being "transactional" in nature, that is, there is an exchange between leader and worker to achieve established goals.	Burns Halpin Barnard Simon Bundel

Grouping/Tracking

Based on assumptions from behavioral theory, students are characterized as differing widely in ability, necessitating homogeneous grouping strategies where similar students are given the same learning "treatment." Teaching efforts are directed at moving students to higher-level groups, although in practice group placement generally remains fixed. Variations in teaching strategies and learning activities are based on the perceived ability levels of students

Thorndike
Binet
Dunn &
 Dunn
Gregoric

Contingency/Situational

Originating in the business literature, leadership is differentiated based on the maturity level or work style of the employee. Teacher supervision by principals has as its aim moving teachers to higher levels of functioning. Leaders are either more or less directive with those they lead so that organizational goals are met.

Fiedler
Bogardus
Hersey &
 Blanchard
Vroom-Yetton
 & Jago
Glickman
Glatthorn
Pigors

Learning/School Effectiveness

Students learn when the curricular goals are clearly delineated and when teaching and assessment methods are aligned with the curriculum. Time spent engaged in active learning is correlated with achievement. The underlying assumptions draw again from behavioral theory, in that a combination of teaching behaviors or school factors can predict learning. Student esteem is believed to be enhanced by academic outcomes. Students evidence growth when teachers hold high expectations and when there is "press" for academic performance. A core belief is that *all* students can learn.

Lezotte
Edmonds
Brookover
Good
Brophy
Weinstein
Murphy
Weil
Hunter

Instructional Leadership/Trait Theory

School level factors contribute to student success, especially instructional leadership by the principal. The principal carries out key instructional functions, including monitoring student progress and serving as a visible presence on campus. Time spent observing in classrooms, participating in staff development, and providing resources for teachers influences both teacher and student growth as well as overall school improvement. Business literature offers parallel traits of effective leaders who achieve organizational goals.

Edmonds
Murphy
Hallinger
Little
Bird
Smith &
 Andrews
Leithwood
Burns
Bennis
Nanus
Peters
Waterman
Deal

Figure 1.1. (continued)

LEARNING	THEORISTS	LEADING	THEORISTS
Communities of Learners		**Communities of Leaders**	
Student learning is enhanced when students work cooperatively and share knowledge. Classroom reward structures are designed to encourage cooperative learning and assessment methods are adapted to determine group and individual progress. The process for learning is valued as highly as the content. Students and their teachers learn together, with group skills and interdependence emphasized. The teacher's role changes from presenter to facilitator of knowledge; classroom processes tend to be more democratic. The role of the educational environment or "ecology" is also seen as interrelated to how students learn and how teachers teach. Student ability or intelligence is believed to be not an innate quality but part of the educational context.	Johnson & Johnson Slavin Cohen Goodlad Oakes Costa Eisner Della Dora Egan Bowers Flinders Sternberg Joyce	Leadership is viewed as a shared process among educators — principals and teachers. The principal is seen as a "leader among leaders" who facilitates the growth of others. Thus the organizational structure is flattened and integrated, and participants share common values and purposes. The interactive nature of a community promotes continuous improvement, with assessment integral to the work of the community. Again, democratic processes are emphasized. This view of leadership has its roots in a number of theoretical constructs, including human relations and systems theory and ecological thought.	Lieberman Little Sarason Barth Vygotsky Sergiovanni J. Gardner Follett Getzels & Guba Garmston Bowers Flinders Glickman

Constructivist Learning

Based on assumptions from community of learners/leaders theory, students construct meaning from personal values, beliefs, and experiences. The development of personal schemas and the ability to reflect on one's experiences are key theorectical principles. Unlike in traditional thought, it is believed that knowledge exists within the learner. The social nature of learning is emphasized: Shared inquiry is a central activity. Multiple outcomes are expected and encouraged, with assessment being integral to the process. Human growth is a moral imperative.

Dewey
Bruner
Piaget
Vygotsky
Feuerstein
Tyler
Resnick
H. Gardner
Scinto
Duckworth
Brooks & Brooks
Leinhardt
Perkins
Brookfield
von Glaserfeld
Lowery

Constructivist Leading

Leadership is viewed as a reciprocal process among the adults in the school. Purposes and goals develop from among the participants, based upon values, beliefs, individual and shared experiences. The school functions as a community that is self-motivating and that views the growth of its members as fundamental. There is an emphasis on language as a means for shaping the school culture, conveying commonality of experience, and articulating a joint vision. Shared inquiry is an important activity in problem identification and resolution; participants conduct action research and share findings as a way of improving practice.

Greene
Senge
Zohar
Wheatley
Foster
Kegan
Barnett
Carlsen
Garmston & Lipton
Lambert
Walker

and expectations and that teachers will perform their role as expected. In either instance, the principal is not seen as a facilitator of teacher growth, nor does the purpose of teacher supervision seem to be the professional development of the teaching staff.

While a central purpose of the first schools was to ensure continuance of our democracy, the theme of the dominance of administrator authority in traditionalism obscured this purpose. Glickman (1993), in his writings about empowerment and school change, notes that schools are perhaps the least democratic of institutions and that attempts to democratize them and share authority in them are often met with disdain from colleagues at other schools and from the central office. Likewise, traditional schools have not promoted shared leadership with teachers, nor have they involved students in making decisions about their curriculum or in evaluating their own progress. In this sense, traditionalism is at the opposite end of the learning/leading continuum from constructivism, especially as envisioned by Dewey in *Democracy and Education* (1916) and his other writings.

Behavioral Approaches to Learning and Leading

Behavioral theories of learning and leading draw from a confluence of thought regarding the nature of the world and the extent to which human phenomena can be measured and predicted. Newtonian science, social theories, and religious dogma advanced the view that the world and the universe are predictable, static, and clocklike. Quantitative research, which to a large extent has shaped education's knowledge base, also derived many of its approaches from a similar set of assumptions: that behavior can be predicted; that intelligence is fixed and innate; that differences in intelligence can be accurately measured; and that based on these measurements, learning "treatments" can be prescribed.

In the classroom, behavioral psychology translates into teachers breaking down large concepts into component parts and discrete skills, often taught in isolation, with drill and practice and large-group instruction favored. Behavioral approaches include increased dependence on standardized measures of achievement, offering rewards for learning as a way of shaping student behavior. The development of the "behavioral objective" concept by Mager (1962), and the more narrow definition given to the idea by Baker and Popham (1973), ushered in a whole generation of educators who learned how to write and apply behavioral objectives. Behavioral approaches are very much alive, especially in special education classes and most forms of remedial programs.

Behavioral psychology's influence extends beyond the classroom to how we in education—and others in business and industry—view organizational behavior. The input/output model favored by behavioral psychologists suggests a direct relationship between resources fed in and results produced: learning, teaching, and leading are based on information, materials, or funds fed in, and they result in outputs, such as test scores achieved, professional credentials granted, or organizational goals accomplished. Milstein and Belasco (1973), in a comprehensive text about systems theory, organized the chapters into input, throughput, and output concepts, which at that time were drawn from behavioral assumptions. This input/output model as a behavioral framework has formed the basis for school funding formulas and traditional approaches to change (see Chapter 3), and it still dominates major arenas of educational practice.

In the behavioral construct for school leadership, the principal is viewed as being responsible for the quality of teacher performance and for using rewards and sanctions to ensure that teachers maintain standards. This view of leadership is not unlike Burns' (1978) conception of "transactional leadership," in which the principal transacts or exchanges rewards for desired behavior that is clearly specified and understood. The principal's role is to "shape" teacher behavior, in much the same way as the classroom teacher shapes student behavior. It seems natural outgrowth of behaviorism to seek to cluster people into manageable and "treatable" groups, based on identifiable and measurable behaviors.

Grouping/Tracking and Contingency/Situational Approaches to Learning and Leading

During the Industrial Revolution in this country, the need to sort people emerged as a societal imperative for two reasons: Unprecedented numbers of immigrants were entering the country who were unfamiliar with the principles of democracy and who often needed to acquire facility in English; and the growth of factories introduced the need for large numbers of production-line workers. The children of the more affluent Americans, who were considered to be superior to the immigrants, attended school to prepare themselves for higher education or to run the businesses and factories; the children of immigrants completed courses to enable them to work in the factories and to function as citizens in a democracy. This early sorting was bolstered by the formulation of statistical analysis as a way of determining intelligence and academic performance. Fueled by a societal belief in racial and ethnic superiority, educators such as Elwood Cubberly used research techniques to justify the sorting of students in preparation for their life's work (Oakes, 1985).

Though we are long past the Industrial Revolution and many believe in a new revolution sparked by the information age, we continue to sort students in school as early as kindergarten, often on bases that reflect socioeconomic status, language, gender, and race. Elementary-age students are grouped by ability for reading and math as well as for other subjects, and secondary students are tracked by ability and placed in academic or nonacademic courses of study. While the last decade has brought increased pressure to revise and eliminate grouping and tracking practices, they still persist, based on educators' beliefs regarding students' capacity to learn or access learning through a second language—and also because teachers often lack the tools to teach in heterogeneous settings. An underlying premise of grouping and tracking remains the belief that student ability is fixed and can be accurately assessed at a young age.

Another prevailing myth related to grouping and tracking is that if students are placed in low-ability groups or in remedial classes, they will eventually acquire the necessary skills and catch up with their peers. Remedial efforts tend to cover the same ground repeatedly; they also teach discrete skills in a sequential manner without providing opportunities for students to put these skills together in a coherent way. The reality is that these students never catch up; in fact, they fall further behind as they progress through the grades (Braddock & McPartland, 1990). The process of grouping and tracking assigns students to fixed tracks throughout their schooling and limits their opportunities beyond school.

The movement that resulted in the grouping and tracking of students also shaped conceptions of leadership and of the formal leader's relationship to teachers in the school. In their training, principals were presented with a variety of contingencies or situations to which they must adapt their leadership style. These situations share common assumptions with the grouping/ tracking of students: that teacher capacity is fixed; that the leader's role is to learn to deal with the different abilities of teachers and manage them successfully; that teachers will naturally sort themselves into high-, average-, and low-performing groups, much like students. Hershey and Blanchard's (1972) situational leadership suggests that leaders need to be flexible in their approach to employee supervision, but it also suggests that employees can be easily categorized and that an appropriate "treatment" exists for each category of behavior. It is important to remember that no theme or movement in learning and leading exists alone, but rather is connected to previous, concurrent, and countervailing movements—in these instances the behavioral movement.

The work on differentiated supervision and teacher development also categorizes teacher behavior, although the goals are more laudable. According to Glatthorn (1984) and Glickman (1990), supervisors can, by varying their approaches, move teachers to higher levels of performance and development. Glickman advances a continuum of leader behavior, from directed to nondirected, correlated with particular levels of teacher development. His work forms a transition from the situational approach to leadership, which has its roots in turn-of-the-century conceptions of fixed ability, to developmental approaches with the belief in teachers' capacity for growth.

Effectiveness and Instructional Leadership Approaches to Learning and Leading

The school effectiveness movement was sparked by the conclusions of the Coleman Report, *Equality of Educational Opportunity* (Coleman et al., 1966). This report attributed student achievement to factors largely beyond the control of the school, namely, parent income and education level. In response, educational researchers identified schools—mostly in the inner cities, with students who were from lower socioeconomic groups and were often minorities—that had produced high levels of student achievement on standard measures in reading and math. These researchers studied these schools, looking for patterns to which to attribute increases in achievement and from which other schools could learn. They found that the mission of the school was generally narrow and focused on basic skill acquisition as measured by achievement tests; there was alignment among the curriculum, teaching methods, and assessment; there was sufficient opportunity to learn in terms of engaged time and success rate; and a "safe and orderly" environment existed (Brookover et al., 1982; Edmonds, 1979).

From these initial findings grew a related body of research known as learning or teaching effectiveness, which focused on classroom practices related to student achievement. Direct instruction (Brophy & Good, 1986; Hunter, quoted in Brandt, 1985) emerged as a style of teaching especially appropriate to basic skill acquisition. It drew from behavioral theory—for example, learning is broken down into small pieces, expectations are made very clear, and approximations of desired behavior are rewarded. While learning/school effectiveness did not necessarily promote active learning and student construction of knowledge, it did establish two basic tenets that still underscore reform movements today: the belief that all children can learn (argued much earlier by Bruner); and the recognition that when teachers hold high expectations for student achievement and press for academic performance, students tend to meet those expectations.

Another important finding contributing to the knowledge bases of learning and leading that is drawn from the effectiveness literature links instructional leadership, particularly on the part of the principal, to student achievement. While the effectiveness research is correlational and not causal, there is corroborating evidence that principal instructional leadership can increase the achievement of those students most at risk (Andrews, quoted in Brandt, 1987). A substantial body of literature exists on "instructional leadership," which proposes that formal leaders pay attention to what goes on in the classroom through direct observation and focused discussion, participate in staff development, be visible on campus, and make instructional resources available to teachers (Hallinger & Murphy, 1987; Little & Bird, 1987).

Parallel to the development of the effectiveness theories of learning and leading was the emergence of the "excellence" literature in business. There are many similarities and one large difference in these approaches. The similarities lie in the emphasis on a well-defined vision or mission (that of the leader), processes aligned with the vision, the importance of training and staff development, expectations for high performance, and involved leaders. Both education and business advanced a "trait" theory of what makes an effective leader: articulating a sense of purpose, keeping people focused on goals, working collaboratively within the organization. The assumption was that if we could observe what highly successful leaders did, and teach it to others, they, too, could be highly successful. Some of this thinking had grown out of notions of "charismatic" leadership, such as in the work of Weber (1947, 1968). The major difference is that the business literature promoted excellence as a way of achieving greater profits, while the education literature promoted equity as a means of increasing opportunities for those students typically underserved by schools.

The theory of effectiveness as applied to both learning and leading was seen as a template one could superimpose on schools, their leader, and classroom teachers to promote equity and increased achievement. The theoretical principles embedded in the research contributed to focused efforts at school improvement, resulting in some statewide initiatives in California, Michigan, Connecticut, Kentucky, Texas, and other states. Application of the template without a recognition of the complexity of school improvement and efforts to change existing practice, however, revealed the limitations of the effectiveness theory. Because effectiveness literature drew heavily on the behavioral movement, it focused on direct teaching and learning and did not adequately address the issues of school culture and established patterns of interactions that dramatically influence both learning and leading.

The Community of Learners and Community of Leaders: Approaches to Learning and Leading

Over the years, schools have struggled with various metaphors to describe their central enterprise. A metaphor that dominated from the turn of the century was that of the school as factory, emphasizing assembly-line production, compliance, and uniformity. During the 1980s the metaphor of the school as a community of learners emerged, calling forth new images of learning. In a community of learners, both individual and collective growth are valued, as are the processes for achieving that growth.

This shift in consciousness ushered in a new synthesis of educational thought and a new set of assumptions. It was a coming together of major countervailing themes from throughout the century: the work of Bruner and Vygotsky in the social construction of knowledge, of Dewey and Combs in democracy in schooling, changing conceptions about the fluidity and scope of intelligences, quantum theory, women in leadership and research, brain research, the emergence into respectability of qualitative research, critical theory, and postmodern thought.

This new "enlightenment" advanced some challenging assumptions; among them were: (1) The capacity to learn is not fixed or innate; (2) the social construction of knowledge actually changes "intelligence"; therefore, learning must be an active and interactive process; (3) student and adult learning are both fluid and linked; (4) achievement is increased when the culture of the school supports learning for both students and adults; and (5) new norms need to be developed that foster collaboration and shared inquiry. This was the first movement to place a high value on teacher growth and to link teacher and student learning. Collaborative teaching methods that promote learning for all students are applied to the organizational processes that characterize the school, so that the school becomes a learning organization (a continually renewing place to live and work).

The community of learners movement reshapes classroom interactions from student as passive listener and teacher as source of knowledge, to learning as an interactive process entered into by both students and teachers. Students take greater responsibility for designing their work, setting deadlines, and evaluating progress in terms of individual and group outcomes. Interdependence and group skills are emphasized along with mastery of content, sharing knowledge, and gaining multiple perspectives (Johnson & Johnson, 1988; Slavin, 1986). Cooperative learning approaches provide a forum for the social construction of knowledge as well as the promotion of democratic practices.

At the school level, this sense of community is evidenced in a commitment to the growth of the faculty as a whole and to activities such as seminar groups, reflective writing, team research, and discussion. Community refers not just to a sense of cohesion among students and teachers, but also to the notion that the educational environment or "ecology" plays an important role in how students learn and teachers teach (Bateson, 1972; Bowers & Flinders, 1990; Eisner, 1988; Goodlad, 1987; B. Joyce, personal communication, 1976). The concept of the school as an "ecology" was thought to comprise the norms of the school, expectations, patterns of behavior, processes, and human and material resources. This integrative view of schooling suggests that an ecology is a complex and interrelated system that influences and supports intellectual growth (see Chapter 2 for a more in-depth discussion). Further, student ability or intelligence is viewed not as predominantly innate, but as a function of the educational context (Egan, 1979).

The roots of the concept of community of leaders run as deep as those of community of learners. Mary Follett's (1924) work in the human relations movement in business led to democratic ways of relating in the workplace, and to Burns' (1978) transformational leadership. This humane and participatory philosophy also influenced Total Quality notions and Senge's "learning organization" in *The Fifth Discipline* (Senge, 1990). Max Weber's systems theory (1947) contributed to our early understanding of the influence of the social and organizational context, and Getzels and Guba's (1957) adaptations of this theory described the relationship of systems theory to roles and personalities.

The community of leaders language was introduced into education by Roland Barth (1988) as an interactive process of shared leadership. Leadership is shared among the professional staff, with the principal seen as a leader of leaders (Barth, 1988; Glickman, 1993; Schlechty, 1990). The hierarchical structure is replaced by shared responsibility for school governance, professional growth, and achievement of agreed-on goals. Because a community is characterized by shared values and hopes, many of the control functions associated with school leadership become less important and even counterproductive. In a community of leaders, it is assumed that all teachers can lead and can contribute to accomplishing the work of the school. Like classroom processes, school-level processes emphasize participation, interaction, and collective growth. In many parts of the country, this movement has manifested itself as shared decision-making and site-based management.

CONSTRUCTIVISM IN THE LATE TWENTIETH CENTURY

Defining Constructivist Learning

Constructivist learning derives from the field of epistomological psychology and describes how people construct their reality and make sense of their world. Its application to the field of education suggests that students make their own meaning and is based in part on Plato's contention that knowledge is formed within the learner and is brought to the surface by a skilled teacher through processes of inquiry and Socratic dialogue. In some ways, it is easier to define constructivist learning by what it is not, rather than what it is. For years, education and learning have been viewed as an external process. Students, whether they are children or adult learners, are "empty vessels" into which knowledge and even wisdom are poured. Meaning is considered to be inherent in ideas, events, experience, knowledge; and students are to learn about the meanings that others have interpreted. The teacher possesses this knowledge and wisdom, which is shared with students through strategies such as telling, recitation, and drill.

Typically the experiences and practical knowledge that students bring with them are not woven into the curriculum or classroom learning activities. For instance, students write about classroom topics primarily in expository form, and even narrative writing is largely based on classroom materials rather than parallel experiences that students have had. According to this theory of learning, students acquire "school knowledge" (Schön, 1987) that is separate from and unrelated to the practical knowledge they have gained at home and in the community. This view of teaching and learning has remained fairly constant since colonial times and persists today in many quarters.

In the opening of this chapter, we described some of the origins of the concept of constructivism in conceptualizing the epistemological processes of "knowing and coming to know." When translated into constructivist learning within the framework of the educative process known as schooling, constructivist learning theory can be distinguished from other theories by the following principles and brief descriptors.

- *Knowledge and beliefs are formed within the learner.* Rather than considering learners as "empty vessels," constructivist learning theory assumes that learners bring experience and understandings to the classroom. Thus they do not encounter new information out of context, but rather apply what they know to assimilating this information; or they accommodate or reframe what they know to match new understandings they have gained. Either way, the process of coming to know is an interactive one.
- *Learners personally imbue experiences with meaning.* Teachers typically explain meaning for learners—what a poem means, what events in history signify, what theme a painting conveys—instead of allowing learners themselves to suggest possible meanings. The values and beliefs they have already formed help learners to interpret and assign meaning, as do their interactions with other students. Meaning is constructed and is shaded by the students' previous experiences. Thus two students may read a poem and hear the same images summoned by the language of the poet, yet the meaning of the images is determined first by each student's personal schemas, and second by the interaction with the perspectives being formed by other students' schemas.
- *Learning activities should cause learners to gain access to their experiences,*

knowledge, and beliefs. Constructivist approaches to learning include those which allow learners to use what they know to interpret new information and construct new knowledge. Teachers often complain that learners have little to write about and, when they do find subjects to address, that their writing is devoid of rich detail or insight. Constructivist learning theory suggests that the questions posed to students must prompt their writing to connect with what they know and believe. When these connections are made, learners draw on what they know and reshape it in new and newly meaningful ways.

- *Learning is a social activity that is enhanced by shared inquiry.* Learners learn with more depth and understanding when they are able to share ideas with others, engage in the dynamic and synergistic process of thinking together, consider other points of view, and broaden their own perspectives. Constructivism advances the idea that learning is a social endeavor requiring engagement with others in order to gain a growing understanding of the world and one's relationship to it.

- *Reflection and metacognition are essential aspects of constructing knowledge and meaning.* Learners clarify their understandings when they are able to reflect on their learning and to analyze the ways they construct knowledge and meaning. Constructivism suggests a more complex and dynamic process for learning than is traditionally described (in which students are thought to absorb information like sponges and feed it back at test time): Students develop as learners when they are aware of the processes they engage in as they "come to know." This awareness enhances their ability to learn and make sense of new information.

- *Learners play a critical role in assessing their own learning.* Traditionally teachers establish learning goals and criteria for success, and they evaluate student progress. A constructivist approach suggests that students can help to determine how much they have learned as well as the processes by which they have come to know. Student self-assessment makes the processes for learning explicit to students, shaping their personal schemas and enabling them to actively engage with new learning in the future. This kind of "authentic assessment" also provides insight for the teacher into how students develop and view their own growth.

- *The outcomes of the learning process are varied and often unpredictable.* Constructivist approaches allow the students to direct the learning and to generate both understanding and meaning. In a sense, the teacher gives up a degree of control over both the process and outcomes. Student interpretations and perspectives may be richer than the teacher imagined and may take a different path than anticipated. Constructivist learning theory holds promise for broadening current definitions of learning to take into account the way knowledge is constructed and to consider the subtleties and nuances that emerge when students, working together, create meaning from what they know, value, and believe.

Based on these principles, a constructivist theory of learning is the antithesis of the factory model that has dominated in education. Learning is not uniform and cannot be specified in advance; it is not assembled like parts of a machine, but rather evolves in nonlinear ways from the experiences and attitudes of the learners.

Dewey and Constructivism

Each era or theme in education is built on preceding themes and is an outgrowth of social, political, and economic forces. Because each era is complex in its prevailing attitudes and growing understandings, notions of learning and leading from early in the century continue to influence current thought. Nowhere is this connection to the past more vivid than in the case for constructivism.

While John Dewey did not use the term *constructivism,* certainly his ideas contributed to the formulation of constructivist theories of learning and leading. Dewey (1916) first gave voice to this view of learning, noting that students must learn and make sense of new knowledge together, based on their individual and collective experiences. He perceived learning as a social endeavor, and his ideas about instruction can be found in current models of cooperative learning that emphasize the social construction of knowledge. He questioned the prevailing wisdom that education was preparation for life, holding instead that education should allow students to experience life, that authentic experience was essential to learning. He believed that the development of the self into a self-directing, inquiring, and reasoning human being was central to education. He invited us to understand that democracy is the chief purpose of education and that the structures of education should model this purpose. Even though he never used the term *constructivism,* Dewey's ideas regarding the centrality of student experience to the learning process have informed the evolution of the theory of constructivist learning.

Moreover, Dewey was eloquent in his plea for teachers to assume a decision-making role in regard to curriculum, instruction, and the assessment of student progress. He believed that teachers should have a determining role in the structure of school. His early notions of shared decision-making shaped evolving notions of schools as communities of learners and leaders and also contributed to the emerging theory of constructivist leadership. His visionary ideas, dating from the turn of the century, planted the seeds that, watered by other theorists and educators, created a soil favorable to the growth of constructivist theory.

Constructivist Approaches to Learning

If Dewey set the stage for the emergence of constructivist thought, we can credit Jean Piaget with expanding our understanding of learning in ways that support and contribute to constructivism. Piaget understood that knowledge is not a static body of information that is passed on to learners, but rather a process. He viewed this process as one of continual construction and reorganization of knowledge, with the learner taking responsibility for constructing and reorganizing (Piaget, 1971, in Brooks & Brooks, 1993; Piaget, 1985). According to Piaget, learners move through stages of cognitive development—from concrete to abstract—prompted by a discrepancy or "disequilibrium" between what they previously believed to be true and their new insights and experiences. As learners mature, they develop new cognitive structures, or schemas, that are more sophisticated, allowing them to make sense of increasingly more complex knowledge. Piaget saw the child as an "active scientist, constructing hypotheses about the world, reflecting upon experience, interacting with the physical environment and formulating increasingly complex structures of thought" (quoted in Bruner & Haste, 1987). During the 1980s and 1990s the work of Piaget has come under close scrutiny for his approaches to the study of the learner and his observations and assumptions about stages of development. He viewed, and therefore studied, the learner from a primarily individualistic perspective, rather than seeking opportunities to view learning in social or multiple contexts. His explanations of the stages of development are now viewed as too linear, sequential, and compartmentalized. These criticisms, however, do not detract from the powerful influence of Piaget's work on the public dialogue about the nature of knowing and learning.

De Vries and Kohlberg (1987, 1990) have pointed out that the first major paradigm shift in learning theory in this country began in the mid-1960s in the field of early childhood education, based on the work of Piaget. Piaget "fundamentally altered our views of the child and the nature of mental development. The central theme of this paradigm is the view of the child as active in constructing not only knowledge but intelligence itself" (1987, p. xi). Piaget's contribution to constructivist thought cannot be understated. His theory of learning, translated by others into new approaches to teaching and learning in the primary grades with very young children, gave rise to a reconsideration of how students create knowledge.

As is often the case with new or different conceptions of learning, a number of educators developed converging theories of learning. Like Dewey and Piaget, Bruner emphasized the learner as constructor of knowledge and the role of prior experience in enriching the learning experience. In addition, Bruner altered Piaget's stage theory, suggesting that simple maturation alone does not account for the development of new cognitive structures or schemas (cited in Brooks & Brooks, 1993). He determined that other factors, including the development and complexity of language in use and prior experiences, contribute to cognitive growth (Bruner, 1966). In *Making Sense,* Bruner reflected on "a quiet revolution" recently taking place in developmental psychology in which the child is once again seen "as a social being. . . . 'Making sense' is a social process; it is an activity that is always situated within a cultural and historical context" (Bruner & Haste, 1987, p. i).

Like Dewey, Piaget, and Bruner, Lev Vygotsky (1962, 1978) assumed a major role as a co-creator of constructivist thought. Earlier we noted the significant role played by the notion of the "zone of proximal development," the space or field among learners and teachers in which individuals negotiate meaning and create knowledge and intelligence. Further, he persuaded us that learning could not be viewed without context, as if independent of cultural or historical influences or significance. Learning is a cumulative experience derived and informed by an individual's and a group's cultural and historical experiences. Bruner, in introducing Vygotsky to educational thinkers in America, understood that this view of learning was vital to the understanding that knowledge and intelligence are socially constructed. Social interaction in the moment could not adequately explain the social processes of learning.

Following World War II, Reuven Feuerstein began to work in Israel with children who had been in concentration camps. In his assessment of these children, he detected major cognitive gaps undoubtedly arising from limited and distorted experiences. He developed a means through which he assessed, taught, and reassessed learning, noting significant changes in cognitive complexity. His teaching approaches involve mediation during learning by teachers and other students so that children can "self-modify" or self-construct themselves as learners. Today, Feuerstein (1990; Feuerstein et al., 1991) is considered one of the most insightful and influential constructivists of our time, the "modern day Piaget" (A. Costa, personal communication, 1994).

CONSTRUCTIVISM AND COGNITIVE PSYCHOLOGY

The work of Dewey, Piaget, Bruner, Vygotsky, and Feuerstein altered conceptions about learning and set the stage for the emergence of constructivist learning theory. For the authors of this book, the recent research by cognitive psychologists regarding how students learn has further clarified and supported constructivist learning theory. This research includes findings related to how students formulate and apply knowledge; the theory of multiple intelligences, which cause students to process knowledge in unique ways; and the learning approaches that allow students to create meaning and reflect on their own learning. While these findings are varied, they have in common an emphasis on the student's role in creating new knowledge, a role characterized by active engagement and personal sense-making.

Cognitive psychologists have thus continued to build on the work of Dewey, Piaget, Bruner, Vygotsky, and Feuerstein, expanding our concepts of learning as a social activity in which knowledge is constructed as a result of interaction and shared efforts to make sense of new information (Brooks & Brooks, 1993; Leinhardt, 1992; Resnick, 1984). Interactive concepts form a stark contrast to more traditional patterns of schooling in which individual learning is emphasized, competition is fostered, and student-to-student interaction is undervalued. Following the line of thinking that learning is socially constructed, teaching strategies such as cooperative learning have gained increasing credibility. These strategies allow students to share knowledge and experience, problem-solve together, and arrive at more complex solutions collectively than they could have individually. Cooperative learning assumes that student interaction results in a richer learning experience in which meaning is rooted.

A key finding from cognitive psychology is the importance of the process of learning. If the student is more than an empty vessel and in fact creates new knowledge, then processes for learning must be valued in the same way that content is valued and emphasized. Perkins' (quoted in Brandt, 1990) work on intelligence builds on the notion of personal schemas (cognitive structures, world views) and suggests that teachers need to find ways to identify some of the basic assumptions embedded in a learner's personal schemas so that they can make connections with those assumptions and beliefs. Teachers also need to assure that learners encounter dissonance or "disequilibrium" in order to help them reconstruct their schemas, accommodating what they currently believe to new and contradictory information. In this way they continue to develop as learners. Schema theory as developed by Perkins provides additional insights into the ways students learn, and it equips teachers with strategies, such as questioning and the sequencing of learning experiences, that assist learners in the process of constructing knowledge.

Earlier in this chapter, constructivist learning was defined in part by the ability to reflect on one's learning. Donald Schön's (1983) work makes a case for self-reflection as central to clarifying one's understandings and making meaning. Starting with adults and making application to learners of any age, Schön suggests that the key to growth and development, whether as a teacher or a student, is the ability to reflect on one's learning, to adapt behavior based on that reflection, and to develop a theoretical workframe, or set of understandings, that takes into account one's experiences. Because schools have traditionally functioned with external controls—teachers grade students, supervisors grade teachers—the idea of self-reflection appears to be at odds with prevailing practice. Yet studies of both teachers and learners have demonstrated that self-reflection is vital to learning and performance and leads to continued growth over time (Schön, 1983).

Further studies of intelligence challenge traditional approaches to learning and suggest why constructivism has captured the interest of many educators. Gardner's theory of multiple intelligences (H. Gardner, 1983, 1991, quoted in Siegel & Shaughnessy, 1994) has caused educators to rethink their most basic understandings about learning and about human capacity. He proposes that, in addition to so-called academic intelligences (logical–mathematical and linguistic), other kinds of intelligences exist that serve as a lens through which students perceive and interpret new experience. These intelligences include spatial, musical, kinesthetic, interpersonal and intrapersonal, as well as logical–mathematical and linguistic. This view of intelligence explains why students learn in different ways and why some students experience frustration when only a few intelligences are addressed by traditional curricula and instructional design. As teachers are becoming aware of the work in multiple intelligences and finding ways to redesign their approaches to instruction and assessment, all students can make better sense of new knowledge, create personal meaning, and learn at higher levels.

Further insights about learning suggest that students do not learn small, discrete skills in sequence and then at some point put these skills together to form large concepts and deep understandings. Instead, cognitive psychologists assert that a focus on discrete skills exaggerates differences in student ability and that many students are never able to fuse these skills into some kind of coherent whole (Oakes, 1985). Learning needs to be focused on large concepts, patterns and themes, with knowledge integrated across disciplines. Researchers now believe that learning is less sequential than previously thought (Resnick, 1984) and are designing what has been labeled the "thinking curriculum." Students are more often successful in working with large, important issues to which they can more naturally assign meaning. Fragmented curricula do not easily connect with a learner's schemas; Learners cannot find relationships and vital linking patterns among disparate bits of information that cannot be seen as readily coherent based on their own experiences. For example, national and local writing projects demonstrate that when students have frequent opportunities to generate and develop ideas, and to write about them, their writing improves. Writing errors are often associated with lack of conceptual control over a topic. As students gain clarity about their intents and ideas through the revising and editing processes, the quality and accuracy of their writing further improves. The traditional notion that writing is sequential and that students must master spelling, grammar, and syntax *before* they begin to write does not hold. Writing serves as a tool for thinking, helping students to organize, reorganize, and construct knowledge in the ways that Piaget, Bruner, and Feuerstein have described.

As the preceding discussion demonstrates, constructivism has evolved based on the contributions of educational theorists and practitioners as well as psychologists whose work influences what we know about teaching and learning. Dewey, Piaget, Bruner, and Vygotsky laid the foundation of important ideas that set the stage for the emergence of the principles of constructivist learning. Further work by cognitive psychologists, including theory related to the nature of intelligence, clarifies the importance of the learners' role in constructing knowledge, making meaning, and enhancing their own intelligence.

CONSTRUCTIVIST LEARNING AND ASSESSMENT

New directions in the assessment of student learning parallel growing understandings regarding constructivist learning theory. Traditional forms of assessment, such as standardized tests, reinforce the notion that knowledge exists outside the student and that the teacher's role is to transmit, and test, the rote acquisition of knowledge. Recent developments suggest that alternative measures of learning, which are rooted in students' authentic experience, evoke meaning-making. Chittenden and Gardner (1991) propose moving from a testing culture to an assessment culture, in which assessment practices are ongoing and cumulative while formats are open-ended and drawn from a variety of settings. Assessment, as envisioned by Chittenden and Gardner and others, both contributes to the theory of constructivist learning and is influenced by it. Their view incorporates assessment into the design of instruction and uses authentic measures to seek to understand what and how each student has learned. Even though individuals construct knowledge and meaning together, the interpretations derived from personal schemas mean that outcomes will be different—so assessment must be different. Perrone (1991) illuminates the paradigm shift implied in constructivist learning theory as it relates to student assessment:

> Trying to instill in students not just the mechanics of reading and writing, but also a love for reading and writing. It means providing them the opportunity to *practice* democracy, not just learn *about* democratic thought. It means encouraging them to *construct* knowledge, not just hear about it. It means making sure

they experience the power of cooperative and collaborative thought, not just the pressures of competition. (p. 164)

Perrone's ideas echo those of Dewey in the early years of this century, suggesting that new ideas about assessment have strong links to the past and to the beginnings of constructivism. They are also indicative of the paradigm shift taking place in education today, which holds that students construct new knowledge and that the meanings they negotiate individually and collectively should form the basis of assessments about their learnings. One form of assessment based on constructivism is student portfolios. The portfolios are compilations of student work samples over time that are selected by the students themselves. The emphasis on student performance events and portfolios as valid measures of student learning reflects constructivist principles, especially in relation to students assessing their own learning, incorporating their own beliefs and experiences, and reflecting on their learning. (A performance event is an assessment activity where individuals or groups of students are asked to demonstrate knowledge, for example by conducting a science experiment or solving a logic problem.) Application of authentic assessment to the work of leadership is occurring through the increasing use of such assessment practices, particularly portfolios, in teacher, administrator, and program evaluation.

MAKING CONNECTIONS TO CONSTRUCTIVIST THEORY

Powerful insights into cultural and sociohistorical differences in ways of perceiving the world have arisen through our understandings of metaphors, particularly iconic and root metaphors, as frames of meaning (Bowers & Flinders, 1990; Lakoff & Johnson, 1980; see Chapters 5, 9, and 10). Root metaphors, which are culturally constructed, create alternative schemas for such basic concepts as family, community, individualism, learning, and democracy. These metaphors arise from social interaction over time and thus represent a historical accumulation of meanings. Therefore, as Vygotsky claimed, we can interpret an individual's personal schemas as not just individual, but as the dynamic among personal, sociocultural, and historical experiences, beliefs, and perceptions.

As we reflect on some of the profound insights about constructivist learning described above, we begin to understand and envision a learner with fluid and multiple intelligences and potential for constructing and reconstructing personal schemas through reflection and interaction with others. Such learners build their interpretations of the world through engagement with their culture and peers, through engagement with big ideas, and by recognizing and forming new patterns. In the process, they self-construct themselves as learners.

Application of Constructivist Theory to Adults

How does constructivist theory apply to adults? Constructivist learning theory is not age- or stage-bound but refers to the processes of cognition for humans. Interestingly, even though the major works on adult learning appeared later than the inquiry into learning in children, we were more quick to accept constructivist notions for adults than for children. In 1970 Malcolm Knowles developed an analysis of pedagogical and adult learning (androgogical) assumptions in which he accepted behavioral learning assumptions for children and constructivist learning assumptions for adults! Why were we willing to accept adults as more self-directing individuals? We seemed to think of adults as more "complete," as beings who had solidified their personal schemas, moral and ego development, and world views.

Now we know that the notion of "completeness" is a myth for any living organism. All individuals have the potential to continually learn and grow. Adults, like children, bring their prior experiences, beliefs, and perceptions to their work with new experiences to construct knowledge and meaning.

Loevinger (1976) constructed stage theory in ego development as Kohlberg (1976), and later, Gilligan (1982), were constructing stage theory in moral development. Each of these bodies of work enabled us to understand factors that influenced the self and world views forming personal schemas. While these ideas provide us with information about the forces influencing the constructivist process, they give us no cause to believe that the processes of cognition themselves are different at different ages. Indeed, in 1957, Festinger's work with "cognitive dissonance" with adults was to parallel Piaget's findings regarding the role of dissonance in creating disequilibrium and the mind's search for consonance and equilibrium. Bateson (1972) related patterns to meaning-making, much as we now relate patterns and big ideas to learning. Kegan (1982) describing meaning-making as developmental in that it propels and influences us, children and adults alike.

TOWARD A THEORY OF CONSTRUCTIVIST LEADERSHIP

Throughout this chapter, we have advanced the notion that learning and leading have been mutually informing concepts, each deriving its assumptions from prevailing schools of thought that have emerged from our social, political, and economic histories and from multiple disciplines, such as psychology and sociology. For each of the eras—traditional, behavioral, grouping/tracking and contingency/situational, effectiveness and instructional leadership, community of learners and community of leaders—we have briefly described both the learning and leading implications. However, as we described constructivist learning theory and its implications for adults, we were *not yet able* to present a theoretical base for constructivist leadership. The next question now becomes: Can we generate a theory of Constructivist Leadership? Such a theory will need to address several criteria related to constructivist learning for adults. This theory of leadership needs to incorporate criteria that involve all adults in the learning and leading processes, create a culture in which reflective and interactive learning can take place, involve structures that allow for conversations from which meaning and knowledge can be constructed, and encourage professionals to seek collective meaning and collective purpose grounded in their practice.

SUMMARY

Throughout this century a number of theories related to learning and leadership have evolved. These theories reflect the social, political, and economic forces at work in the larger society. They also build on each other so that, as we formulate new ways of examining learning and leading, our knowledge is enriched by what has come before. This raises an obvious question: What will come after constructivism, and is this theory merely a fad?

Without the perspective of history, it is difficult to answer this question authoritatively. Constructivism does possess a richness of thought, a different world view, that offers a sense of possibility rather than limitation to human growth and development. An important test of its durability will be whether it can generate a theory of leadership that will bring lasting change to education as we know it. In the next chapter we advance a theory of constructivist leadership that builds on the community of leaders and constructivist concepts in this chapter and ushers in what we hold to be our next stage of educational history.

CHAPTER 2

Toward a Theory of Constructivist Leadership

Linda Lambert

The development of collective meaning is an essential characteristic of a learning organization.

Peter Senge
The Fifth Discipline (1990, p. 241)

During this century, concepts about learning and leading have been influenced by similar historical and philosophical ideas. Constructivism has
emerged as an important educational perspective that is changing how educational researchers, writers, and practitioners view the world of teaching
and learning. A constructivist perspective requires a reexamination of the
concept of leadership as well, since it is central to our argument that the
relationship between learning and leading philosophies is a dynamic one,
each view changing as it is influenced by the other. The constructivist learning perspective has given rise to expectations that constructivism is critical to
adult learning. This book examines the relationship between adult learning in
schools and the role and function of leadership.

All humans bring to the process of learning personal schemas that have
been formed by prior experiences, beliefs, values, sociocultural histories, and
perceptions. When new experiences are encountered and mediated by reflection and social interaction, meaning and knowledge are constructed. Learning takes place, as does adult development. When actively engaged in reflective dialogue, adults become more complex in their thinking about the world,
more tolerant of diverse perspectives, more flexible and open toward new
experiences. Personal and professional experiences require an interactive
professional culture if adults are to engage with one another in the processes
of growth and development.

Yet rarely are adults members of coherent, dynamic educational communities in which they develop "collective meaning together." Bound by
rules, schedules, policies, hierarchical roles, and time-worn practices, educators often experience cultures that limit interaction and mitigate against professional growth. They have few opportunities to engage in the reciprocal

processes that would call forth their ideas and successful experiences and enable them to make sense of their world together. Nor do they experience the supported encounters with discrepant information about teaching and learning that are essential for moving toward significant change. Hurried interactions of the sort that often characterize faculty room encounters and faculty meetings tend to draw on the sameness of teaching, reaffirming and reiterating similar educational practices. "Business as usual," the business of schooling, protects us from differences and therefore from challenges to our old ways of thinking while it "protects" us from growth.

Leadership that would change our schools and our communities must be cognizant of the essential actions needed to alter the lives of teachers in schools. It must address the need for sense-making, for coherence, for seeing educational communities as growth-producing entities. Leadership must be formed around the principles of constructivist learning for adults that capture these possibilities for learning. Leadership must be redefined.

This new conception of leadership is based on the same ideas that underlie constructivist learning: Adults learn through the processes of meaning and knowledge construction, participation, and reflection. The function of leadership must be to engage people in the processes that create the conditions for learning and form common ground about teaching and learning. Schooling must be organized and led in such a way that these learning processes provide direction and momentum to human and educational development. This chapter explores and seeks to interpret the influence that the constructivist perspective is having on our notions about leadership. We will refer to Constructivist Leadership as

> the reciprocal processes that enable participants in an educational community to construct meanings that lead toward a common purpose about schooling.

In this text, *leadership* is defined as a concept transcending individuals, roles, and behaviors. Therefore anyone in the educational community—teachers, administrators, parents, students—can engage in leadership actions. In the development of a theory of leadership, we combine and interpret assumptions regarding reciprocal processes, participation in educational communities, construction of meaning, and common purpose about schooling that lead us toward an explanation of Constructivist Leadership.

Constructivist Leadership can be distinguished from current notions of leadership that are influencing education and business in a number of ways, particularly in reference to who leads, the role of constructivist learning, and the need for community.

NOTIONS OF LEADERSHIP

Never before has society struggled with notions of leadership in such interesting and complex ways. Rost (1991), in his extensive historical review of leadership, argues that it is a concept that is rarely defined, a concept that often eludes those who work in the field. According to Hodgkinson (1991), there are over a hundred "serious" definitions of leadership.

Recent definitions of leadership that have influenced work in schools contain both the best promises for a new conception of leadership and the constraints and contradictions that limit their views. Among the numerous current writers influencing the practice of leadership in education and business are Peter Senge, Michael Fullan, Roland Barth, Phillip Schlechty, Steven Covey, Thomas Sergiovanni, Diane Dunlap, Harold Hodgkinson, John Gardner, Margaret Wheatley, William Foster, Joseph Rost, and Warren Bennis. Many of them are educators, yet a significant number, such as Senge, Gardner, Bennis, Covey, and Wheatley, have entered the field of leadership through business or organizational development.

Definitions of leadership have often been confused with definitions of *leader,* and the terms are often used interchangeably. "The problem with the organization is leadership," an analyst might claim when referring to a specific person, the "leader." Most writers in the field interchange the two notions, viewing leadership as the work of the leader.

There are persistent patterns of process that characterize what leaders do or leadership is. Whether a writer is describing leadership or leader, definitions inevitably fall into three categories: (1) what the leader does, (2) for or with whom the action is taken, and (3) toward what end the actions are taken. A few illustrative definitions from the work of these authors will clarify this three-dimensional analysis:

> Peter Senge (1990): *Leaders* design learning processes whereby people throughout the organization deal productively with issues and learn the disciplines. (Michael Fullan [1993] uses a definition that is similar to Senge's.)
>
> Phillip Schlechty (1990): *Leaders* invite others to share authority. Others are those who accept the invitation and share responsibility.
>
> Stephen Covey (1991): *Leaders* foster mutual respect and build a complementary team in which strengths are made productive and weaknesses become essentially irrelevant.
>
> Roland Barth (1992): *Leaders* make happen that in which you believe while working with all in a community of leaders.
>
> William Foster (1989): *Leadership* is the reciprocal processes among leaders and followers working toward a common purpose.

John Gardner (1990): *Leadership* is the process of persuasion or example by which an individual (or leadership team) induces a group (followers) to pursue objectives held by the leader or shared with his or her followers. (In 1991, Sergiovanni's definition was essentially the same as Gardner's.)

Joseph Rost (1991): *Leadership* is an influence relationship among leaders and followers who intend real changes that reflect their mutual purposes.

Margaret Wheatley (1992): *Leadership* is context-dependent and relational among leaders and followers, with an emphasis on the concepts of community, dignity, meaning, and love.

In most of these conceptions, the processes of either the "leader" or of "leadership" are summed up by a single verb: *design, foster, invite, persuade, influence.* Leaders typically do things to or for others—for instance, "design learning processes" (Senge and Fullan), "invite others to share authority" (Schlechty), "foster mutual respect" (Covey), or engage in "an influence relationship" (Rost) or a "process of persuasion" (Gardner and Sergiovanni). The strong implication is that someone is designing for or acting on another or others. This action is directional and hierarchical, the process being applied to a group of followers who may work as individuals or as members of a team. A sharp distinction from this traditional view may be seen as Foster's (1989) characterization of leadership as "the reciprocal processes," although he does not explain the meaning of these processes.

Those "others" who are the subject of the action are most often referred to as "followers." For instance, the "for or with whom the action is taken" portion of current definitions usually refers to relationships among leaders and followers or individuals who choose to be recruited. Barth, Rost, Foster, and Wheatley present patterns that are communal and relational, suggesting that reciprocity might be possible—for instance, "all in a community of leaders" (Barth), "a complementary team" (Covey), "among leaders and followers who intend real changes" (Rost), "relational among leaders and followers" (Wheatley). However, Foster, Gardner, Sergiovanni, Rost, and Wheatley proceed to use the language of followership, a constraining concept that imposes a mind-set of inequitable participantship. The follower, as a root metaphor, conjures up images of walking behind, being alert to the cues of the "real" leader, waiting one's turn. Even those who seek to bring enlightenment to the dim concept of followership assume that a conscious shift in power and self-perception would be necessary in order to move from the role of follower into the role of leader.

The third element of leadership definitions—"toward what end the action is taken"—generally refers to the product or outcome of the influence or power relationship. Senge, Fullan, Covey, and Schlechty suggest that the quality of the working relationship might be an "end" in itself, and their writings are rich with additional values and purposes for learning organizations. One can infer from their works that they understand and trust that, when a learning organization (an organization that is continually renewing itself) is built, people will be increasingly able to commit themselves to a larger purpose. Foster looks "toward a common purpose," while Schlechty anticipates "shared responsibility" and Wheatley identifies "community, dignity, meaning, and love" as laudable outcomes. These "ends" represent the outcomes to be achieved or produced by the followers working together. Most of these definitions are behavioral in character: The leader designs a process, which acts on the followers in order to produce a certain outcome.

Rost (1991), in an extensive analysis of influential writers from 1900 through 1990, found a consistent picture of the conceptions of leadership:

> Leadership is good management. . . . Leadership is great men and women with certain preferred traits influencing followers to do what the leaders wish in order to achieve group/organizational goals that reflect excellence defined as some kind of higher-level effectiveness. (p. 180)

Rost refers to this composite definition as the "industrial leadership paradigm," which is hierarchical, individualistic, reductionistic, linear, mechanical—ideas which are worlds away from the ideas in this book and the needs of today's schools and society.

TOWARD A NEW CONCEPTION OF LEADERSHIP

Above we examined three dimensions of the definition of *leader* or *leadership*. The definition of Constructivist Leadership that we are proposing is initially most closely aligned to "the reciprocal processes" proposed by Foster. The major distinction that can be made from current definitions of leadership lies in the "for or with whom the action is taken" dimension: "participants in a educational community to construct meanings." This distinction is at the heart of the constructivist nature of leadership: that adults in a community can work together to construct meaning and knowledge. The balance of this chapter examines each dimension of this definition in turn:

> The reciprocal processes that enable . . .
> participants in an educational community to construct meanings . . .
> that lead toward a common purpose of schooling

Since leadership is viewed as essentially the enabling reciprocal processes among people, leadership becomes manifest within the relationships in a community, manifest in the spaces, the fields among participants, rather than in a set of behaviors performed by an individual leader. The school culture, the field in which we work, is permeated with opportunities for exercising leadership of this character. This culture, or field, among us is imbued with our histories, energies, emotions and thoughts, conflicts and affections. Greene (1988) finds in these spaces among us the possibilities for creating an authentic presence with each other . . . being real and vulnerable with each other in ways that engage us in genuine conversations. Hannah Arendt, Greene reminds us, called these spaces the "in-between" (quoted in Greene, 1988, p. 17). Vygotsky (1962) understood well the value of those fields, the in-between, as present in the "zone of proximal development" through which participants negotiate their own meanings, knowledge, and intelligence, influenced by social, cultural, and historical forces. He envisioned these spaces between and among people as being the central arena through which individuals in interaction make sense of what they think and believe and create new ideas and information. This is not unlike Kegan's (1982) "zone of mediation" for meaning-making, through which individuals labor toward new understandings. To this extent, leadership provides us with a "third dimension"— a set of untapped opportunities that exist within the culture of the school. There are the individual minds of educators in the school community, the minds of others in that community, and the richness of ideas and questions as yet unexplored or unasked that exist among us.

The authors of this text propose that leadership inhabits these spaces, fields, or zones among educators in a professional community. Leadership, like energy, is not finite, not restricted by formal authority and power; it permeates a healthy school culture and is undertaken by whoever sees a need or an opportunity. Occupying these "zones," leadership is different from an act of leadership, for it can be omnipresent among and within all participants. Leadership possibilities permeate our interactions and inform our actions. A new teacher is having trouble? An experienced teacher might intervene, provide assistance, secure other resources and ideas, mentor. In a culture rich in leadership connections, this experienced teacher does not have to be recruited; he or she is a fully functioning professional leader. Barth (1988) seems to have this notion in mind when he talks about a "community of leaders." Lieberman (1985, 1988, 1992, 1994), in her extensive and continual discussions of the relationships in collaborative work, understands the criticalness of human interaction and the emergence of professionalism.

The Reciprocal Processes That Enable . . .

Constructivist leadership involves *the reciprocal processes that enable* participants in an educational community to construct meanings that lead toward a common purpose of schooling. It is important to understand that the capacity for reciprocity is the result of long years of meaning-making with others (Kegan, 1982). To be able to move outside oneself, to differentiate one's perceptions from those of another, to practice empathy, to move out of the self and observe the responses and thoughts of another—all are prerequisites to reciprocity. Reciprocity, or the mutual and dynamic interaction and exchange of ideas and concerns, requires a maturity that emerges from opportunities for meaning-making in sustainable communities over time. As adults, we need to be able to engage in processes of meaning-making as we live and work together in educational communities if capacities for reciprocity are to be developed. "Knowledge is not *extended* from those who consider that they know to those who consider that they do not know," pointed out Paulo Freire in 1973; "knowledge is built up in the relations between human beings" (p. 109, emphasis added).

Judith Warren Little (1982) saw multiple forms of relationships in schools more than a decade ago. She identified differences among congenial and collegial and thoroughly individualistic relationships, findings that have recently been echoed by Michael Fullan in his work with Toronto schools. These relationships shift as the collegial nature of the professional culture alters over time. Reciprocity tends to be a spiraling experience, gathering strength as it is practiced. Wheatley (1992) attributes further meaning to relationships when she explains that individuals generate information in their interactions with each other, information that becomes a feedback spiral enriching and creating additional information.

The reciprocal processes that enable us to construct meaning occur within the context of relationships. The creation and expansion of our possibilities and capacities for reciprocity occur in communities rich in relationships. We need to stop thinking of roles or people as fixed entities and instead view them as relationships, as patterns of relationships that involve one another: "Patterns do not 'contain' one another, but rather 'involve' one another" (Wheatley, 1992, p. 71). "Patterns that involve" is reminiscent of Bateson's "patterns which connect" (1972), which encompasses both the relationship and the pattern of meaning. These consistent, repetitive forms reveal patterns of relationships that evolve and deepen over time.

A pattern of relationship can reveal itself in governance structures in schools. Many schools and districts have separated and fragmented governance processes, such as a leadership team, school site council, curriculum committee, PTA, professional development committee, and so forth; these tend to operate in isolation, neither involving nor connecting with one another. As a result, decision-making is time-consuming and parallel, redundant and perfunctory, disengaged from the information and feedback systems that could bring a grounding in values. The fragmented processes deny coherence of practice and the building of the school communities. These governance groups can be coordinated so that they become connected by information, products, and people. Integrated structures are essential to connecting relationships. When people are connected together, the opportunities for conversations and meaning-making become self-evident.

A recent study by the Claremont Graduate Schools' Institute for Education in Transformation (Poplin & Weeres, 1993) was published under the title *Voices from the Inside*. Three qualities make this study report profound: (1) Both lead and associate researchers were teachers; (2) it was conducted as a series of dialogues; and (3) it discovered that the most important factor in schools is *relationships*. Speaking eloquently about their work, the researchers write:

> For it is in the coming to know that we came to want to act. It is in the listening that we changed. It is in the hearing our own students speak, as if for the first time, that we came to believe. This is what we heard. . . . Relationships dominated all participant discussions about issues of schooling. No group inside the schools felt adequately respected, connected, or affirmed. (p. 19)

All participants in the Claremont study—students, parents, teachers, administrators, classified staff—felt a deep absence of authentic relationships in which they were trusted, given responsibility, spoken to honestly and warmly, and treated with dignity and respect. In reference to this last statement, it is important to note that perceptions of caring varied among groups. For teachers, dedication to their work indicated caring; for students, caring on the part of teachers was shown more directly and personally—touching, using their names, being asked about or told personal things, laughing with them. A middle school teacher observed: "Our data is contrary to the way most of us traditionally have thought about schooling in which curriculum is at the center of the model and measures of school productivity are there. And here we're saying we have to put relationships at the core of what we're doing." (p. 20) *Would teachers have questioned that myth if they had not discovered it themselves?* Not likely.

Teachers and administrators in *Voices* further realized that their relationships were dominated by rules, regulations, and contractual agreements. Administrators admitted that changes are often unsuccessful because preliminary dialogue is rushed. Those who survive in spite of arid, impersonal environments devoid of meaningful relationships often go elsewhere for what they need, as explained by one middle school student:

> If I talk to my parents sometimes they get mad at me because of what I say to them. Or maybe they're too busy. If I talk to teachers I can't tell them that I said a bad word or something because they suspend me. So I guess the only people

that understand are gangsters. They always understand and they always help me solve it too. (p. 13)

Reciprocal relationships, the meanings of which must be discussed and commonly construed in schools, are the basis through which we make sense of our world, continually define ourselves, and "coevolve," or grow together. With relationships, we give up predictability for potentials. Potentials are those abilities within us that can develop or become actual, those personal passions and personal schemas that enable us to construct meaning and knowledge. They exist in possibilities; they are unpredictable, yet limitless; they are built on relationships and connecting patterns; they are dynamic and paradoxical; and they are continuously renewing themselves. We must evoke or provoke potential (Wheatley, 1992)—it does not appear on command (or through "persuasion, recruitment, or enlistment").

While the chapters ahead provide a more detailed look at reciprocal processes along with practical examples, it is essential here to portray what is meant by these processes. These portrayals are examples and will undoubtedly give rise to thoughts of other processes as the reader ponders them. *Reciprocal processes* are understood as those that:

- Evoke potential in a trusting environment
- Reconstruct, or "break set," with old assumptions and myths
- Focus on the construction of meaning
- Frame actions that embody new behaviors and purposeful intentions

Those processes that *evoke potential in a trusting environment* are those that enable individuals to call forth memories, perceptions, and assumptions that underlie and inform their work. These recollections may be elicited in the form of stories, discussions, brainstorming, writing, or even reenactment. These evoked ideas create an essential foundation for constructing meaning and knowledge together, for making our schemas explicit and public enables us to understand how we and others are making sense of the world.

Those processes that *reconstruct, or break set, with old assumptions and myths* necessitate a reexamination of accepted ideas and traditional interpretations. (To "break set" is to loosen one's attachment, adherence, and dependency on the assumptions that formed current schemas in order to consider or entertain new assumptions. Confronting and processing new information or experiences that are different from those that formed the original schemas can cause an individual to "break set," or disconnect from, old assumptions. This process can lead to the formation of new schemas and to changed perceptions and behaviors.) This aspect of the conversation involves gathering new data, posing questions that cause dissonance and disequilibrium between the held beliefs and new information, and reconceptualizing or re-designing the ideas in question. This "redesign" function may involve specu-lation, reframing, visioning, or imagining possibilities. As assumptions are reexamined, we can begin to make sense of new information and ideas.

Those processes that include the *focus on the construction of meaning* involve many of the same evocation processes described above (discussion, stories, writing) and entail combining or recombining these ideas so that they make sense to those involved. "Making sense" (constructing meaning) also requires the creation of new symbols or images (examples, metaphors, pat-terns) that form the basis for construal and interpretation. As adults share common experiences and common inquiry, assigned meanings converge, be-coming more common than uncommon. Teachers begin to agree on—or at least to understand—the interpretations that they are making about teaching and learning.

Those processes that *frame actions that embody new behaviors and pur-poseful intentions* involve the most practical aspect of the reciprocal pro-cesses. These undertakings may include establishing new criteria, planning approaches, identifying emerging goals and objectives, implementing new ac-tions, evaluating progress, and redesigning or reframing the actions in re-sponse to the effectiveness and additional information generated by the pro-cess. These are the specific actions that emerge from the conversations.

These are spiraling processes, involving and building on each other and circling back upon themselves. New actions become the means through which other potentials are evoked, new information is generated, and deeper meanings are constructed.

The following scenario from a school we will call Evergreen Middle School describes how these processes may join together: As a staff that has deliberately planned to build a more collaborative working culture, they meet together for a professional development day. Two teachers are facilitating the work of the day, aimed at "designing working agreements for ourselves." The leadership team and the professional development committee have planned this day together.

> *First activity:* In small groups, staff are asked to recall their best memory of a working group in which they felt energized by the pro-cesses and exceeded their goals. They share experiences. (*Evoking poten-tial in a trusting environment*)
> *Second activity:* They discuss as a whole group: What made these experiences so powerful? Could we re-create these experiences here? How would our experiences here need to change in order to re-create our work together? (*Reconstruct, or "break set," with old assumptions and myths*)

Third activity: They discuss in groups: What would these experiences look like if we were to create them here? What were the qualities or characteristics of these experiences that we would want to re-create here? Why? (*Focus on the construction of meaning*)

Fourth activity: The last activity asks: Based on our conversations this morning, what work agreements shall we establish? Small groups generate four to six ideas. All groups post work; whole group forms consensus. (*Frame actions that embody new behaviors and purposeful intentions*)

The above example combines four phases of reciprocal processes involved in constructivism so that a staff can create together the parameters for their future work.

These processes involve rethinking our structures as well: "We must invent organizations where process is allowed its varied-tempo dance, where structures come and go as they support the process that needs to occur and where form arises to support the necessary relationships" (Wheatley, 1992, p. 68). These forms that support relationships are nodes of connections, channels of energy flow. We will call them "enabling structures." For instance, these places or intersections where people and energy converge might include groups, such as leadership teams, study or action research teams; places, such as a professional library, faculty research and development center, even open supply closets or "user-friendly" faculty rooms; and events, such as workshops, district dialogue sessions, or parent conversations.

The essential criterion for enabling structures involves an element of high synergy, which Carlsen (1988) explains as the positive reaction and interaction that occur when people do things for themselves and at the same time do things for others (reciprocity). Carlsen recalls Buckminster Fuller's 1978 work, *Operating Manual for Spaceship Earth,* in which he explains, "Synergy is the only word in our language that means the behavior of whole systems unpredicted by the separately observed behaviors of any of the system's separate parts or any subassembly of the system's parts" (quoted in Carlsen, 1988, p. 71). Larger than the sum of the parts, synergy in schools is the interaction dynamic arising from opportunities for joint conversation, work, and action. It is the by-product of true collegiality. We provide additional examples of school and district collegial structures in later chapters.

Participants in an Educational Community to Construct Meanings . . .

In Chapter 1, we discussed the process of *meaning-making* as constructivism; above we discussed leadership as the "reciprocal processes that enable . . ." participants in an educational community to construct meanings. By participants we mean *all* members of the educational community, not segregated as leaders and followers. At any given time, roles and behaviors will shift among participants based on interest, expertise, experience, and responsibility. In more advanced school cultures, as in good marriages, roles are integrated or transcended.

Together we create and engage in experiences that we imbue with meaning, meanings informed by common experiences and also by our own personal schemas. The above example of the Evergreen staff working through a process for creating common work agreements is illustrative of these undertakings in schools. In Chapter 1, we discussed Kegan's concept of meaning-making as motion; this understanding is critical to the role of constructivism within the context of community. This motion, born of negotiating experiences together, gives force and purposeful direction to community. The Evergreen staff will never be quite the same; meaning-making together changes us and creates momentum (motion and direction) for our work together.

Bateson's (1972) concept of meaning as a synonym for "pattern" adds another rich dimension to our communal work: meaning-making for common patterns of understandings. When the Evergreen staff members have practiced their new agreements for a few months, the pattern of their understandings will deepen and further interpretations of their work will evolve from these new and common patterns, or practices. They will be "pulled into the future" (Land & Jarman, 1992) by this shared intention. Land and Jarman use this notion to mean that the realization of our hopes and goals becomes increasingly inevitable as we share intentions and work together in ways that exemplify these intentions. There has been set in motion a patterning process that gives rhythm and purpose, force and direction, to the educational community.

Experiences with educational communities that have evolved from sustained collaborative work have created an understanding of communities as the primary context for professional growth. "The constraints of constructed knowledge," point out Bransford, Goldman, and Pellegrino (1992, p. 116), "come largely from the community of which one is a member. In the absence of any community, we suppose that it would be possible for an individual to have an idiosyncratic view of the world—but then, because there is no community, the idiosyncrasy is irrelevant." In a community, views are brought into harmony or we agree to disagree—either way, we consider the other.

Since constructivist learning is a social endeavor, community is essential for learning to occur. In our definition of constructivist leadership, the educational community is considered the medium for meaning-making, for human growth and development. In this chapter community is defined in terms of its natural ecological qualities and its relationship to constructivist leadership.

Fritjof Capra, author of *The Tao of Physics* (1975) and *The Turning Point* (1982), has recently turned his attention to education through his work with the (now) Center for Ecoliteracy in Berkeley, California. The Center has two major goals: to expand ecoliteracy as part of school curricula and to apply the principles of ecology to our work with whole-school cultural change. By "ecoliteracy," Center staff mean literacy in environmental principles and practices; by "ecology" they mean the guiding principles informing the development of all organisms and systems (see Figure 2.1). Capra has become interested in translating the concepts of ecology into social systems, in the tradition of Gregory Bateson in psychology and anthropology; Bruce Joyce, Elliott Eisner, John Goodlad, and C. A. Bowers in education; Robert Kegan in psychology; Robert Bellah in philosophy and political science; and, more recently, Theodore Roszak in political and environmental philosophy. In Figure 2.1, the principles of ecology are described by Capra (1993), and each statement is followed with my social interpretation that relates to communities that serve as settings for meaning-making and human development.

In order to create educational communities that function as ecological social systems, members of these communities work in *interdependence* with one another. They rely on and trust one another to provide the support and skills needed by the whole group. In order to evolve as educational communities, they must be *sustained* over time, since it takes time to deepen the spiral of meaning-making, seek common purpose, and develop interdependent professional cultures in schools. *Ecological cycles* require a fluid flow of information and feedback, spiraling processes that are essential to engagement with the disequilibrium that causes us to break set with old assumptions and construct meaning.

The biological systems described in Figure 2.1 are propelled by the *energy flow* of the sun. The energy driving the social systems is meaning-making, which we have described as developmental, as motion. These energy sources keep communities in motion. To understand meaning-making as the primary energy source of a community is critical to the understanding of constructivist leadership, which relies on communities in motion.

Partnerships with parents and the broader community are essential if information and learning opportunities are to enter and leave the culture of the school. *Flexibility* is basic to communities in motion if fluctuations, feedback, and surprises are to lead to change rather than disorientation in schools.

Diversity brings a complexity to the network of relationships that contains multiple perspectives and multiple resources and talents. Static, homogeneous relationships cannot challenge the thinking of its members, since

Figure 2.1. Principles of Ecology

BIOLOGICAL	SOCIAL

Interdependence

All members of an ecosystem are interconnected in a web of relationships in which all life processes depend on one another. The success of the whole system depends on the success of its individual members, while the success of each member depends on the success of the system as a whole.

All members of a community are interconnected in a web of relationships in which all processes are *reciprocal.* The success of the community depends on the success of its individual members, and the success of each member depends on the success of the community as a whole.

Sustainability

The long-term survival (sustainability) of each species in an ecosystem depends on a limited resource base.

The long-term survival of a community depends on a limited material resource base, shared talents and ideas, and sustained purpose.

Ecological Cycles

The interdependencies among the members of an ecosystem involve the exchange of matter and energy in continual cycles. These ecological cycles act as feedback loops.

The interdependencies among the members of a community involve the exchange of energy and information in continual cycles. These ecological cycles act as feedback spirals (spirals, because they never return to the same place [Costa and Kallick, 1995])

Energy Flow

Solar energy, transformed into chemical energy by the photosynthesis of green plants, drives all ecological cycles.

Human energy, experiences, and beliefs, transformed into *meaning and knowledge,* drive purposeful communities.

Partnership

All living members of an ecosystem are engaged in a subtle interplay of competition and cooperation, involving countless forms of partnership.

All members of a community are engaged in a reciprocal interplay of competition and cooperation, involving countless forms of partnership.

Flexibility

In their function as feedback loops, ecological cycles have the tendency to maintain themselves in a flexible state, characterized by interdependent fluctua- tions of their variables.

In their function as feedback spirals, ecological cycles in communities have the tendency to maintain themselves in a flexible state, characterized by interdependent fluctuations of their variables. Flexible communities give open rein to fluctuations and surprises, from which they derive innovations and change.

Figure 2.1. (*continued*)

BIOLOGICAL	SOCIAL
Diversity	
The stability of an ecosystem depends crucially on the degree of complexity of its network of relationships; in other words, on the diversity of the ecosystem.	The stability of an community depends crucially on the degree of complexity of its network of relationships; in other words, on the diversity of the ecosystem.
Coevolution	
Most species in an ecosystem coevolve through an interplay of creation and mutual adaptation. The creative reaching out into novelty is a fundamental property of life, manifest also in the processes of development and learning.	Most members of a community coevolve through an interplay of creation and mutual adaptation. The creative reaching out into novelty is a fundamental property of life, manifest also in the processes of development and learning.

individual and group thinking will stem from experiences and biases that are too similar. Diversity introduces the opportunity for participants to think and act in more complex ways. Such cognitive complexity involves the ability to understand and work with multiple perspectives; the capacity to think systemically; and the ability to access, generate, and process vast sources of information. Diversity in the learning environment improves our possibilities for developing such complexity and therefore the possibilities for variance and dissonance.

Coevolution refers to the idea that as we work together in collaborative professional cultures, we grow together. This book focuses on the multiple means of learning in a professional culture, including shared leadership, conversations, common language, and the use of narrative. Bransford and colleagues (1992) describe knowledge as "a dialect process": "By continually negotiating the meaning of observations, data, hypotheses, and so forth, groups of individuals construct systems that are largely consistent with one another" (p. 116). This dialectic is an essential aspect of coevolution.

A composite narrative of a social ecological community might be interpreted in this way:

> A community is an interconnected and complex web of reciprocal relationships sustained and informed by their purposeful actions. Complexity is manifest in the diversity of the system; and the more diverse, the more rich and complex. Such communities are flexible and open to information provided through feedback spirals, as well as unexpected fluctuations and surprises that contain possibilities. The coevolution, or shared growth, of the participants in this community is propelled by

the joint construction of meaning and knowledge and involves continual creation and adaptation.

To borrow generously from Carl Rogers' (1959) concept of the "actualizing tendency" in individuals, these ecosystems are "actualizing communities," in the process of becoming more coherent and more growth-producing for both individuals and social groupings. In the process, these communities are responding to the dual nature of human beings to be both independent and interdependent, self-directed and interconnected. However, Bellah, Madsen, Sullivan, Sidler, and Tipton (1985) would remind us that to focus too deeply on the nature and needs of human beings may lead us to narrowly therapeutic interpretations of community, designing communities that are aimed primarily at meeting the needs of the individual. Rather, we must seek communities that serve the needs of the broader society as well as the needs of the individual. Educational communities of this character concurrently attend to the professional development needs of the individual, to the professional culture of the group, and to the outcomes of the students. Bakan (1966) refers to this challenge to bring together the dual natures of humans as a moral imperative: to try to mitigate agency with communion. Costa and Garmston (1994) use the enticing word *holonomy* to refer to achieving the dual goals of independence and interdependence. "Some," comments Della Dora (personal communication), "call this 'democracy.'"

Such educational communities have coherence, a wholeness and an integration that characterize sense-making. Carlsen (1988) and Zohar (1990) agree on the centrality of coherence. For Carlsen, synergy and systems theory are the most appropriate conceptions within which to understand that a belief system serves as the lens through which we construct coherence and meaning. For Zohar, a world view is that organizing theme running through a life that gives it meaning and coherence. "If, at this personal level," claims Zohar, "one fails to sense some coherent world view, then life itself fragments. . . . If, at a social level, one fails to sense some coherent world view, the sense of self and others breaks down" (p. 232). Belief systems, world views, and personal schemas that are coherent require continually constructed meaning within the context of shared and created experiences. For many children and adults in our schools, both the sense of self and the sense of others have broken down. According to the children's voices in *Voices from the Inside* (Poplin & Weeres, 1993), coherence seems unlikely without caring, sustaining relationships.

Some schools are now reaching for these communities through which they can address society's most compelling dilemmas. Two major changes herald a new view of schools as meaning-making communities, both involving the creation of common experiences that lead to "zones of mediation" for the construction of meaning. A common experience creates the opportunity for shared meaning-making as children and adults (or children with children or adults with adults) join together at the same time and place to discover what they know and think. They can talk about and mediate their histories within a common experience so that the journey occurs together. These two most promising of practices are the building of a collegial, professional culture for educators and the work in authentic assessment for children (and, increasingly, for adults as well). The collegial culture involves common agreements, study, planning, and inquiry; authentic assessment creates real opportunities for performance and product development. In order to meet the criteria for development that we are proposing in this chapter, authentic assessment must involve the children in establishing their own criteria for choice, interpreting their own progress, reflecting on their own thinking processes and talents. These are prerequisite behaviors for participation and leadership, as well as for cognitive complexity. Both authentic assessment and professional culture are shared, authentic, thoughtfully chosen, and mutually designed. These experiences help to create educational communities and are encouraged and enhanced by learning in a context of community.

In spite of the promise of educational communities that are based on ecological principles, communities can become fragmented and incoherent without leadership. Leadership is the factor that enables meaning to be constructed together in that it engages people in the essential reciprocal processes. Without value-driven, purposeful leadership, communities can become Balkanized, or focused on the self-serving purposes of an individual or a few individuals. Studies of cult communities such as Synanon (Lambert, 1982) recognize that even though many of the aspects of community may exist (interdependencies, purpose, feedback loops, support, and security), individual and societal growth can be dramatically restricted, then reversed. If flexibility and diversity are disallowed by acts of leadership by an individual who focuses on control and conformity, the rewards of community can become counterproductive. Hodgkinson (1991) similarly reminds us that organizations can be equally value-neutral, that the structures of organizations do not naturally support ethical behaviors. Organization and community can be amoral concepts.

Cult-type communities may articulate a purpose, usually the designated leader's purpose; however, this would not produce a moral community. What is it that creates a common purpose of schooling to which people freely commit?

That Lead Toward a Common Purpose of Schooling

Before the middle of this millenium, the Gutenberg printing press found itself esconced in a warehouse in Victor Hugo's Paris. In one particularly powerful scene in *Notre-Dame de Paris* (1831/1978), a church archdeacon, on learning the purpose of the cumbersome machine, observed in outrage: "Alas and alack, small things overcome great ones! A tooth triumphs over a body. The Nile rat kills the crocodile, . . . the book will kill the building!" Hugo goes on to explain: "It was the terror and bewilderment felt by a man of the sanctuary before the luminous press of Gutenberg. . . . It was the cry of the prophet who already hears the restless surge of an emancipated mankind, who can see that future time when intelligence will undermine faith, opinion dethrone belief, and the world shake off Rome" (pp. 188–189). His prediction proved remarkably keen, for a fundamental shift in access to knowledge gave rise to the Protestant Reformation and the Enlightenment.

For most of the last three centuries, the schools have been the center of knowledge for the "common man." Today, American schools have not only lost their monopoly on knowledge—even their corner on knowledge has shrunk.

Several educational figures had been paddling swiftly against the tide. In 1979, Goodlad published a small work entitled, *What Are Schools For?*, in which he set forth the knowledge and competencies that schools should teach. Hirsch (1988) claimed the centrality of a common knowledge base (albeit European), and Adler laid out his *Paideia Program* (1984) for "essential" knowledge. These statements and arguments for a common knowledge base gave additional credence to the role of the schools as knowledge dispensers—purveyors of the canon—at a time when this ancient role is necessarily under scrutiny. Goodlad, Hirsch, and Adler are persuasive figures in American education and therefore have been significant forces in interpreting the purposes of schooling. While Hirsch was questioned on the accuracy of the chosen content in his proposed cultural literacy, few questioned the assumption that such content should serve as the foundation of schooling.

Children today can see the world and its people on television's National Geographic series, experience news as it is made, observe re-creations of history, have access to the Library of Congress, and observe and fall victim to the conflict and violence on America's streets. In schools, we can teach children how to access, process, and challenge knowledge (roles we are still struggling with), but we are no longer the major knowledge provider.

We agree with our colleagues from Dewey (1916) to Glickman (1993) that our major purpose in schools remains the preparation of children for democratic citizenship. However, our track record here is as wanting as our role in the knowledge business. It is not surprising that when we do not offer democratic learning opportunities for children and adults, as we generally do not, we cannot expect democratic actions. However, in those rare schools and institutions in which we seek to teach democracy through experience, we tend to seek our goals through individual involvement in decision-making. Focusing on such summative actions as the polling booth and the moment of decision-making does not engage the prerequisite lived experiences essential for democratic life. As Bellah and colleagues (1985) remind us so vividly, individuals remain individuals in this country; they have vague understandings of community but virtually no conception of interconnected, pluralistic communities or social vision. Rost (1991) resurfaces this insight as central to the demands of rethinking leadership. On the topic of leadership and civic virtue, he frames some essential aspects of the dilemma:

> Leaders and followers need to develop a new language of civic virtue to discuss and make moral evaluations of the changes they intend for organizations and societies. This new language of ethics must center on an integrated concept of the common good, of our social ecology as a community. (p. 177)

"An integrated concept of the common good" or common purpose can only be found in interconnected, ecological communities. We propose that *the purpose of schooling today* is to engage children and adults within patterns of relationships in school communities that serve as centers for sustained growth. Experiences in ecological communities can produce a common purpose for schooling, encompassing aims that extend beyond self-interest to the growth and well-being of children, their families, and society. Moral educational communities come into existence as people learn to grow together. The purposes referenced in our definition of constructivist leadership involve a commitment to the growth of children and adults as well as a commitment to communities and societies that sustain such growth.

If participants are constructing their own meanings and knowledge, how can we be assured that the common purpose of schooling will entail such a moral commitment? This confidence arises from a faith in ecological communities as enabling their participants to coevolve morally. As this coevolution takes place, caring, equity, and justice seem to surface as guiding values (Gilligan, 1982; Kohlberg, 1976). Poplin (1994) claims that in the work *Voices* the process created shared meanings that led to larger moral purpose—"teachers reconnected with their reasons for going into teaching."

Participation in ecological communities softens and makes fluid and permeable the lines between "self" and "other." Since the development of the self is interdependent with the evolution of the other, Zohar and Marshall argue (1994): "The mechanistic perception of the 'other' as threat gives way to a perception of the other as one who evokes my own latent possibilities. . . . *The . . . other is my necessity*" (p. 193; emphasis added). When individuals and others share a common experience of growth in an educational community, they experience an increased responsibility for others. We become committed to "a cause beyond oneself" (Glickman, 1993, p. 15).

Within the context of these lived experiences, diversity opens up possibilities, helping us to see the multiple perspectives and world views of others.

This revised purpose of schooling demands a rethinking of all aspects of our educational institutions, a commitment to a new set of goals. Knowledge now serves as "grist for the mill" for both students and adults, a basis for framing big questions, for conversations, and for learning the thinking and collaborative skills essential to a democracy. Purpose, like vision, emerges from the conversations. Educators, in turn, can become "constrained by purpose" (Wheatley, 1992, p. 115) rather than by institutionally defined boundaries. This sense of renewed purpose can be made possible through the processes of constructivist leadership.

ACTS OF LEADERSHIP

An "act of leadership," as distinguished from role leadership, is the performance of actions (behaviors plus intention) that enable participants in a community to evoke potential within a trusting environment, to reconstruct or break set with old assumptions, to focus on the construction of meaning, or to frame actions based on new behaviors and purposeful intention. Everyone in the school community can perform an act of leadership. Leadership is an inclusive field of processes in which leaders do their work.

Those who perform acts of leadership need

- A sense of purpose and ethics, because honesty and trust are fundamental to relationships
- Facilitation skills, because framing, deepening, and moving the conversations about teaching and learning are fundamental to constructing meaning
- An understanding of constructivist learning for all humans
- A deep understanding of change and transitions, because change is not what we thought it was
- An understanding of context so that communities of memories can be continually drawn and enriched
- A personal identity that allows for courage and risk, low ego needs, and a sense of possibilities.

As Poplin and her colleagues found, educators generally enter life's work with *a sense of purpose and ethics*. Perhaps it is primitive and sketchy, certainly it is vulnerable. Recently, I heard a young teacher, Susan, in her third year of teaching, say that she had entered the profession because she wanted to make a difference with kids. Midway through the second year, she had begun to question her options, her possibilities. Yet as she sat in an initial meeting to plan for a professional practice school, she reported that this feeling of purpose began to resurface. So easily lost; so easily regained. So vulnerable.

Perhaps all educators were Susans at one point. What has happened? Do educators still possess that sense of purpose with which they began their work? Can it be recaptured? We believe so. Those who initiate an act of leadership are usually those who have held on tight to their purposes or who have been reawakened, experiencing a pattern of relationships that has helped to resurface and perhaps redefine and extend those original compelling purposes into ethical behavior. For them, a sense of coherence and authenticity contributes to the establishment of trust in communal relationships.

Those performing acts of leadership find *facilitation skills* essential to creating engagement in reciprocal processes among leaders in a community. These skills are vital to everyone in "Leading the Conversations" (Chapter 4). When I entered my third year of teaching, I discovered in the interview that all teachers and administrators in my new school were expected to participate in 30 hours of training in open communication, shared decision-making, problem-solving, and accountability. The school was genuinely founded on these four principles, and everyone was a leader expected to facilitate the processes. What a phenomenal experience—one that influenced me dramatically later as a principal, and one that helped me to negotiate the next 25 years of educational experience through a unique lens.

An understanding of constructivist learning for all humans enables leaders to pose questions and to frame actions that cause self-construction and collegial interaction as well as the design of constructivist curriculum, instruction, and assessment. Constructivism is not an evolutionary understanding that has naturally emerged from our training and experiences in behaviorism. Constructivism is a significantly different paradigm that enables us to frame new questions and create learning based on passion, unique learning gifts and perceptions, community, and authentic work and assessment.

A *deep understanding of change and transitions* is also essential to jointly designing the sequencing, timing, and duration of reciprocal processes. Change that is constructivist in nature emerges from the meaning-making process and is therefore unpredictable and evolving. Preset objectives, as well as predetermined strategies and techniques that are too tightly drawn, violate the very nature of constructivism. Constructivists have goals, outcomes, and a repertoire of change strategies that focus talent and resources toward a common purpose. Attempting to harness real change that is being pulled by intention, not pushed by prediction, is so complex that its understandings can only be constructed in the conversations among co-leaders in a learning community. The next chapter explores that which we metaphorically refer to as "sea change," a process in which the sea moves in upon itself as the entire sea shifts forward.

An *understanding of the context* is essential to the unity of "communities of memories," which must be drawn forth and enriched and reinterpreted. Bellah and colleagues (1985) invite us to consider this intriguing concept,

> Communities, in the sense in which we are using the term, have history—in an important sense they are constituted by their past—and for this reason we can speak of a real community as a "community of memory," one that does not forget its past. In order not to forget that past, a community is involved in retelling its story, its constitutive narrative. (p. 153)

These composite and shared memories take on expanded meanings when retold together. These memories constitute a vital part of the meaning construction (and reconstruction) that goes on in schools. When a new principal enters a school, we always advise him or her to talk with people, find out about the memories, "the men and women who have embodied and exemplified the meaning of the community" (Bellah et al., p. 153). Embedded in these stories are the values and intentions that drive the work in the school, as well as the fears and lost hopes that form barriers to creativity and innovation. We must "contextualize" our work for each other; and this entails sketching out a frame of memories, values, assumptions, and promises that create a forum for dialogue and a stepping off place for action.

Emerging leaders are construing and interpreting themselves as they construct meaning and knowledge with others. Their *sense of personal identity* allows for courage and risk, low ego needs, and a sense of possibilities. Personal identity has been forming in reflective interactions with others. They seek not only to explain, but to listen and to understand. These individuals have outgrown the need to "win" in the traditional sense, understanding that reciprocity and high personal regard reframe "winning" into concern for moving toward a common purpose. With a growing clarity and confidence in the grounding values that guide their lives, these emerging leaders are able to cut through the cumbersome morass that sometimes envelopes our lives and ask the next essential question. Since personal efficacy is evolving in a trusting environment, these leaders work with others to create human possibilities for all children and educators. Possibilities are as diverse as the web of their relationships, since diversity arises from multiple perspectives, multiple framings.

This vision of the potential of educational leaders may not only seem ideal; it *is* ideal—and it is possible. Constructivist Leadership enables human growth that was previously reserved for the few. Others were followers, relegated to second-class citizenship and second-class growth. In our traditional systems, growth was a limited resource; in ecological communities, interdependence and reciprocity require equal partners.

Who Can Lead?

Since leadership represents a possible set of actions for everyone in the community, anyone can choose to lead. Participantship, rather than followership, is full engagement, as Wheatley (1992) described:

> We need a different pattern, one in which we engage fully, evoking multiple meanings.... The more participants we engage in this participative universe, the more we access its potential and the wiser we can become. (p. 65)

Full participation leads to acts of leadership; being fully engaged in meaning-making activates one's drive toward purpose and community. One cannot help but lead; one is compelled to do so by the self-directed drive toward self-renewal and interdependency. Responsibility toward self and others surfaces as an essential developmental process. Paulo Freire's ideas (1973) have long been persuasive: "Humankind emerge from their submersion and acquire the ability to intervene in reality as it is unveiled" (p. 44). We would add strongly, "*to intervene*" *and to construct and to reintervene* in their realities. We have seen this over and over as staff emerge into the leadership arena: The next essential question is asked, ideas and traditions are challenged, people volunteer to lead, groups form, curiosity is aroused, verbal and nonverbal interactions change. My experiences in tough-to-change schools and institutions is that these actions begin to emerge during the first year and gain momentum about 18 months into the process. It is the participation processes that create the meaning and the understandings (the reality) to which people then commit themselves. Without these participatory opportunities, commitment is not possible, only obedience.

Students as leaders; teachers as leaders; parents as leaders; administrators as leaders. Crusty old paradigms might warn us that "too many cooks spoil the stew"; new paradigms are making a different stew. The patterns of relationships in this new "stew" connect in synergistic ways that are rich in possibilities and exist outside traditional lines of authority, roles, established norms, rules, and policies.

"Why do we continue to believe in administrative expertise?" queried Bill Foster at the American Educational Research Association gathering in April 1994. "Perhaps we lack a meaning system for administrative actions." Constructivist leadership provides a meaning system and a system of meaning making for leadership actions.

WHY CALL IT LEADERSHIP?

The kinds of educational communities described in this book are quite rare; the understandings, knowledge, and practices cited in this book are not as unique. Many centers, projects, networks, and partnerships function on notions of community, reciprocity, and purpose. The social implications of ecosystems, systems theory, and quantum physics are increasingly understood. Schools are beginning to focus more directly on student outcomes and collegiality. Why call it leadership? Why not call it the work of community, or restructuring, or reculturing, as many do?

We call it leadership because these noble conceptions are isolated and fragmented: They are known, but they are just not happening. Something is missing—the glue, focus, integration, unity of spirit. Barth uses a simple, yet elegant and weighty, phrase—"making happen." Constructivist Leadership that entails

The reciprocal processes that enable . . .
participants in an educational community to construct meanings . . .
that lead toward a common purpose of schooling

is making things happen.

CHAPTER 3

Constructing School Change

Linda Lambert

I do not know what I may appear to the world, but to myself I
seem to have been only like a boy playing on the sea shore, and
diverting myself in now and then finding a smoother pebble or a
prettier shell than ordinary, whilst the great ocean of truth lay
all undiscovered before me.

Isaac Newton
(Quoted in More, 1934, p. 664)

But doth suffer a sea change
Into something rich and strange.

William Shakespeare
The Tempest, Act I, Scene 2

In Chapter 2 we described constructivist leadership as the reciprocal processes that enable participants in an educational community to construct
meaning toward a common purpose of schooling. We now view another aspect of constructivist leadership, namely, as the means through which participants in an educational community construct school change. Schools or organizations change as participants make sense of their work and find
challenging possibilities together. We believe change to be a natural, inevitable set of processes. One of the chief myths with which change agents have
been burdened is that change comes only from a felt need, a discomfort, an
unbearable pressure that forces us to change. While this is often true, it has
veiled a primary reality of change: Within communities that foster human
growth and development, change seems to be a natural result of constructing
meaning and knowledge together—an outgrowth of our conversations about
what matters. Change, under these conditions, becomes more difficult to resist than to participate in, more discomforting to ignore than to embrace.

In spite of its recent sacrifice on the altar of the popular press and its
overuse in economics and politics, "sea change" is an apt metaphor for this
process of constructing change in schools and districts. Unlike the Shake-
spearean use of "sea change" as acting on a foreign body placed in the sea,
this metaphor asks us to imagine change as a process in which the sea moves

in upon itself as the entire sea shifts forward. Feedback spirals, formed by critical inquiry, action research, and other forms of information, resemble the sea moving in upon itself. The shift forward of the entire sea results from the motion of meaning-making, of interpreting new information together. This is what is meant by a "self-organizing" system and this is what is meant by "systemic change"; "positive feedback seems to be the *sine qua non* of change, of surprise, of life itself" (Waldrop, 1992, p. 34).

In discussing Prigogine's discoveries and works, Waldrop provokes us to understand that systems have an incredible capacity to "spontaneously organize themselves into a whole series of complex structures. . . . a tendency for small effects to become magnified when conditions are right" (pp. 33–34). In schools and districts, the most interesting examples lie in the moments in change when people begin to re-form themselves into collegial clusters (complex structures), usually around approaches that respond to new understandings of the nature of professional work. These might include peer coaching pairs, study groups, action research teams, leadership teams, ad hoc planning groups, and on and on. *As professionals find new meaning in their work together, the patterns of relationships and the structures change.*

In this chapter we compare traditional change approaches with constructivist approaches, identify a few compelling change principles or guidelines, describe 3 years of change at Evergreen Middle School, and seek to understand the meanings of some of the occurrences there.

CONSTRUCTING "SEA CHANGE"

Our understandings of change have made major strides forward in the past 8 to 10 years, largely due to a new, or at least newly respected, research paradigm. To brave the danger of seeming simplistic, this simply required a "new eye." The new eye of ethnographic or qualitative research seeks to see things as they are, instead of as they are planned or "should be." For years, change was measured by the extent to which goals and objectives were achieved and sustained. This "eye" seemed to assume that the appropriate change strategy was in place and that the role of research was to find out if it had succeeded as planned. Once in the hen's house, we looked for only chickens and eggs.

The new eye of research, keenly applied by Little, Lieberman, Sarason, McLaughlin, Fullan, and Scriven, among others, looks for what is actually occurring in schools without predetermined assumptions about what is there to see. The approach interprets and helps us understand how change actually occurs, evolves. This recent research has shed light on multiple myths of systematic change and led us to systemic change.

Figure 3.1. A Study in Contrast: Project and Process

PROJECT STRATEGIES	SEA CHANGE PROCESSES
1. Intention is to implement specific content change.	1. Intention is shared meaning and values among peers.
2. Predetermined knowledge base; source is school and education.	2. Pluralistic, emerging knowledge bases informed by action research, observation of teaching and learning, and multiple disciplines.
3. Problem is predetermined, assumed; solution finds problem.	3. Problem-finding is central to inquiring stance; understanding deepens through time.
4. Predetermined objectives based on 1–3.	4. Objectives emerge naturally as discrepancies are addressed; objectives cannot be preset since problems are not initially understood.
5. Innovation not mediated with current practice.	5. Changes evolve from current practice, knowledge bases, and problem-finding.
6. Predescribed skills needed by leaders in content area.	6. Everyone is a leader; skills in reciprocal processes needed by all.
7. Participation by those who agree to apply innovation.	7. Multiple, sustained opportunities for participation.
8. Training in content only for those who will apply innovation.	8. Participation involves multiple professional development opportunities.
9. Parameters are limits (regulations, guidelines, budget, personnel practices, contracts). See also, Chapter 7.	9. Parameters serve emerging goals, rather than being limited by them; teams challenge and redefine parameters.
10. Partnerships, where they exist, are hierarchical, assigning education as the junior partner.	10. Partnerships exist among equals.
11. Monitored and evaluated by external criteria and agent.	11. Self-monitoring based on internal criteria.

Although traditional, systematic change has fallen into disrepute in many arenas, we still find ample examples of "project-related" and categorical changes. Projects are often, but not always, added to the margins of the schools or applied as a "post-hole," driving an innovative stake through a few recruitable classrooms (see Figure 3.1). These approaches avoid interventions in the regular classrooms of the school where business proceeds as usual.

Project strategies are often based on the assumption that the children, not the system, carry the malady. Therefore the task is to "fix the kid" and place him or her back into the (dysfunctional) system. Such approaches as study halls before and after school, gang counseling, homework clubs, remediation, and Saturday schools are based on this assumption. It is not that some of these approaches are not useful supplements to fundamental change, but when they are used as a substitute for changes in teaching and relationships, they seem to say, "Preserve the core of the system for business as usual."

A project's intent is usually to implement a specific change that has a predetermined knowledge base. Recognition of a problem has been predetermined; so are the solutions. Based on the known solutions to similar problems, goals, objectives, types of involvement, necessary training, and evaluation can also be preset. Staff development is seen as an "outside-in" process (Lambert, 1988) in which valid knowledge is assumed to lie outside the person. Parameters, regulations and guidelines, budget, personnel requirements, contracts, and rulings serve as limits and are monitored closely. On the surface, traditional change processes appear quite rational since they can be laid out in the sequential, logical manner that has characterized planning in the past.

The right side column of Figure 3.1 provides a sharp counterexample of change as it is constructed by the participants in a community. Successful change is built on shared meaning and values among peers. As peer participants regularly participate in inquiry, knowledge bases in the school are forming and re-forming continually. Problem-finding is central to such an inquiring stance, with the interpretation of findings and understandings deepening over time. Rather than being firmly preset, objectives and goals emerge naturally from the investigative processes, allowing issues to reveal themselves so that they can be addressed. As issues are addressed, it becomes clearer when new knowledge, perhaps from outside the school, is needed. Setting objectives before the problems are understood can point the school onto an artificial path to contrived change. When objectives are preset, project coordinators and others are compelled to monitor their set direction, therefore continually *correcting ourselves away from the natural direction of change*. Changes evolve in a spiraling pattern from current practice, knowledge bases, problem-finding, and continuing conversations. The changes are context-driven and context-appropriate, emerging from the constructivist conversations.

Participation and professional development are seen as one organizing concept: Learning means having access to multiple, sustained opportunities for participation. Staff development is an "inside-out" process (Lambert, 1988, 1989), which includes participation in leadership processes, governance, observations and inquiry, co-planning and coaching, and new information—all of which are opportunities that involve authority, choice, and responsibility (Lightfoot, 1983).

As we construct change, parameters can serve emerging goals rather than being limited by them. Teams can challenge and redefine parameters, hopefully working with an increasingly flexible and responsive district (see Chapter 7). Regulations, guidelines, resource allocations, personnel practices, even contracts emerge from, rather than being boxed in by, change.

Partnerships and networks provide increasing elasticity and expanded visions to assist in school change endeavors. The partnerships, as in ecosystems, exist within a framework of equals who are learning reciprocally from one another. In Chapter 4, we expand on the nature of reciprocity among coequal partnerships, arrangements through which both partners are learning and changing together.

And, finally, school and district participants in the change process establish internal criteria according to which they can assess their own progress and make in-flight corrections. Assessment that is consistent for students, adults, and programs promotes coherence and understanding among all participants. Change themes are more fully developed in the section that follows, leading to a scenario of Evergreen Middle School that describes one school's experience with constructing change.

THEMES IN CONSTRUCTING CHANGE

In *Change Forces* (1993), Michael Fullan draws from the works of Pascale, Stacey, and Senge to describe the new paradigm of change as a "dynamic complexity" of unpredictable forces and relationships that characterize systemic thinking about change. We agree and we would suggest four *lenses,* or perspectives, that we believe integrate, and give additional coherence to, understanding the nature of change in organizations. These perspectives are essential to understanding a constructivist approach to change, for each of these lenses employs essential aspects of constructivist learning. These lenses are:

- The leadership lens
- Patterns of relationships
- Inquiry and the role of information
- Breaking set with old assumptions

The Leadership Lens

Failure to understand the nature and role of leadership may well be the "missing link" in our change efforts today. When we interpret constructivist leadership to mean the reciprocal processes that enable participants in an educational community to construct meaning toward a common purpose of schooling, it brings into being a conceptual framework through which we can more clearly understand new change paradigms. Constructivist leadership takes into account the wholeness or ecological nature of community, full participantship (including teacher as leader and teacher as change agent), and the momentum and natural undertaking of change.

Numerous centers that work with change, reform, and restructuring are struggling with defensible conceptions of systemic thinking. These include processes for examination of student work and other data; meaning-centered curricula; reorganization into smaller, untracked units for acquiring personalization with diversity; school-to-work transition paths, and other fundamental improvements. These are among the most promising of practices. However, rarely do they involve the "leadership factor" or the "leadership lens" as a way of thinking about bringing the pieces together into a cohesive whole and moving that "whole" forward as a natural evolution of a self-organizing system. Such a perspective brings into focus the third dimension in the school culture, the set of opportunities for exercising leadership embedded into the spaces among us. This systemic view of the school urges us to engage one another in the reciprocal, constructivist processes that bring coherence and focus to our work. Otherwise, the workings in a school remain fragmented, lacking the linkages that are essential to integrated thinking about school change.

Patterns of Relationships

In the Introduction, and again in Chapter 2, we discussed the centrality of patterns of relationships, for this is one of the key ideas in this book. This is a design insight that is central for children, adults, and systems as well: We have come to realize that these patterns are the system synapses through which meaning and knowledge are constructed and the basis through which we integrate emotion, identity, and cognition.

Patterns of relationships in schools are the visible manifestation of meaning-making; their absence contributes to fragmentation in the lives of children and adults. This fragmentation, we believe, prevents self-organizing systems from forming and being sustained. Facilitating the creation of patterns of relationships in school is an act of leadership. The following examples were chosen because they tend to fuse people into patterns that depend on an interdependence around goals, naturally sustain themselves through an investigative process, serve as a forum for constructivist learning, focus teaching and learning, and are interrelated with other school endeavors. Each of these processes can serve as an entry to school change.

- *Action research team:* This team may include a leadership team member, a team teaching partner, and a core teacher, all concerned about, say, female performance in 8th-grade science. They investigate, share data with others, make sense of the information, identify areas that are problematic, and seek more ideas. The pattern of inquiry will continue and become linked to the interests of the whole faculty, parents, and student assessment.

• *Parent/student learning group:* The interest group may organize themselves around a question such as: How can students play a leading role in assessing themselves, teaching their parents, and guiding plans for their own improvement? The group, with parent, student, and teacher members, plans a 3-year pilot for student-led assessment conferences. The group may stay together and become linked to the PTA, the school site council, and the whole faculty. From such beginnings, multiple opportunities for student-led learning can emerge.

• *Guidance planning group:* This interest group may be captured by a question such as: How can student–teacher relationships be sustained and deepened over time? This group proposes to the leadership team, faculty, students, teachers' union, and district that students stay with the same teacher for a minimum of 3 years. The group designs a study to observe the changes in relationships and academic learning engendered by prolonged connections among students and teachers.

These are only a few examples of how patterns of relationships can be created and sustained. Once educators are conscious of the need to build and sustain such patterns, the opportunities for enabling structures become self-evident. Patterns are social, academic, creative, investigative, and overlapping. When this *lens* is applied to our work in schools, the patterns reveal themselves, for *individuals see what they look for.* As community participants become committed to patterns of relationships, it is useful to keep a few things in mind: (1) Engage with one another in the reciprocal processes; (2) commit yourself to the relationship as a peer; (3) share work together; (4) talk often about your common purpose; (5) laugh together.

Inquiry and the Role of Information

"Consciousness," writes Wheatley (1992), "is a property that emerges when a certain level of organization is reached . . . the greater the ability to process information, the greater the level of consciousness" (p. 102). Information is the substance that feeds back upon the sea, shifting it forward; pieces of information, processed together, evoke diversity and coevolution. Information is the basis for constructing new meanings and knowledge. It opens a system to fluidity, flexibility, and air. "Educators cannot teach students how to gain entry into the knowledge and power of the profound discussions of a democracy," asserts Glickman (1993), "unless they themselves have gained entry into the knowledge and power of the profound discussions of their schools" (p. 28).

Professional literature is one obvious form of information, as are letters, memos, newsletters, budget printouts, or written district mandates. However, the forms of information that are most vital to providing enabling structure for our relationships, constructing meaning and knowledge, and opening our minds to diverse possibilities are *gathered, generated,* and *interpreted* from within as well as from outside the school. It is this information that is central to the creation of an inquiring stance in the school. Information emanates from observing and talking with children, from talking about student work, from observing one another's work, from conversations we hold with one another and with parents, from reflection on our own practice and experiences, from disaggregating school-based data (e.g., D, F, & I lists, grades, expulsions, referrals, mobility factors), from visiting other schools, from employing critical inquiry, and from carrying out action research. This is the information that causes disequilibrium in our thinking, that enables us to break set with old assumptions about teaching and learning.

These inquiring processes are not new. Kurt Lewin originated the term "action research" in the 1940s. In 1967, Robert Schaefer published *The School as a Center of Inquiry,* in which "he argued that teachers should become scholars, students become active learners, and schools should be learning organizations" (Reed, Mergendollar, & Horan, undated). Finally, these processes are being used in schools and in networks and consortia with increasing frequency. Processes of inquiry are becoming central to administrative preparation programs (see Chapter 8). Major networks and organizations, such as the California Center for School Restructuring, the Coalition of Essential Schools, and the international action research community are using these strategies as centerpieces for school change.

I describe four of these processes in more detail: disaggregating school-based data, the critical-study process, action research, and the restructuring protocol from the California Center for School Restructuring. These approaches represent the more frequently used inquiry strategies that we have observed. Each involves gathering, generating, and interpreting data.

Disaggregating School-Based Data. In 1994 I asked administrators from four San Francisco Bay Area high schools to disaggregate information from their D, F, & I lists (grades and incompletes). In each case, the vast majority of the students on the list either had Spanish surnames or were African American males. It is not news to note that urban high schools are failing to reach these children. Information such as this, directed back to administrative teams, departments, and faculty, speaks far more eloquently than admonitions; more importantly, staff interpret the meanings of these data, thereby becoming invested in the resolution of current and emerging problems.

Critical-Study Process. Glickman (1993) refers to a critical-study process as beginning with what he refers to as "the school covenant" (the
adopted principles of teaching and learning) as its boundaries; in other
words, how do we know if students are able to do, to be, to meet this expecta-
tion? Information is gathered from (1) within the schools, including readily
available compiled information, student work, and the findings of site action
research; (2) other schools and programs; and (3) the research literature.
These data are discussed, interpreted, and used to inform actions. "How
else," queries Glickman, "would a school know where to focus resources,
time, and human energy?" (1993, p. 50).

Action Research. The international action research movement is taking
a number of different turns. In many cases, it has centered on classroom-
based research conducted by one or more teachers in a school. Often, this
process and even the findings are not fed back through the school. In some
cases, the principals are not informed. This is a particularly unfortunate con-
dition, since it isolates the teachers (Lieberman, 1994) and does little to improve the school for all children and other staff.

A more promising movement is embraced by collaborative action research, which is whole-school based and more closely resembles the critical-
study process described above. "Action research," points out Sagor (1992),
"is conducted by people who want to do something to improve their own
situation . . . because they want to know whether they can do something in
a better way" (p. 7). He describes the major steps as problem formulation,
data collection, data analysis, reporting of results, and action planning (see
Chapter 4 for a more complete analysis). It is the collaborative and school-
based aspects of action research that enable it to work as a major catalyst in
the creation of self-renewing schools.

*Restructuring "Protocol" from the California Center for School Re-
structuring.* This protocol was designed collaboratively by center staff and
teams of teachers in 1993 as a means through which teams within a school
or among schools enter into critical dialogue about student work and student
outcomes. One team presents its findings about student achievement to a
second team and then receives reflective feedback from the other team, which
they publicly consider before the process is reversed. Each team has an opportunity to enter into a public dialogue about teaching and learning. The
protocol provides a powerful learning opportunity for educators in the network of California schools whose restructuring efforts are being supported
by funds from Senate Bill 1274 passed in 1992. In the spring of 1994 and
1995, a statewide symposium engaged all 144 schools in using the protocol.

The essential undertaking in the examples above is to pose the questions that create and frame the dissonance, often the discomfort, between our current experiences and beliefs and those suggested by the new information; to seek information from which to interpret and understand the observed phenomenon; and to design alternative options and possibilities while continuing to observe and reflect. This spiraling movement represents both constructivist learning and constructivist change. Since working with new ideas and information is essential in the meaning-making process, an inquiring stance is essential to constructing change in a school or district.

Breaking Set with Old Assumptions

While this *lens* is also one of the four reciprocal processes described in Chapter 2, it is so significant to our work that it is being singled out in order to emphasize its role in change. Breaking old assumptions is not a new idea; indeed, it has been around since the discovery of religious conversion, since Festinger (1957) wrote about cognitive dissonance, and since writers of the past century talked about world view, mind-set, cognitive structure, schemas, cognitive maps, paradigms, frames of reference, and, more recently, "mental models" (Senge, 1990) and "breakpoint" (Land & Jarman, 1992). These terms, when used in reference to breaking with old assumptions, refer to being fixed in our own perceptions of the world; our embeddedness, "stuckness" in old assumptions; our accumulations or myths, habits, and expectations—and the need to break through or "convert" persons from ways of thinking that get in the way of change. Often we seek not to eliminate old assumptions but to broaden the boundaries, to allow in more possibilities. In the meaning-making process, individuals shape their own coherence in interaction with others, thereby mediating the old ways of thinking.

Why must constructivists take on this challenge? Criticisms of a constructivist approach to change have included many of the same words as those used in the frequent criticisms of collaboration and shared decision-making:

> "How can people imagine that which has not been a part of their experience?"
> "Teachers working together? I call 'consensus' agreeing on the most mediocre idea."
> "The past will never bring us to the future!"
> "Talk, talk, talk. I don't have the time, and we usually arrive at an impasse. You make the decisions. I'm here to teach."
> "Teachers, and kids, don't want to commit themselves to anything."
> "Reality begins when I leave school."

Insightful—and painful—criticisms! And, in too many settings, they might be true. They seem to claim that educators will never be able to break from the past, to carve a new path, to take a creative jump. We do not believe this, but we do believe that the danger must be confronted head-on. We must deliberately build in processes that cause us to break set with old assumptions if we are to consider new ways of working with teaching and learning. Even with that agreement, there are differing opinions on whether this can be done, and if so, how. Land and Jarman (1992) claim that we must make a clean break with the past, that the past will never bring us to the future. Yet our "communities of memories" would remind us that many school staff share common experiences that need to be considered and appreciated before we can put away old ways of thinking or evolve those ideas into new understandings about children. Most vitally, a "clean break" approach is not unlike a "blank slate" approach: Ignore our experiences, beliefs, perspectives, world view; let's start anew. Constructivism will not allow us to "start anew," but we can "break set" while acknowledging the power and contributions of our past in creating what we have today. This lens is about breaking set.

Before talking about breaking set within the context of our work in this book, let us set forth a few old assumptions worth breaking. Some of the toughest are:

- The child carries the malady; fix the child, not the system.
- Ability and potential are innately fixed.
- There is a high and unalterable correlation between poverty and low achievement.
- We must teach to standards rather than to the child.

We have discovered, not surprisingly, that these assumptions can only be challenged and broken within the context of trust, relationships, and self-discovery. Without this trusting, supportive environment, we more often encounter defensiveness. When engaged in the reciprocal processes of constructivist leadership, the following approaches can be very powerful in breaking set with old assumptions:

Seek to understand: Instead of explaining, describing, and defending, when we seek to understand we are genuinely interested in the other's experiences and points of view. Often, in this context, individuals open up to alternative information and perspectives.

Find out: When people are involved in their own inquiries, they can more easily commit themselves to their own discoveries. This is true even when the information is counter to old beliefs.

Create; imagine: Nothing breaks set like creativity! There are multiple strategies for creating new ways of addressing old problems and

imagining shared futures. This can be as simple as an essential question or a synectics exercise, or as involved as multiday planning
sessions. This also includes "visioning," a group process that involves imagining a possible future together.

Storytelling; literature: Stories carry patterns of perspectives and alternative myths that access the emotional aspects of our old ways of
thinking. This can open us up to dialogue about new ideas, new
dreams, and "what ifs."

Liminality: Meaning "threshold," this anthropological concept enables
us to enter experiences in which we shed our roles, authority, and
expectations, and share new experiences. A faculty retreat is a
good example.

Humor: When we laugh together, we often challenge, then reframe old
perspectives. "Laughter can be more satisfying than honor; more
precious than money; more heart-cleansing than prayer" (Schaef,
1990).

In Chapter 5, Zimmerman offers a detailed look at the linguistic moves and
patterns that enable us to break set with old thinking.

The four lenses through which change might be viewed—the leadership
lens, patterns of relationships, inquiry and the role of information, and breaking old assumptions—are central to a systemic change perspective. Below,
the story of 3 years of change at Evergreen Middle School provides a context
in which to understand more specifically what many of the factors look like
in practice.

THREE YEARS OF CHANGE AT EVERGREEN MIDDLE SCHOOL

The following story of Evergreen Middle School is a composite drawn
from true events and occurrences, critical moments and incidents, all of
which did not happen at the same time and place. The frame of the story
comes from one real school. The additions are actual experiences from other
middle schools struggling with similar issues. The story is guided by the perspective of constructivist leadership using the change lenses or perspectives
discussed above. The overall process was emergent and evolving, although
common themes wove themselves throughout the experiences.

Year 1

It was a hot, August day, but Jan had decided to wear a suit to her
meeting with the district superintendent. As a new principal and a new district employee, she hadn't a clue about district norms for hot days when chil-

dren and parents weren't around. She was in the building only a few minutes when she wished she had made another decision. Oh, well. The superintendent welcomed her with warmth and an eagerness to talk. This was Jan's first principalship, although she had taught for 8 years, served as a program coordinator for two change initiatives, and worked as a middle school vice principal for 4 years, all in other districts.

"I thought I'd fill you in on a little history," began the superintendent, and proceeded to describe his perceptions of the past decade at Evergreen. During the past 11 years, Evergreen had been under basically "autocratic" rule. Many of the teachers had never worked under any other conditions. There were many talented staff there, some of whom had found ways around the system. A particularly clever group of teachers would present a completed plan for a workshop, visitation, new resources or set of materials to the principal, and he would okay it. A few others, equally talented, had disengaged themselves, working only with students, staying in their rooms at lunch, and leaving right after school. Another group had found it important to please the principal; they were the ones who conducted the after-school and noon sports, agreed readily in faculty meetings, and decorated their rooms for back-to-school night. There were no school discretionary funds, since the school had never applied for any programs.

"We hired you to bring the staff and the community together and to get the school started toward improvement," he concluded. "It will be quite a challenge." The suit felt particularly confining as Jan walked to the car.

Once in her office, she began a series of phone calls that would be her first conversation with many faculty. "I want to get to know you before school starts," she said, "I want to know what you consider important to our school. And I'd like for you to begin to get to know me." No one refused to come in for the special visit, although three staff were out of the country.

These opening conversations were eye-openers. People had really thought about the questions, and they were ready to talk about what they valued, what they thought was important to keep—and to change. Equally importantly, each person took on a face and a life.

The week before school started, the PTA President, Martha, returned Jan's call and suggested that they go to lunch. "Sounds great," she replied, and it was. During that memorable lunch, Jan heard about the lack of parent communication, particularly responsiveness to questions and concerns. She heard about "favored" parents who were "kept in the loop." She heard about the lack of clarity about what the school stood for, what it wanted for kids. Martha knew what parents wanted, but she didn't know what the teachers and principal wanted. "Where should we start?" queried Jan. Together they began to brainstorm possibilities. Before they parted, Martha warned, "It won't be easy. Teachers are bound to resist a closer working relationship with parents."

The first faculty meeting felt like a theatrical opening night. Nervous but excited, Jan shared some of the overall impressions that she had gotten from her conversations with staff—those things worth keeping, those things needing change, some of the shared (but rarely spoken) values, and most of what she had heard from parents. She knew all but 3 faces in the crowd of 35 faculty and 6 classified staff. The counselor and vice principal shared information about the logistics of getting school opened, and there were a few district announcements. As the meeting ended, Jan asked for volunteers to help plan the district staff development day in mid-October. "Don't move too quickly," said a voice from behind as she moved to the door. She turned to see a middle-aged teacher whom she didn't recognize from the interviews. "Thank you," Jan replied, "when are we going to get our talk?"

Everyone at Evergreen was busy with getting school underway: Jan spent short periods in most classes and conferred regularly with her administrative staff. Whenever possible, she continued her conversations with faculty in hallways and during preparation periods. She was learning a lot about what made this school tick.

By early October, she proposed to the staff the selection of a leadership team. "But you have an administrative team," one teacher replied quickly. "Yes," acknowledged Jan, "but my vision of how schools work is much more inclusive than that. By choosing teachers for a leadership team, decisions will reflect the continuous voices of the staff." "Sounds like choosing favorites to me," said another. "I'm not doing the choosing," said Jan, "you are."

Reluctantly, the staff agreed to work in small groups to identify some criteria for team members. In a secret, written ballot, each person wrote down three names for the four positions. The counselor collected the ballots, and a week later the names were announced. Fortunately, the selection included two members of the informal subculture that had been primarily responsible for any professional undertaking in which the school had been involved: Ann Thompson and Jack Murphy. A newer teacher, energetic and constructive, Garth Williams, was also selected for the team.

The leadership team agreed to meet on Tuesday afternoons and had had only one meeting before the first staff development day was upon them. They reviewed the agenda, met with the ad hoc planning committee, and prepared to explain how they might communicate with the staff between meetings.

The warm-up for the staff development day was a little less playful than Jan would have liked, but not inappropriate for the group. Humor was not a prevalent quality in this staff. "I hope that changes," she thought. A woman named Judy Roake from the county office had agreed to facilitate the process to identify common work agreements (see the complete activity in Chapter 2). As people began to recall their best group working experiences, few examples came from education; rather, they came from a community activist group, Boy Scouts, a group planning a senior show, and the like. The day ended on a relative high. "Perhaps we're on our way," Jan shared with a new teacher.

The leadership team set aside a part of each of its meetings for its own training and discussion of roles and responsibilities. The group began to explore the question of what might be the right time to actually create a school vision and identify student outcomes. Feedback from discussions with staff and their own sense of timing told them that perhaps the end of January might be a good time. "Trust is growing," observed one seasoned faculty member, "and people are talking more openly with each other; let's wait until after the holidays."

It was mid-November when data began coming in from the first quarter. Jan sat at her desk eyeing the D, F, & I grade printout. It was 5:00 and getting dark. She could not believe what she was seeing: 40% of the 7th-graders had received two or more failing grades. Tomorrow was the faculty meeting. "Surely we have come far enough to confront this together," reflected Jan. She placed the pages to be copied on the secretary's desk and went home.

Since the staff had agreed to rotate the meeting location on their staff development day among the rooms of faculty members, this meeting opened in Jack's room. Jan asked for a few minutes on the agenda in order to share some information, handed out the 7th-grade information, and explained what they were looking at. It was clear that teachers had never seen these printouts before. Silence was heavy in the room. Jan could feel her breathing slow down. Finally, a teacher said: "Are you suggesting that this is our fault?" "The students who come to us are just not prepared! The elementary schools are not doing their jobs," said another. Then everyone began to talk. All hell had broken loose. People were angry; they were defensive. Jan listened, struggling to maintain her composure. "I think we need to talk about the meaning of these data. How about if we place this on the next agenda?" She sat down. Several moments went by; Jack continued the meeting.

By the next afternoon, at the leadership team meeting, Jan was more curious than upset. "What happened?" she began. "You should have consulted with us first," said Ann. "There wasn't time," Jan responded, "and I didn't realize it would cause such a reaction. Fill me in." The members of the team began to give their ideas. "You see," said Ann, "this staff has never had information like that. And they've been complaining for years about poor articulation with the elementary schools and poor communication with parents. We've been isolated here, and I guess we've turned inward to protect ourselves—from the administration, the parents, and eventually even the kids." "I agree with Ann," continued Garth, "we're just not ready to examine our own responsibilities in this situation." Nods came from around the table. "Then where do we go from here?" asked Jan. "Do you think I've undermined our trust to the extent that we won't be ready to talk about our vision by January?" "I think the situation can be salvaged," continued Garth. "Let's think about our next meeting."

Nearly 2 weeks later, early in December, the faculty met again, this time in Ann's room. During those 2 weeks, leadership team members had been holding brief conversations with staff, mostly listening. "I think the question before us," began Jan, "is how we respond to this information. The leadership team would like to suggest a process." Everyone was listening. This is the process: "We identify the questions that these data raise and the possible sources of information. We then ask a small study group to investigate the questions and data and come up with their findings and some possible courses of action. Would you talk among yourselves for a few moments before we begin?"

Staff talked among themselves. Some voices were louder and more rapid than others; some were defensive and accusatory. A few resented the assumptions of staff responsibility that underlay the inquiry. The debate was difficult. After several moments, someone said, "We're unclear why we need such a process. We know what the problems are." Ann intervened, "We agree that we know what most of the problems are, but there may be possibilities that we've not considered, and we'd like to treat this like a professional investigation." Ann was a respected voice in the room. Others seemed to concur, although enthusiasm in the room varied dramatically.

Ann walked to the board; Jan recorded. Ann began: "What questions does this situation raise? I'll start with one of my own: Are the causes for poor performance consistent among 7th-graders?" Others followed, and there was soon a list of nine questions on the board. The issue of further data was puzzling. "Let me give you a few examples," began Susan, the school counselor, "test data, interviews with teachers, students, and parents." "And research literature," added Gretchen, a fourth-year teacher getting her master's degree in curriculum and instruction. Kelly was the first volunteer for the 7th-grade study group. Three others added their names, as well as Jan.

On the second day back from the winter holidays, Susan stood in Jan's doorway. She looked pleased. "Have you noticed," she asked, "that things are feeling a little different around here?" "I'll admit that I feel it," replied Jan. "How do you interpret the feelings?" "It's as though there is a shift in energy," replied Susan, "people seem a little less tense, guarded. They respond to me in a more open way." "I feel it, too," observed Jan, "I hope it isn't just wishful thinking!"

The next Tuesday the leadership team met to plan the visioning workshop for the end of January. "Hey," stated Garth, "have you noticed that things are a bit more relaxed around here?" Susan and Jan exchanged glances, smiling. "I think our timing is right for the visioning meeting," observed Jack. Ann, Garth, and Susan concurred. "I've been reflecting heavily over the holidays on our first semester together," began Jan. "I'm persuaded that whenever we've started with the staff's experiences, perceptions, and values—and listened respectfully—we've worked through most issues." "You're right," observed Jack, "I'm remembering the October workshop when we established our work agreements. How can we create a visioning workshop that accomplishes the same thing?" "We've done a lot of the groundwork already," Jan responded. "As you'll recall, my August conversations included issues of personal vision. This has remained a part of our frequent talks since then." "And, we've been doing the same," added Ann. "Our conversations with the seven staff with whom we agreed to keep in touch—often those talks are about values." "We've been stirring the pot," noted Garth. "Where do we go from here?" "If we are agreed that we start with personal vision," commented Jan, "then our purpose for the day would be to move from personal vision to school vision." "Easier said than done," laughed Jack, "but let's give it a try."

The last Friday in January was a second district staff development day (students not in attendance). The meeting was held in a community recreation room a mile from the school. Each member of the leadership team and Bob, the vice principal, had agreed to facilitate a part of the day's agenda. Three representatives from the PTA joined the gathering. Jan had distributed two articles on visioning a week before. Food was abundant, and the music teacher had brought some tapes. It promised to be a good day. (See Figure 3.2.)

The day did go well. There were a few cynical remarks and moments of disengagement; but there were also laughter and moments of high energy. The team members stayed around a while to debrief. Overall, they were pleased. "It was useful to have the agenda out ahead of time," observed Jack. "It gave people time to think through their roles in the day, as well as the plans to give this information back to students and parents. That could have been a rough spot."

Gretchen and Sam, an 8-year veteran science teacher, seemed to be the natural leaders for the 7th-grade study group. Throughout February and March they conducted a review of research literature on early adolescence and some of the successes that middle schools were having. They were able to engage three other teachers in the interviewing of students and parents and to work with Susan to obtain additional school-based data (test scores, referrals, absences). Several teachers offered samples of 7th-grade student work. By early April, the group was ready to report. The leadership team had advised them not to report and ask for action at the same time, so they were on the agendas for the first and third meetings in April.

By mid-April the student outcomes group would have finished their writing (based on two faculty meetings in which staff identified student out-

Figure 3.2. Creating the Evergreen Vision

1.	Overview of the day; the agenda	Jan
2.	Warm-up: Sharing a great teaching moment, in trios	Garth
3.	Revisiting our personal visions. Reflective writing—each person spend 10 minutes responding to: "What is my personal vision/dream for children at Evergreen?"	Susan
	In small groups (4), each person shares ideas from their writing. The groups identify three areas or concepts that they think should be part of the school vision; post on the wall for viewing.	
	Break	
4.	Clarifying the visions. Posted concepts are read by a representative from each group; groups clarify, combine, discuss.	Jack
	Lunch	
5.	Small discussion of key concepts; whole groups advocacy. Choices among key concepts (3 each). Tally. Discussion: "What do our choices mean to us? To our school?"	Ann
6.	Where do we go from here? Parent and student involvement. Select a writing team. Next step: creating whole school student outcomes.	Jan
7.	Reflections of the day and closure.	Bob

comes based on the school vision) and would be ready to report as well. During the winter, the leadership team continued to disaggregate student and school data, which served as portions of each discussion.

Jan asked for another meeting with the superintendent. This time she had a couple of requests in mind. "The 7th-grade study group has been working very hard," she began. "They will be recommending a core program for next year. We envision this as three periods with the same teacher teaching language arts and social studies. I want to be able to offer them an opportunity to work during part of the summer to plan the core program." The superintendent smiled, "I can't say that I'm not delighted. How much do you have in mind?" "Perhaps 2 weeks for four people," asserted Jan. "I'm aware that some of the other school improvement–funded schools have agreed with the teachers' association on a flat summer stipend rate." "Should I hear your second request before I respond?" laughed the superintendent. "Perhaps," agreed Jan. "Perhaps . . . we think that the staff might be receptive to the idea of a retreat to open school in the fall. We'll need support if this happens.

Please be thinking about it." "Alright," said the superintendent, "and, in the meantime, let's plan to move ahead with the summer core planning."

Gretchen and Sam had prepared the 7th-grade study group report thoroughly for the first faculty meeting in April. They gave a sketch of the typical 7th-graders at Evergreen, what their day was like and the expectations from both home and school. They provided additional data: test scores, referrals, and a summary of interviews, including comments from 6th-grade teachers. The picture they presented was as follows:

- Many 7th-graders report that they are confused by having many teachers and many different sets of expectations.
- Parents are unclear about homework expectations; sometimes students lose things before getting home.
- Most students are doing poorly because they are not handing in the work.
- Seventh-grade boys who had no elementary school infractions are being referred to the office.
- Students feel intimidated by older students, particularly around the lockers and in the bathrooms (some boys report not going to the bathroom all day).

"Does this make sense to you? Does this fit with your experiences?" began Gretchen. Teachers talked among themselves, agreeing that this was not an atypical description of 7th-graders.

"We took a look at the research literature from two perspectives," noted Sam:

(1) Are the experiences of our 7th-graders similar to those of students in other schools? (2) What are some successful strategies for working with 7th-graders? This is what we found. Yes, most schools have found that the life of 7th-graders can be very difficult; at least these were the findings in schools that have undertaken to make major changes. And these are some of the things that seem to be working: advisement, core classes with a small group of teachers and a constant group of students, active learning, numerous and active electives, performance-based assessment, leadership opportunities, inventive programs for involving parents, and middle schools (moving in 6th-graders, although the 9th-graders usually do more poorly in the high schools).

Sam briefly described each option and handed out written descriptions.

Sally, the third member of the 7th-grade study group, said, "We are going to propose to you that we undertake the implementation of a 7th-grade core program for next year. We will return to discuss this recommendation on April 15." "Meanwhile," continued Gretchen, "we've planned four conversations during the next 2 weeks to discuss these ideas further, one at lunch tomorrow, two after school, and one at breakfast. Here are the dates—if we need more, we'll plan more. Thank you."

During the next 2 weeks, most staff attended one of the conversations. Each discussion began with the school vision and outcomes, seeking to draw out parallel issues.

On April 15, the staff decided to support an alternative proposal, put forth by John Macy, a veteran math teacher and a respected, though low-profile, colleague. The pilot proposal was for an initial core program involving four teachers and 120 students. John volunteered to be a part of the team that would do a formative evaluation of the pilot.

The leadership team held a Saturday retreat in May centering on their own development, reflecting on the year, and planning the last faculty meetings of the year. "How are you feeling about the year?" queried Ann of Jan during one of the reflective conversations. "Very optimistic," began Jan. "I believe that the staff are closer together. This team has provided thoughtful leadership and support. The 7th-grade data fiasco seemed to turn around into some promising ideas for rethinking our work with 7th-graders. We have a vision and student outcomes, which still need to become central in the discussions of the life of the school. I hope we can undertake serious, focused conversations about student learning next year." Before the team retreat ended, Jan said, "I'd like to suggest a retreat for the opening of school. I've talked with the superintendent about it, and I believe we can get some financial support." "Talk to us about how you see this working, Jan," said Jack. "The retreat can serve several purposes," began Jan. "It can build on the strengths from this year, provide reflective time away from school, and move our relationships to a more interdependent level. The social, informal time, mixed with work time, can do wonders. Also, we need a substantial piece of time to take our vision and student outcomes and build a strong improvement plan for the school. I'd like to see us apply for school improvement funds, and we need a substantive plan."

"I think I can support the idea," said Jack. Ann and Susan nodded. "Sounds great," observed Garth.

At the late May faculty meeting, Jack presented the idea of a fall retreat. All members of the team gave their ideas. A couple of people took exception, one because of young children at home. The idea carried, although there were several questions about both logistics and content.

Ann asked the group to reflect on the year in small groups and share a couple of ideas from each with the whole group. Susan noted that sheets of paper would be posted in the faculty room for additional comments, suggestions for next year, and so forth. Jan promised to compile the information and get it back to people before the retreat.

As the year drew to a close, several faculty dropped by Jan's office. The general message: "Things have gone fairly well, Jan, congratulations. There have been some glitches, but in general, they were handled well. We are feeling that we have a voice here, and fewer of us are reluctant to use it." A few teachers didn't drop by.

As soon as school was out, Susan, Bob, and Jan finished the master schedule, giving the four core teachers the same preparation period. Where possible, preparation periods were clustered around teachers with similar teaching interests.

On June 20, Martha, the PTA president, called to set up two appointments—an end-of-the-year luncheon with Jan and a small-group discussion with a group of concerned parents: "They are concerned about a few teachers, Jan; I think you need to see them." On June 24, the discussion took place. The concern encompassed more than a few teachers—it was also one of style, Jan's style. "We appreciate, Jan, that you've taken on a tough situation," began Clare, one of the parents, "teachers weren't talking with each other or with us. Things seem to have improved. But are the children your key concern? We think you've capitulated on a few issues, and we don't see much change in the few teachers whom we're concerned about." "I see," said Jan, "would you expand a little on those issues?"

The four parents began to talk, giving specifics and elaborating on their concerns for their own children. "Let me share with you a few things that we've done and others that we're planning. Then I'd like your ideas for additional directions and your involvements for next year." Jan pointed out that the vision and outcomes had been developed with all members of the community and would be turned into a strong plan at the fall retreat. Further, she described her approaches in working with teachers and the plans for a district undertaking for a new teacher evaluation system. She explained the core planning sessions for the summer and how they had come about. Her tone was open and nondefensive; each person talked, each person was heard. "I've found," ended Jan, "that if teachers don't talk to one another about their work, that they don't talk about improving learning for children. We need for you to participate with us in those discussions." The parents were animated and positive as they left Jan's office. They felt they had been heard but said they would reserve judgment for several more months. "Don't forget lunch on Monday," called Martha over her shoulder as she left the room.

The core teachers had chosen the last week of June and the first week of July for the planning workshop. Gretchen had arranged for a few visitors who could share their experiences—a teacher education professor from the nearby university, two language arts teachers from a middle school in an adjoining district, and a county office curriculum specialist. They all came on the first day, and then returned on separate days to work along side the team; department chairs, leadership team members, and Jan and Bob dropped in whenever possible. The results promised to be exciting; they were planning to report at the retreat.

Year 2

Following the completion of the core workshop, the balance of July was a mixture of reflection, family, and work for Jan—and others as well. She wrote in her personal journal: "On balance, I'm feeling fairly good about this year. I think it proved wise of the faculty to include some of the accepted teacher leaders in the leadership team. This bridge was invaluable, and yet I'm beginning to feel that we must expand the base of leaders this year by discovering other structures for participation."

In mid-August, a call came from John Macy. "I'd like to set up an appointment to see you," said John, "I'll need about an hour." They scheduled the meeting for August 18. John seemed self-conscious. "Not like him," thought Jan, "this must be serious." "What I have to say is serious," began John after a few moments. "I've thought about this for weeks." Jan was listening intently. "This new approach . . . your new approach . . . just isn't for me," admitted John. "What do you mean?" asked Jan. John continued, "I believe I am a competent and professional teacher. I enjoy my work and do the best I can by students. I keep up with my profession, and I'm active in the state and national mathematics associations. I read the journals regularly. You see, I've thought a lot about how I improve my work. Talk and working together doesn't do it for me. I'm considering asking for a transfer." Jan was quiet and thoughtful for several moments. "Can you understand what we're trying to do here?" asked Jan. "I think so," said John, "I notice that for several people, working together seems valuable. I'm just not sure that I can do it."

"I've been thinking a lot about these dilemmas and my role in them" began Jan. "This summer, I've needed to reexamine some of my actions and ground them once again in my values. Let me share with you some of my thoughts. I truly believe that we are, and must be, a community. That means to me that we must be both independent and interdependent, that we must stretch ourselves in both directions. Communities, like families, work for both adults and children—we need sustaining relationships, for people who care about us to hang around. We need to make sense of our work together. I understand and deeply appreciate your independence and your professionalism. And I would ask that you remain open to exploring your own possibilities for interdependence. I would ask that you give us a year and that you help me understand what you need in order to be able to make that commitment."

John reflected, for what seemed like a long time. "I think I can do that," he began. "Also, I think I would like to come back to you in a month and respond to your second request, to tell you what I personally need from this situation." "Thank you," said Jan. "About the third week in September?"

A few days later, the leadership team met to finish the planning for the retreat. Jan shared some of the ideas emerging from the management retreat she had attended, particularly on teacher evaluation. The fall retreat held great promise—and apprehension. Would everyone show up? What if they didn't? Team members agreed to help anyone who wasn't there to "catch up" by spending time with them. The agenda built on the vision and outcomes developed in the second semester of the previous year.

The retreat began on Thursday morning of the week before Labor Day. As each person arrived, it was clear that they were relaxed and positive, seemingly trusting the 2 days to the planning of their colleagues. Two teachers were not there; one had a family emergency, the other "just couldn't get back."

During these 2 days, the group played and laughed, had quiet reflection time alone and together, and developed a plan for implementing their vision and student outcomes. Most striking among their accomplishments were agreements regarding essential questions that they would ask one another as they went along and interdisciplinary work groups, as well as plans to look at "some kind of student work" and to watch one another teach by second semester. The core planning group shared their plans, and there seemed to be much interest in them. There were moments when John got up and took a walk by himself and when a few others looked disengaged. "But I think we're making great progress as a community," said Susan to her tablemates at breakfast on the following morning.

The opening of school was positive and surprisingly uneventful. The new core began with a few days of getting-acquainted activities, reminding each other of cooperative learning skills, becoming oriented to the school, and recalling "what we learned last year that we bring with us to our learning together at Evergreen." Parents were invited in for all of these activities, and they appeared to be a group that the school could consider 3-year partners.

The greatest undertakings of the leadership team, now augmented by one parent, one student, and the library aide, was to do some of the detailed designing of the ideas agreed on at the retreat. Finding time for interdisciplinary planning groups to meet was a real sticking point. "We are going to have to have an early release day, like the elementary schools," noted Jack emphatically. "Or a late start day!" added Garth. "We will need to prepare a request to the board," observed Jan. "Would you work on drafting that for us, Jack?" "Sure," consented Jack, "but I'll need some assistance with the format." Meanwhile, the team decided to propose that the planning groups meet every other week for breakfast. "The contract could be a problem here," noted Bob, as he sat in for part of one meeting. "What do you mean?" queried the parent, Cynthia. "The teacher's contract with the district," explained Bob, "permits two required staff meetings per month." "These aren't required," insisted Ann. The issue felt unresolved.

In the third week in September, John Macy came to see Jan for their scheduled appointment. "I've been thinking a great deal about our conversation, Jan," started John, "and I think I'm ready to tell you what I need. I won't cut myself off from the group, and I'll carry my share of the responsibilities, but I would like to do so on my own whenever possible." "I'm relieved, John, and eager to find ways to work with you on this. I want you to know that I've learned a great deal from you about how teachers get better at their work. I do feel that it's important that you design the formative assessment of the 7th-grade pilot with the core teachers, but I can envision other undertakings that could be done solo." "I think you're right about the 7th grade, and I'll plan on that. Meanwhile, I'd like to submit professional goals that reflect my actual work, instead of the pro forma goals that I usually submit." Jan smiled, "That's the least that we can do, John. I wouldn't have wanted it any other way. Actually, I have an idea for an undertaking that could be very useful to our work with team learning and our look at new assessment processes. There's a professor at U.C. Berkeley working with metacognition and mathematics. Could you get us some specific information on this?" "I do know of his work," said John, "and I'd be glad to."

The interdisciplinary teams began to focus on student outcomes, building in action research around the questions that were forming: Are our students accomplishing this outcome? How do we know? What other information do we need? What are the sources of that information?

Each faculty meeting included discussion of the group work, time spent learning facilitation skills, and examination of the pressing issues of the day. Information was made available through a weekly memo, a posting board in the faculty room, and individual contacts from leadership team members. "By second semester, we'll need to broaden the governance structure," thought Jan.

Jan had begun to regularly place the district and school budget printouts in the faculty room. Faculty had never been privy to this information before; demystifying the process seemed essential to countering the charges of secrecy and favoritism that had been leveled at authorities in both the school and the district. At one faculty meeting, she had explained the accounting codes, and she regularly discussed allocation of resources with the department heads and leadership team. The distribution of school resources was made jointly.

On the second day after the winter break, Jan found a letter on her desk. It had been written by Gretchen, but was signed by six teachers. It read:

Dear Jan,
You know how excited we are about what has been happening here, and we are glad to be a part of it. We are learning a great deal and enjoying a closeness with the staff that we've never experienced before. However, we are beginning to feel overwhelmed. We can't seem to do enough, to work enough hours in the day. We are undertaking so many new skills and feeling less competent than we did before. Perhaps we won't be able to do this; perhaps we do not have adequate preparation or talents! We need to talk with you. This letter is just our way of opening the discussion.
Sincerely,

| Gretchen | Carrie | Kelly |
| Sam | Katherine | Warren |

Jan spent a lot of time on the school grounds that day, talking with kids and clearing her head—talking with kids had that effect on Jan; it always brought with it a sense of perspective. In mid-afternoon, she dropped by Gretchen's room. Gretchen looked a little embarrassed but also pleased to see Jan. "Before all of us talk, I want to ask your permission to share this with the leadership team," Jan began. Gretchen thought for a few moments. "Sure," she said. "We realized that we needed to be ready to share our feelings with the whole staff." "Will you let the others know that we've talked?" asked Jan.

On the next afternoon, Jan shared the letter with the leadership team. They asked what Jan had done. She explained. A few members said that they were beginning to feel the same way. "I haven't noticed that my teachers are becoming less competent," observed Eric, the 9th-grade member of the team. "In fact, classes are getting more interesting." Team members watched Eric with interest as he spoke. "One of the things that we've failed to do adequately," observed Susan, "is to let people know what to expect from change." "I'm not sure that we know!" remarked Garth. "There must be a great deal of research on this topic, isn't there, Jan?" He turned to Jan, who nodded. "I think that is one important piece of the puzzle," began Ann, but we may also need to set more priorities and eliminate a few things that we continue to do." "I hear some promising possibilities," summarized Jack. "Eric reminded us that reassurances might be in order; and, as Susan has noted, we haven't adequately talked with people about the natural consequences of change; and we do need to let go of some things." "While these are good options," observed Jan, "we need to hear from the authors of the letter first. Only then will we understand what this is about." The team agreed that another person, Ann, would join Jan as she talked with the six teachers.

The conversation with the six teachers revealed a surprisingly high degree of frustration. Among the comments:

> "We let our excitement carry us away. Then 4 days before Christmas I realized that I hadn't even found time to do my own shopping. I called Gretchen."
> "I was a good teacher, already—I think. I wanted to get better, but that isn't happening."
> "I can't decide what's important to do. There's too much."
> "In spite of my busy schedule, I still don't feel like I'm reaching the most needy kids in my classes."
> "Parents are as demanding as ever. What do I tell them? Be patient?"

Ann and Jan listened intently, asking questions, clarifying, trying to put ideas together. "We need to talk with the staff," observed Ann. "Yes, I agree," acknowledged Sam. "How will we go about this?" "Would you meet with the leadership team so we can plan this together?" asked Jan. They agreed.

On the following Tuesday, the 11 people met together in the conference room. Gretchen summarized their conversation with Jan and Ann. Together, they developed a plan for the next staff meeting, during which time all staff would talk in small groups and as a whole about the issues presented here. Jan would lead a discussion about change and transition, and what is normal to expect. Jack would lead a process for deciding what to "let go of" and further prioritizing their uses of their own energies and resources. Before the meeting, all of the people involved in the planning would have small conversations with staff, alerting them to the agenda and the recent history leading up to this plan. This gathering was planned as a dinner meeting. Everyone attended.

The staff seemed to make a leap forward as a community after this historic meeting. Priorities were reset, and several traditional undertakings were dropped (for example, fundraisers during school time, finishing some texts cover-to-cover, submitting daily lesson plans). A staff development day, set for late February, would reflect this focus; and the agreement about examining student work would still remain at the top of their agenda. They had become committed to finding out together whether students were learning. The funding of the school improvement program meant that late-start days could be made available for collegial work.

The leadership team proposed that each interdisciplinary planning group choose one of its members as a representative to an expanded governance group, along with a few parents and older students. The proposal was accepted, and the leadership team members were reelected as well. Ann and Garth moved to the larger leadership group, and Gretchen and John Macy moved onto the leadership team. The new leaders met after school to orient themselves and plan the fall retreat. The larger governance group would be called the school council. Both the leadership team and the school council reflected together on the evolution of participation at Evergreen and focused their discussion on the patterns of relationships in the school and how these could be extended and strengthened.

Year 3

July journal entries,

Ann: I have been a leader at Evergreen for a long time. Of course, the requirements of a leader were different, more subversive and manipulative. I didn't like myself then. Could I have always been the kind of leader who supported the growth of others??

Jan: Did I have these plans in my mind? Have I been acting out a script all along? I don't want to think so. No, I can't accept that. There are some recurring themes and values, and things feel right. I, too, am changing in the process.

The retreat agenda included discussions on the extended core and some additional research findings as well as the newly proposed teacher evaluation system. The interdisciplinary groups, led by the representatives to the school council, structured conversations on three of the key student outcomes: democratic citizenship, written communication, and self-reflection. In each case, samples of student work were discussed as a means of interpreting the range of performance and the range of criteria that had been identified in each area. A work session established procedures for designing student rubrics for portfolio assessment. A "weaving" activity posed questions designed to test the interconnectedness of school programs and how they relate to the school vision and student outcomes ("How is this connected?" is repeated and responded to as the conversation identifies and describes the school's undertakings).

By the third week of school, a small group of parents had called for an appointment with Jan. "We want you to know that we represent a group of parents who are concerned with the quality of progress that our students will make here at Evergreen," began one parent. "Tell me what you mean by 'quality of progress,'" responded Jan. "We understand," continued another, "that students are deciding what 'good work' looks like, in other words, they are deciding what is good enough."

"I'm beginning to understand," said Jan. "We have begun to implement an alternative assessment program through which students will help decide on and select their best work. Over time—a year, 3 years—students will be able to observe and understand their own growth. They are involved in developing a range of criteria, sometimes called a rubric, through which they can reflect on and make choices among their own works." With an edge of impatience, one parent suggested, "this seems very complicated for junior high school. Frankly, I'm not at all persuaded that they can be that responsible."

"We have increasing faith and solid evidence that the children have the capacities to do this work, Mrs. Allen," continued Jan. "We have observed improvements in many forms of performance: fewer students are doing poorly in their grades, achievement has improved on the district criterion-based tests, children are evidencing more cooperative behavior in and out of class. But I'm not expecting you to be convinced so quickly. I'd like to invite you to any of our next two school council meetings and to our staff development day in October. I'd like for you to see for yourselves what we're attempting. And I believe this topic will be on the next parent group agenda as well." The parents requested more information in writing, including the dates and times of upcoming meetings. "Other schools must be struggling with these same issues," thought Jan, "I'll raise it at the principals' center meeting."

Year 3 at Evergreen saw a consistent pattern in the conversations and meetings: student work, the teaching and learning process, and action research findings that enabled staff to interpret their own teaching and to identify new skills that were needed. Tough issues were still there: a couple of teachers who were experiencing new teaching difficulties, community and family issues centering on latchkey children, variations in parent expectations. Jack, Ann, Gretchen, Garth, Sam, and John increasingly led the conversations and the reflections. Values were affirmed; assumptions continued to be challenged. Jan's, Bob's, and Susan's roles changed. Jan worked more directly with issues of teaching and learning; Bob played a more prominent role in administrative issues; Susan reframed her work as facilitating evolving relationship patterns and designing new structures for cooperation among students and adults.

Involvement in the regional and state networks for school improvement enabled staff to learn new ways through which they could talk about student work and their own teaching as well as to engage students and parents in talking about the products and performances of students.

Not everyone at Evergreen had been persuaded and engaged by the new turn of events. By the beginning of the third year, two teachers had requested and received transfers to one of the high schools in the district. By the end of the third year, two other teachers had been persuaded to take early retirement. The work at Evergreen was demanding, and it broke down protective barriers that had kept students and parents at arm's length. For most faculty, the discomfort resulted in professional and personal growth; for four faculty members, the dissonance was too sharp, prompting a "moving away from" the fields of change.

Discussion of Evergreen Middle School

The incidents and processes described above do not represent a complete picture of Evergreen during these 3 years; they were chosen to portray the themes and rhythm of evolving change and relationships. The process was fluid and inclusive, expanding its boundaries in response to the diversity of thought and needs of the education community. However, the boundaries were strongly informed by the prevailing values of participation, diversity, teaching and learning for all children, collegiality, and informed systemic change.

The patterns of relationships formed around the conversations that were initiated in response to the need to lead the change processes, the feedback spirals among leadership team members and other staff and parents, the attempt to make sense of discrepant information, visioning and student outcomes, professional planning, and shared work.

At first, the leadership team served as a support group and sounding board for Jan, a bridge between Jan and the rest of the staff. Eventually, team members gained the understandings that enabled them to become thoughtful leaders in their own right. Would a leadership team be needed after the fourth year? Perhaps not, depending upon the size of the school and the other structures that have formed around new tasks and roles. Or perhaps it would continue to change form or function.

Incidents that brought dissonance and fluctuations to the school played a critical role in the rhythm and movement of change at Evergreen. These occurrences included the presentation of 7th-grade data in the fall of the first year and the subsequent inquiry, parental critiques and questions, the vision and outcomes as a means of framing new questions, and the letter from Gretchen. The system response to dissonance became: dissonance, processing and conversing, redefining, and moving on. Whenever the dissonant information looked as though it might be particularly disturbing, small conversations were held first.

The school staff was also confronted, initially by Jan, with a few *insis-*

tencies, which became part of the "grammar" of change. These were ideas and structures that she felt would play a central or "turnkey" role in moving the school: the formation of the leadership team, working through the issues raised by data, visioning, the acquisition of needed resources, the retreat, student outcomes and a school plan, collegial structures, talking about student work, and expanded governance. As teacher leadership increased, roles shifted and shared language became a regular part of the conversations; the processes seemed to take on a life of their own.

It is important to understand the symbolism and reality of John Macy. John represents one of the most challenging dimensions of school change and a major fluctuation in the system. He is a self-directing individual, competent and concerned as a teacher and professional. Yet, because he has a clearly defined professional life, he can be resistant to changes that bring with them processes he views as distracting. It is critical that the change process be flexible and inclusive enough to benefit from John's strengths and invoke his own potential for contributing to the community. He is able to redefine himself and his world view in order to include relational work, but only if his individual needs are also given room for acknowledgment and development.

Did the school become a self-organizing system? After the first major fluctuation (the 7th-grade data), there was a shift in the system; certain interaction patterns were forming and re-forming themselves. New collegial groupings began to arise spontaneously after each fluctuation or discrepant event (new planning processes, ad hoc groups, small teams of teachers sharing a curiosity or interest). There was a time when dissipation was considered to be deterioration and loss; however, the "dissipative structures" of natural systems reframe this notion as a "part of the process by which the system lets go of its present form so that it can re-emerge in a form better suited to the demands of the present environment" (Wheatley, 1992, p. 19). Gretchen's letter activated a dissipative process by which the staff were compelled to make sense of what was happening to them and let go of some old ways of doing things. This "release" actually diffused the press of growing frustration and confusion that was accumulating from the change efforts. The processes for "allowing" dissipation to take place required listening, processing new information, and providing continuous support and presence. The staff, by letting go of some old patterns, made a major leap forward in their relationships and their progress.

By midway through the third year, Evergreen had become a self-organizing system; that is, the patterns and structures were in place that enabled the school to function as a self-renewing organization. The school was no longer primarily dependent on the principal's understanding of systemic change, for those understandings had become "holographic" in nature—

each staff member held a substantially complete understanding or image of what he or she was trying to accomplish at Evergreen.

Jan had not had firm outcomes in mind. However, her world view, relationships, and actions were strongly informed by her constructivist philosophy and her strong core values, which formed a perspective from which she could genuinely interact and create knowledge and meaning with others.

CONCLUSION

Constructing school change is an emergent process driven by constructivist learning and leading. Professionals make sense of their work as they consider information that is gathered, generated, and interpreted in interaction with others. The reciprocal processes of constructivist leadership evoke potential, enable participants to construct meaning, break set with old assumptions, and frame actions based on new behaviors and purposeful intention. These processes are propelled by meaning-making, because meaning-making is *motion*. It is the motion of "sea change," the whole system moving in upon itself and shifting forward at the same time. And it is deliberate, not the serendipitous outcome of an "anything-goes-as-long-as-we-have-consensus" stance.

Constructing school change is a function of "the conversations." In the next chapter, we look more closely at the nature of conversations and what it means to lead them.

Leading the Conversations

Linda Lambert

"What is the use of a book," thought Alice, "without pictures or
conversations?"

Lewis Carroll,
Alice's Adventures in Wonderland, Ch. 1

In the story of Evergreen Middle School, we encountered more than 26
different kinds of conversations. Evergreen staff, parents, and students con-
versed in small groups and one-on-one about all issues affecting the school;
they processed new information in meetings, planned and problem-solved;
they sought to understand each other and interpret these new understandings; they talked about values, vision, and student outcomes; they reflected-
in-action and upon action. Eventually, they talked about student work and
their own teaching. This chapter explores the concept of conversations and
what it takes to lead them. *A primary role of the constructivist leader is to lead
the conversations.*

Conversations give form to the reciprocal processes of leadership that
make up the sum of the spaces or fields among us; they create the text of our
lives. In Chapter 2, we discussed the concept of spaces, or zones, among us
that constitute the texture of our relationships. The conversations serve as
the medium for the reciprocal processes that enable participants in a school
community to construct meanings toward a common purpose about teaching
and learning. Conversations are fractals of communities; that is, they re-
create on a smaller scale the ecological processes of the larger community.
Conversations are the visible manifestation of constructivist leadership,
thereby encompassing the reciprocal relationships that make meaning and
community possible.

THE CONVERSATIONS

We are referring to all forms of talk or dialogue as "the conversations,"
even conversations with self. That does not mean, however, that all talk is
conversation. Conversations that are constructivist in aim and nature have

some common qualities or characteristics distinguishing them from talk that has undeclared agendas or agendas that are directed by persuasion through power. By undeclared agenda we mean talk that appears to have a public purpose, but instead stems from a private purpose of manipulation. We speak of the qualities of dialogue, for "anti-dialogue does not communicate, but rather issues communiques" (Freire, 1973, p. 46). Talk that is directed by power involves those discussions through which individuals holding hierarchical authority over another are declaring a demand, or "request." This does not mean that there will never be a role for this latter type of discussion; it does mean that we would not consider this interchange to be a constructivist conversation.

In a constructivist conversation, each individual comes to understand the purpose of the talk, since the relationship is one of reciprocity. Each person is growing in understanding; each person is seeking some interpretation of truth as he or she perceives it. My colleague, Jan Huls, principal of Jefferson School in San Leandro, California, finds that there are two enabling elements to such conversations: a nurturing environment and a mutual search for truth. Habermas (1973) placed "communicative competence" at the center of his work in hermeneutics, such competence referring to the genuine pursuit of truth.

What does this mean—"truth"? "Truth," in the sense that we use it here, refers to the intention to bring to bear to the interpretation of the current experience our past experiences, beliefs, and perceptions so that we can come to understand. It is the genuine pursuit of understanding as it exists in the moment and within the context of the conversation, the relationship, and the community. This means, of course, that this understanding will be context-influenced and developmental; therefore it will change with time.

Carlsen (1988) describes a provocative meaning-making process that is strikingly similar to collaborative inquiry. She presents four elements that she thinks are central to meaning-making interactions: the presence of a "holding environment," the gathering of data or information, a search for patterns and processes, and reinforcement of new abilities to think about one's own thinking. The gathering of data and the search for patterns are also at the core of collaborative action research conversations (Sagor, 1992). Carlsen's fourth dimension, metacognition, will be explored in more depth in the following chapter. Below, we compare these descriptions with the reciprocal processes described here as a means of further understanding dialogic conversation.

The idea of a "holding environment" as described here was first advanced by Kegan (1982) and is similar to our use of the phrase "trusting environment" (the first reciprocal process, evoking potential in a trusting environment). According to Kegan, there are a series of holding environments, of cultures of embeddedness, which hold onto and support us, stick around through the changes and afterward during the processes of integration, and eventually let go. Every community and relationship has its "holding" qualities, the most healthy of which support us in the processes of coevolution. Trusting is especially important in constructivist learning, since, as Kegan points out, "there are few things as intimate as constructing meaning in the presence of another" (1982, p. 16).

The conversations described in this chapter are characterized by *shared intention* of genuine "truth-seeking," *remembrances and reflections* of the past, a *search for meaning* in the present, a *mutual revelation of ideas and information,* and *respectful listening.* Participants share an intention to seek "truth" together. Remembrances and reflections are evoked by the genuine interactions in a meaning-making arena. As participants search for meaning, they try to make sense of what is being talked about together, revealing to one another their ideas, experiences, and insights. These rich processes are made possible by really listening to one another, listening for words, expression, emotion, and meaning.

A conversation may not include all of these elements during each interaction, for some conversations are short and informal. However, all of the elements are usually implied or understood, based on prior experiences with the relationships of the conversants. These conversations occur within the context of a trusting environment. We consider these elements to be central to constructivist conversations, although the content and goals of the conversations will vary, as will the entry points into the process.

A TAXONOMY OF CONVERSATIONS

Whenever the word *taxonomy,* or classification, is used, qualifications or caveats are required. The idea is being employed here to embody the common elements discussed above while revealing different initial purposes or entry points (see Figure 4.1). No category is self-contained; they are fluid, overlapping, and informing of each other. Sometimes they are one and the same; for instance, a one-on-one dialogic conversation can be both inquiring and sustaining.

A principal colleague, Rick Rubino, uses a trust-building activity in which a long piece of nylon rope, about 40 feet in length, is shaped into a square by four blindfolded people. The shape takes form as they talk together. While the rope may become a four-sided figure, it can also take on any other shape. This taxonomy of conversations is the nylon rope.

Figure 4.1. Typology of Conversations

DIALOGIC
One-on-one
Mentoring, coaching
Relationship building
Reflection narrative writing

COMMON ELEMENTS
Shared Intention
Search for sense-
    making/understanding
Remembrance & reflection-
    beliefs, experiences
Revelation of ideas,
    information
Respectful listening

PARTNERING
Parent involvement
Community
    participation
Professional networking
Activism

INQUIRING
Problem-finding
Action Research
Critical inquiry
Information
    sharing
Problem-
    resolution

SUSTAINING
Visioning
Conceptual work
    of whole community
Resource discovery
Communities of memory
Sustaining direction

Illustration by John E. Antis

Dialogic Conversations

Dialogue is conversation in a reciprocal relationship, in this case, with oneself (realizing that this is not an accepted definition) or with one other person. We often use the term *reflection* to denote the processes that can be activated in the dialogic conversations. When calling forth our own experiences, beliefs, and perceptions about an idea, we are simply remembering or recollecting; when we also assess and reevaluate the assumptions underlying our remembrances (we stop and think), we are reflecting (Dewey, 1938; Schön, 1987). Reflection and self-construction are the central purposes of the dialogic conversation, and this requires that we consider "conversations" with the self in this domain.

Schön (1987) likens the conversation to musical improvisation. "Conversation is verbal improvisation. . . . the participants are making something . . . an artifact with its own meaning and coherence. Their reflection-in-action is a reflective conversation" (pp. 30–31). Conversation is discovery, constructed in interaction with one another.

Dialogic conversations take many forms; they can be the complete conversation of two colleagues talking through an idea, a preplanned conversation about teaching, an informal moment when we lift a cup from the stream of conversation that is ever-present in a relationship.

"So, what did you think of the idea?"
"You mean the advisement discussion?"
"Uh-huh."
"I see a need, but I'm not sure this is how to go about it. I was trained
   as a teacher, not a counselor."
"How else could we tackle it?"

Or it might be as formal as a postobservation conference within a cognitive coaching process. Cognitive coaching brings a strong constructivist approach to the "supervision" table. The purpose of the postobservation of teaching conference, particularly, is the construction of meaning, of self-reflection and sense-making. Because the process is reciprocal, both individuals are seeking to understand the teaching episode. This purpose is not shared by all approaches to clinical supervision; many forms of supervision cast the supervisor in the role of teaching the teacher about "good teaching," using the conference as a forum. Under those circumstances, the supervisor is the expert, the teacher is the student. The following brief excerpts were chosen from the Association for Supervision and Curriculum Development tape, *Another Set of Eyes,* by Costa and Garmston for their text, *Cognitive Coaching* (1994):

Marilyn: Well, how do you think it went, Lloyd?
Lloyd: I'm not sure yet. I think I have to talk it through a little bit. I think it
   went well. During the first three minutes of interaction, I got back from
   the student what I expected to get back from this group—that they
   wouldn't have any specific gross misconceptions about the two concepts.
   When we started to do the exemplars, however, I felt as though, at least
   at one point, that I was losing them. I had the feeling I was talking with
   or working with only about five or six students.
Marilyn: What did they do that made you feel that way? (p. 24)

The following slice of conversation (featuring Diane Zimmerman) focuses on the same portion of the postobservation conversation, during which teachers are struggling to make sense of their teaching:

Diane: How did you feel about the lesson in general?

Ellie: Well, if I had it to do over, I would leave out the part about multiplying and have it be eight times bigger because that just seemed like one extra thing for kids to think about. And when I planned it, I thought that the ones that are really into art and math would choose that. But there were all kinds of people making, I thought, bad decisions about doing that. (p. 25)

And, we might ask, "What do you mean by 'bad decisions,' Ellie?" When self-reflection reaches this quality of construction, it is clear that there is a high degree of trust in the relationship and that both individuals understand the nature of their work together. The power of questioning within conversations will be developed by Diane in the next chapter.

Another powerful relationship context for dialogic conversation can be that of mentoring and mutual or co-mentoring. While the mentoring relationship is initially uneven, it is nevertheless imbued with a caring investment in the growth of each other. Three years ago, as a teaching intern at James Logan High School in Union City, California, Stacy Kopshy entered into an unexpected set of mentoring relationships:

As a beginning teacher I was excited to know that Ms. Sklavos would teach me to plan interesting lectures and show me ways to easily create multiple-choice tests. Instead of the lesson plans I envisioned, Ms. Sklavos [a recent California Literature Project graduate] challenged my own concept of the classroom. She encouraged me to think beyond the prepared lessons I could present to the students and, instead, to coach the students as they *discovered* literature.

The following year I shared a common prep with Ms. Nelson. In the same manner as Ms. Sklavos, Ms. Nelson never just presented information to the students. Instead she modeled lessons that caught the attention of each student as he/she was forced to interpret the literature on an individual basis. (letter to the California Literature Project, June 20, 1994).

These teachers taught Stacy to be a constructivist teacher and a constructivist learner; they altered her view of herself as a teacher and her world view about teaching and learning. The relationship of a new teacher to an experienced teacher or a new administrator to an experienced administrator can provide for these fundamental processes in the construction process: a reexamination of the self and world view within the context of a supportive relationship (Lambert, 1986). The process can also be similar to a cognitive coaching conference: Personal experiences and perceptions are elicited; feedback or information that causes dissonance can be introduced; the discussion and self-reflection centers on trying to make sense of any discrepancies that are encountered. Often the process is a coevolutionary one; both mentor and mentee are redefining themselves and their world views. Eventually the relationship evolves into one of co-mentoring, or, if the mentor cannot make a shift to equity, the mentee tends to move out of the relationship.

Many of the qualities being described here as part of a mentoring relationship can also be found in the current term "critical friend." A critical friend, writes Costa and Kallick (1993, p. 50),

> is a trusted person who asks provocative questions, provides data to be examined through another lens, and offers critique of a person's work as a friend. A critical friend takes the time to fully understand the context of the work presented and the outcomes that the person or group is working toward.

The friend is an advocate for the success of that work. He or she observes, joins in the research process, provides feedback and data, questions and probes. The critical friend, like the mentor, must be invited into life.

Clearly the dialogic conversation processes underlie the conversations that follow, for the reciprocal processes of dialogue evoke potential in a trusting environment, reconstruct or break set with old assumptions, focus on the construction of meaning, and help to frame actions that embody new behaviors and purposeful intentions.

Inquiring Conversations

It is the inquiring conversation that distinguishes a self-renewing school from a stagnant or declining one. Just as personal inquiry is at the heart of the dialogic conversation, organizational inquiry is at the heart of this cluster of conversations. These are the conversations that occur around inquiry processes such as action research, critical inquiry, disaggregating school data, the protocol, and planned conversations around student work. In Chapter 3 we described these inquiry modes and the significance to whole school change of information that is gathered, generated, and interpreted.

Above, we noted the interesting parallels between Sagor's "steps" in collaborative action research and Carlsen's phases of meaning-making interactions. A closer examination of these two works and the concepts in this book are presented in Figure 4.2.

These processes are even more similar than they appear in Figure 4.2. For instance, Sagor's "problem formulation" phase includes constructivist processes of preliminary investigation, including discovering what teachers already know and think about the topic under question. The collection of

Figure 4.2. Three Approaches to Inquiring Conversations

CARLSEN: *Meaning-Making*	SAGOR: *Collaborative Action Research*	LAMBERT: *Constructivist Leadership-Reciprocal Processes*
Establishing a holding environment	Establishing of trust as a prerequisite	Evoking potential in a trusting environment
Data collection	Problem formulation	Challenging old assumptions (data focus)
Seeking patterns—examining old cognitive structures	Data collection Data analysis Reporting results	Constructing meaning/sense-making (metacognitive)
Reinforcing ability to examine one's own thinking (metacognition)	Action planning	Framing action for new behaviors and intentions

data is central in all approaches, enabling participants to analyze, reexamine, construct meaning, and challenge old assumptions. The understanding of personal patterns is made more explicit in Carlsen and in this text, as are reflection and metacognition.

Carlsen begins with data collection, acknowledging that a nonlinear approach that allows us to deduce the issues or problems at hand can be as powerful. This is also true of disaggregating student data and examining student work. Although the impetus for seeking these data is supported by strong hunches, data collection is a journey of observation and discovery. We are not certain of the problem, of what we will find; therefore, there is the possibility of being surprised. "Surprise" is becoming recognized as one of the great gifts of community, a gift that tickles the static qualities of our work and activates dynamic thinking. Like curiosity, surprise provokes synergy.

Let's listen in on a meeting of a high school leadership team,

George: As you will recall, we agreed to look at the available school data and disaggregate those data for race, ethnicity, and gender. Here is what we have: attendance (daily and period), suspensions, expulsions, district test scores, grade analysis sheets.

Joan: We separated the data into columns so that we can look at the patterns that arise in all categories. We've enlarged each sheet and posted it, and you each have your individual copies. Let's take some time to look at it.

Lillie: A number of patterns are beginning to form. Look at the consistent

patterns for Latino and African American males; more suspensions
and expulsions, but not necessarily poorer attendance! Latina girls
have the best attendance, yet . . .

Gary: What?

Lillie: Their test scores are slightly above average, but their grades reveal
that they are getting D's or F's in more than half of their classes. I won-
der why?

The discussion continued to discover patterns and possible interpretations.

Joan: How will we present this to the faculty?

George: They need to go through exactly the same process that we did. The
most powerful aspect of inquiry is discovering the patterns yourself.

Joan: Agreed?

After the staff engaged in a similar process, they were ready to frame actions
around these discoveries. This is an area of inquiry that often requires breaking set with old assumptions, perceptions. The analysis took place over two
meetings involving facilitated small-group discussions. Defensive stances
were challenged and redirected (see the next chapter).

The faculty at Bryant School in San Francisco regularly use their faculty
meetings for protocol discussions. Barbara Karvelis, former principal, describes a shift in the dynamics of professional inquiry, at first initiated and
directed by the principal (personal communication, August 27, 1994):

> It was agreed that all teacher information that was normally dissemin-
> ated (verbally) at a staff meeting be placed in a binder where staff
> could read it at their leisure. In place of one of the monthly staff meet-
> ings, a protocol session took place in which a teacher team prepared a
> burning question and shared information centered around the examina-
> tion of student work. After several protocol sessions, two teachers
> came to the meeting somewhat confused about the task. At this point,
> the staff took over the session and helped the teachers rethink their
> question and place it in the proper context. A shift in thinking oc-
> curred whereby the process was no longer driven by the principal but
> was owned by the staff. From that point on the staff took charge of the
> protocol process.

The dynamic described by Karvelis centrally involves teachers moving into
leadership, exercising the options that had become available in the school
culture.

Morgan Lambert reports the following portion of a turnkey conversation among two schools at the May 1994 Symposium of the California Center for School Restructuring. The focus on student outcomes and student work is central to inquiring conversations.

Teacher A (Analysis team): As you can tell from our presentation, we're having trouble with our "risk-taker" outcome. We're not sure we can get solid evidence that a student is becoming a "risk-taker."

Teacher B (Reflector team): You know, I wasn't sure what you meant by that term. It almost seemed like you were looking for an "impulsive gambler" type of behavior, but you weren't sure.

Teacher C (Reflector team): Yes, and I think you're going to have to collect more than one kind of data to make that call.

Teacher D (Analysis team): Those are helpful comments and they confirm my own hunch that we've got to do some rethinking on that student outcome—maybe re-phrase it—and certainly have the assessment need in mind as we revise it.

Teacher A: Yes, let's bring that up at the next restructuring committee meeting.

As we have noted elsewhere, the constructivist process of meaning-making is motion, it is developmental. Unless experiences are created and negotiated together, this development usually does not take place. Conversations in school often cease when conversants encounter discrepancies, opposition, rough spots—people back away, become silent, divert their interests elsewhere. "Effective collaboration is not always easy," point out Fullan and Hargreaves (1992), ". . . to bite the bullet of fundamental, deep and lasting change, improvement efforts should move beyond cooperative decision-making and planning, sharing experience and resources, and supportive interpersonal relationships into joint work, mutual observation, and focused reflective inquiry" (p. 57). As we saw in the last two examples above, establishing processes and posing questions that draw forth new information are essential to leading the conversations.

Sustaining Conversations

The idea of "sustaining" conversations is drawn from the concept of "sustainable development" in ecology. Sustaining conversations are those that continue, endure, over a period of time and are essential to sustaining the development of the community. Changes can be made, but we have to ask whether those changes represent true developmental changes in the staff and school. If the individuals are becoming different, that is, taking on new assumptions about teaching and learning, this is sustainable development, and it emerges primarily from sustaining conversations.

Clearly, dialogic and inquiring conversations can be sustaining as well. We are beginning to see an image of conversations more like this:)))—a pattern whereby each conversation is a part of another one because they share common elements. Sustaining conversations need to be tied to enabling structures and real work; it is almost impossible to contrive sustainability. Such structures might include the talk of leadership teams, team-teaching groups who share the same preparation period, regularly scheduled portions of staff meetings, action research teams, and shortened-day staff meetings of various forms. The structure that allows for sustaining conversations includes a specific time set aside with predictable regularity, a group understanding of the purposes of these times, and someone to facilitate the conversation. When I was a junior high principal, I assumed that once we had managed to schedule teachers into common preparation periods for team planning, the teachers would know how to talk with one another. Not so. We found that teachers still talked narrowly about individual children and instructional materials. It took a facilitator (during the first year, a facilitator from outside the group; subsequently a facilitator from within the group was chosen) to enable the teachers to develop an agenda for their work and keep it moving toward conclusions.

Although this may appear to be what Fullan and Hargreaves (1992) call "contrived collegiality," such enabling structures are essential to sustainability and should be designed by teachers and administrators in response to emerging work needs. They also need to be enveloped by dialogic conversations that are informal and persistent. Chuck Bowen, the principal of Broadmoor Junior High School in Pekin, Illinois, who was first a facilitator with the Coalition of Essential Schools, was aware of the need to work with collegial processes. He describes a joint staff undertaking:

> We set a standard early on in terms of process, about how decisions had to be made. . . . Over time, we learned how to work through conflicts, how to disagree and not take it personally. (Quoted in Prager, 1993, p. 2)

"Sustaining" is the key element through which polite interactions work themselves into authentic talk about real work.

"Authentic talk about real work" is usually tied to the processes of teaching and learning, although we observe that some programs seem to define these too narrowly. Teaching and learning are, and are affected by, all the experiences that children and adults have in and out of schools. In some programs, incoherence grows out of separating discipline, guidance, extracurricular activities, and parent involvement from the teaching and learning conversations. Conversations worth having need to connect the philosophy and actions of the school to all learning opportunities.

All groups and all cultures that engage in sustaining work and change together go through phases of transition. William Bridges' work in *Managing Transitions* (1991) has been very helpful to educators in numerous schools and districts as a way of understanding the processes that people encounter as they undertake substantive change. The phases of *letting go* of old ways of thinking and acting, *experiencing the neutral zone* of transition, and engaging with *new beginnings* has much relevance to sustaining conversations.

During the "letting go" phase of change, participants need to listen to the losses that each is experiencing. Letting go of old ways of thinking and acting is painful and may not occur unless we go through a "grieving" process. Fortunately, when we work through a constructive mode, people do take a piece of the past with them; their selves are carried forward as they redesign their work. However, when new data challenge old ways of thinking, we need to help each other to be explicit about what we are leaving behind.

As we let go, we enter what Bridges refers to as the "neutral zone," a time of disconnectedness before we take hold of something new. It may be a short time, or it may last several months, depending on the magnitude of the change. Grieving continues during this period, but, intriguingly, creativity is also high. We need an abundance of accurate information, because rumors run rampant. It is a time to envision new ways of working and to ask ourselves: How does all of this fit together?

"New beginnings" can coalesce around purpose and vision. At this time, we need concrete images of what this new work can look like. What does this purpose look like in practice? How will my teaching be different? What student work can we expect? For example? Feedback is even more important now as we formulate new images of a practical vision. Roles that have been emerging and changing now become more explicit. Specific knowledge and skills are brought to bear, and it becomes more clear what additional knowledge and skills are needed. We can develop policies, procedures, and new parameters to fit the new changes. And we are able to reflect on the processes that we have experienced. This awareness of the effects of change on each of us can become an enlightening journey.

This knowledge of transitions is vital to all participants in a school and needs to inform our conversations together. It is particularly important to our sustaining conversations; otherwise we get stuck in transition and are handicapped in our own development. Making sense of what is occurring to ourselves allows us to make sense of what is occurring to others.

Partnership Conversations

Partnership conversations engage individuals and groups who are physically outside of the school into a reciprocal relationship—parents, community, universities, governmental agencies, businesses, professional organizations, networks, cultural organizations, other schools and school districts. Reciprocity (see Chapter 2), or the mutual and dynamic interaction and exchange of ideas and concerns, requires a maturity that usually emerges from opportunities for meaning-making in sustainable communities over time. We need to enlarge the circle of community to be more inclusive than we have been in the past if we are to develop reciprocal partnerships with parents and members of the broader community so that together we can improve learning for children and adults.

A school's relationships with parents and community are notoriously nonreciprocal, with the lack of equity moving in both directions. A few examples:

1. Parents are recruited to serve the school—sponsor fundraisers, work in classrooms, donate time to a school beautification effort, set up for the science fair.
2. Social agencies are called on in emergencies to handle problems that schools are unequipped to deal with.
3. Student outcomes may include community-related goals, but usually as a means of meeting an individualistic outcome.
4. Businesses contribute to schools as a function of their charitable work.
5. Other schools, regional education agencies, and professional networks are sought out to provide training or when they host a program or possess expertise thought to be superior to that in the initiating school.
6. Universities seek out schools in which they can conduct research on human subjects.

In the first three examples, the school's stance is often one of usage; it seeks to "use" parents, agencies, communities, to the perceived welfare of the school. In the next three examples, the one-way relationship points the other way; now we have the school as "subject" or "object" of charity, expertise, and research. Some key questions arise:

What does each entity have to give as well as receive?
What knowledge can these partners construct together, thereby creating

something that did not exist before—something that each had to learn?

If the conversations with these agencies involved a shared intention, a search for sense-making and understanding, remembrances and reflections on their own experiences and beliefs, an openness to ideas and information, and respectful listening, how different would the relationships be? Below are examples in each of the six areas that hold potential for co-evolution.

The *relationship of schools to parents* has probably been the most problematic area of school work because of the centrality of the parent–child–school relationship to learning. Many educators eagerly accept the research findings telling us that student achievement is directly linked to parent involvement; however, in many schools we have not changed our paradigm about the notion of "involvement." Hollins (personal communication, 1994) challenges us to understand that parents have much to teach us about how their own children learn. And if we ask the questions and listen for the answers, we might be able to create a new joint pedagogy (not necessarily a joint curriculum).

Perhaps the most hopeful conversations I have experienced have been in schools in which parent–teacher conferences were thoughtfully organized and planned through advisement programs. This conversation was conducted by the student, Tom.

Tom: I want to thank you both for coming to this conference today. Let me show you some of my work and tell you how I think I'm doing.
Parent: I'm very eager to see it. Do you have any examples of your writings?
Tom: Yes, here are three that I've chosen because they represent my best work.
Parent: What do you mean, "best work"?
Teacher: Tom used criteria that we developed together as a basis for choosing his work.
Parent: I'd be interested in seeing those criteria. Would they help us at home when you're doing homework?
Tom: I think so. They've helped me to understand what's good about my work.

Deborah Meier (Central Park East) once commented that parents ought to feel better about themselves as parents when they leave the school. In a reciprocal relationship, each partner becomes *more* clear about his successes and his common courses of action.

The new work of schools and regions in *interagency collaboration* has great potential for redefining partnerships. In California, the Healthy Start Program is designed to enable elementary schools to develop partnerships with social service agencies (e.g., child protective services, probation departments, housing authorities, community health groups, welfare agencies) so that planning, thinking, and serving can be coordinated and focused around agencies and organizations. Santa Cruz, California, County Superintendent Diane Ceres has worked with regional school districts to provide a countywide coordinating structure of social service agencies.

Heretofore, *student outcomes that are community-related* have been one-way and individualistic. In other words, we figure out how to use the community to accomplish student outcomes that are not reciprocal in nature. If we arrange for students to work in senior centers, the outcome may say: Students will perform community service and experience the rewards of contributing to the lives of individuals from different age groups. *A reciprocal outcome might read:* Students and senior citizens will contribute to the lives and learning of each other through the sharing of their stories, ideas, interests, and time.

In order to develop outcomes such as this, we need to let go of a felt need to control all of the named participants in the outcome and to involve the community members in writing the outcomes. We have designed outcomes narrowly and thus missed the vital interconnectedness of children's lives with those of all others in the community.

Businesses have generally been seen as the senior partner in their connections with schools. We have not talked with many businesspersons who have thought about what they have to learn from schools. Those business leaders who have been involved in "shadowing" principals come away with a new understanding and respect for the work of schools. Perhaps this bridge of observing and understanding each other's work needs to be crossed before full reciprocity can be undertaken. Many businesses do articulate their understandings of the connection of their involvements to societal goals: preparing students for successful performance in the workforce and in the democratic process. The fertile field of partnership might include common questions to be explored as well, the answers to which will improve both businesses and schools. For instance:

- What are some of the many ways in which students and adults learn together in their work?
- What democratic practices do individuals and groups need to experience in the workplace?
- How can education's work in authentic assessment inform business?
- What does it mean to have "clients"? How does it change your relationships toward those who become identified as clients?

- How can education's understandings about diversity and equity inform business policies and practices?
- Can we design a common vision that is oriented toward the betterment of society and to which we could all commit? What would that mean for our work together?

Education agencies and schools are in constant connection with each other. Demonstration sites boast the implementation of programs that are of interest to other schools. Counties, regional education centers, and academies often view themselves in a service role, which in translation means that "we have expertise with which to serve you." The one-way relationship has been even more problematic for the serving agency, since the lack of interconnectedness hinders its own efforts for self-renewal. The recent move toward networks holds much promise for enlarging the self-renewal potential for education as a whole. The Leadership Network—a new partnership among Alameda and Contra Costa County Offices of Education; California State University, Hayward; the Bay Area School Leadership Academy; and the Association of California School Administrators—worked through the changing conception of partnerships (Figure 4.3). The California Center for School Restructuring protocol process (see Chapter 3) and reciprocal team coaching (see Chapter 7) offer further examples of the shift toward reciprocity in professional organizations. "The Coalition of Essential Schools metaphor of change assumes," points out Watkins (1993, p. 1), "the possibility, and, in fact, the necessity, of a substantive *conversation* among professional colleagues." Ann Lieberman (1992), in her AERA presidential address, invited us to rethink partnerships as reciprocal networks to the future. The networks offer vital connections for schools and districts as they enlarge their circles of work.

The school–university partnerships of professional development schools are altering the historical relationship between universities and schools. There are now more than 125 schools in this international network, which focuses on "simultaneous renewal"—both institutions are re-forming as a result of their dynamic and reciprocal relationship. Research is joint action research that explores questions of common interest. Dilemmas provide arenas for joint struggles. Conversations emerge from common dilemmas and curiosities.

The changing nature of partnerships is altering the course of our conversations together. As the ripple enlarges and unfolds we continue the image of))))—dialogic, inquiring, sustaining, and partnership conversations moving out from a common set of understandings and interpretations about our interconnectedness. These newer conceptions of partnerships are essential to educational communities, since reciprocity and interdependence create equi-

Figure 4.3. The Leadership Network—Characteristics of a Partnership

TRADITIONAL	RECIPROCAL
Fragmented	Coordinated, Collaborative, Focused
Dependency	Capacity-building
Competitive	Cooperative, Complementary
Agency-dominated	Partnership, Member-driven
Centralized	Decentralized
Parallel work	Network
Expert-based	Constructed, Facilitated
Training	Conversations, Connections
Service-oriented	Leadership and support
Unequal	Reciprocal

Developed by representatives of the Leadership Network, 1993.

table relationships that form the patterns that give rise to learning for children and adults alike. The search for reciprocal partnerships can be hindered by naiveté, however, if educators do not understand the need to attend to issues of authority and seek to shift power relationships.

Authority and Power in Relationships

Schools and school districts are among the more hierarchical of organization. Such structures of domination and control have been considered the backbone of modern "efficient" organizations for several centuries. The larger and more complex the organization, the more complex and tightly drawn is the organizational chart. We particularly see this form of organizations in our large, urban school districts. Hierarchy and roles establish and maintain authoritative power, that is, power and control over the decisions and behaviors of others. While there is a legitimate role for authoritative power, professional cultures created exclusively or primarily by such arrangements have resulted in uneven power relationships, unilateral flow and control of information, fear of reprisal, and censure for overtures made across hierarchical levels. The invisible bonds that hold hierarchies in place imprison the inhabitants of each level, fragmenting their lives and their work and making it difficult to construct a common purpose for teaching and learning.

Dunlap and Goldman (1991) propose an alternative to authoritative power that they believe more accurately describes how power should be exercised in schools. They define facilitative power as "the ability to help others achieve a set of ends that may be shared, negotiated, or complementary without being either identical or antithetical" (Goldman, Dunlap, & Conley, 1993, p. 70). Dunlap and Goldman suggest that facilitative power in schools involves acquiring or arranging material resources, such as budgets; creating synergy by grouping staff together; providing feedback; and using networks (rather than hierarchies) to link with the outside world. Goldman and colleagues (1993) added three dimensions to the above factors: "(1) collecting and distributing information to allow greater control over the conditions of work and methods of teaching, and broader participation in decision making, (2) lobbying informally to cause movement toward goals, as opposed to exercising authority in the context of formal meetings; and (3) serving as a role model of the organization's vision" (p. 70). These authors have asked us to shift our perspectives about the kinds of power and the exercises of power that work in schools. Clearly, constructivist leadership is based on facilitative conceptions of power. An objection that we would lodge with the interpretation of facilitative power by Goldman and colleagues is the notion of "working through people." This suggests that preset goals are in the mind of the leader and that facilitative actions is being taken to maneuver professionals toward these goals. We are comfortable with the idea of "working *with* people," seeking goals that emerge from the constructivist process.

Communities based on facilitative power and the principles of ecology are marked by networks (webs of relationships) rather than hierarchies (Capra, 1994). These networks are characterized by feedback spirals bringing information and knowledge to everyone in the community, thereby breaking the "cult of expertise." Such human communities require leadership that engages participants in the reciprocal processes described in this book. We have found that these conversations bring with them the familiarity and regard that can shift the meaning and definition of roles and authority. However, as powerful as these respectful and sustained conversations can be in building equitable partnerships within professional culture, they must be accompanied by district and school structures that replace hierarchy with networks and redefine roles, practices, and policies that have historically created and protected uneven power relationships (see Chapter 7).

LEADING THE CONVERSATIONS

In order to lead conversations that can lead to professional cultures, educators need to construct understandings about the nature of constructivist conversations and acquire facilitation skills in order to convene, move, and deepen our talk together.

Leading the conversations is not a neutral role; it is a role of active involvement through which leaders insist on the convention of conversations, facilitate the reciprocal processes, and connect participants to the vision, values, and established norms of the group. Conversations such as we envision here do not occur naturally, at least at first. Yet they do not have to be scheduled in usual ways. Conversations can hold "strange attractors" (the design created by the magnetic pull of random data in chaotic systems), that is, inherent incentives that pull people into common talk. For instance, such attractors might include constructivist approaches that engage individuals in learning; conversations that do not insist on closure but encourage continuance to deeper levels ("let's continue this talk at lunch tomorrow"); and decision timetables by which one can anticipate closure and some resolution. These processes and forms result in complex networks of relationships. Professionals who are participating as constructivist leaders need to pose the questions and convene the conversations that invite others to become involved.

Those who engage in acts of leadership also serve as a catalyst in the work of bringing participants together. They create climates of expectancy, observing for expected leadership behaviors in others, responding to these evoked behaviors and thereby assisting in the process of self-construction, and acting as a catalyst by connecting performances of leadership. Waldrop (1992) reminds us that in chemistry one sees "this sort of thing all the time: one molecule, a catalyst, grabs two other molecules as they go tumbling by and brings them together so that they can interact and fuse very quickly" (p. 123). These acts of connecting are central to forming ecological communities, since the processes bring participants into contact so that the conversations can be held. In Chapter 2, presuppositions, understandings, and skills that are embedded in the reciprocal processes and acts of leadership are described. To briefly recap, we argued that those who perform acts of leadership need:

1. A sense of purpose and ethics. This includes an understanding of community, reciprocity, relationships, learning, and participantship.
2. Facilitation skills. This includes the linguistic skills discussed in Chapter 5 and skills in facilitating the reciprocal processes:
   • evoking potential in a trusting environment

- reconstructing or breaking set with old assumptions (including working with conflict and creativity)
- focusing on the construction of meaning
- framing actions based on new behaviors and purposeful intention.
3. An understanding of constructivist learning for all humans.
4. A deep understanding of change and transitions.
5. An understanding of school context.
6. A personal identity that allows for courage and risk, low ego needs, and a sense of possibilities.

Leading the conversations is the work of everyone in the educational community. In order for leaders and potential leaders to actively convene, frame, and move the conversations, these predispositions, understandings, and skills are highly important. These can be learned in a number of settings, including preservice education, professional development within a district, working in a culture in which these processes are regularly experienced; regional workshops, site-based workshops, and observing, modeling, and coaching. It is vital that all participants eventually have these or similar skills; otherwise, it is difficult to be a full participant in the processes of creating communities together. In Chapter 7, M. Lambert and Gardner discuss the professional development of constructivist leaders within a school district; in Chapter 9, Walker describes university programs and strategies for leadership preparation.

We are persuaded that plans, approaches, and strategies for leading the conversations need to originate initially from some group such as a leadership team. Otherwise, the principal is apt to attempt to go it alone, and this greatly limits the early construction of knowledge around school change that needs to occur in a group as well as the potential for teacher leadership. Further, it eliminates the "multiplier effect" of the patterns of relationships through which team members create feedback spirals by consistently interacting with a particular group of participants. Spirals gather others into the leadership arena.

CONCLUSION

Leading the conversations is at the heart of constructivist leadership. It is the facilitation of the reciprocal processes that enable participants in an educational community to construct meanings toward a common purpose for teaching and learning. It is a skilled undertaking for which each participant needs to be prepared; it is a shared responsibility.

In this chapter, we described a taxonomy of conversations that include dialogic, inquiring, sustaining, and partnership conversations that are informed by common elements. These common elements involve shared intention, a search for sense-making and understanding, remembrance and reflection, revelation of ideas, and respectful listening.

In the next chapter, Zimmerman makes explicit and examines linguistic moves embedded in conversations. This dimension of the reciprocal processes plumbs the depths of interaction and reciprocity.

CHAPTER 5

The Linguistics of Leadership

Diane P. Zimmerman

Union pickets in front of a school can be the source of self-serving criticism or the beginning of a reflective conversation about the issues. Chaotic and irrational events in school life can often be reframed into messages that support the meaning-making process. One conversation can lead to defensive or protective postures such as placating, distracting, or blaming (Satir, 1972); another can lead to meaning-making and an attempt to understand and learn from life's events. This chapter is about the second kind of conversation.

The constructivist leader's goal is to explore meaning with others as a way of deepening understanding. By using linguistic moves and being conscious of language choices, a leader creates spirals of meaning that are continuously formed and re-formed. Common knowledge about linguistic moves allows any participant to perform an act of leadership. In this chapter we propose some new ways of thinking about these moves and choices that enhance a constructivist leader's capacity to facilitate conversations. We begin by viewing linguistics through the lens of the new sciences.

LINGUISTICS—THROUGH THE LENS OF THE NEW SCIENCES

Like all complex systems, linguistic systems are unstable. In conversation one cannot predict exactly what will be said. As with the weather, only general patterns are predictable. For example, one might expect a friend to add humor to a serious discussion or to bring up a topic of common interest. One can never predict exactly what will be said, how it will be said, or what its effects will be on the listener.

A key concept discussed in earlier chapters suggests that self-organizing systems are feedback systems that are so complex that the traditional notion of cause-and-effect relationships is no longer relevant. It is the interaction among people, not cause and effect, that creates the cultural coherence and self-organizing phenomenon in an organization (Stacey, 1992). Linguistic moves and language choices bring fluid form to the meaning-making process.

Just as systems have form that create a set of boundaries, so do conversations (see Chapter 4). It is the field created by the conversations that serves as the medium for the reciprocal processes of understanding and meaning-making. A few simple rules can frame, deepen, and move the conversation to facilitate the construction of meaning. The purposeful application of linguistic processes by all group participants creates a basis for shared conversations that are meaningful in context and focus and that begin to shape the school culture.

Group members can deepen their understanding of a concept by reflecting, summarizing, or inquiring about the field of meaning. Lakoff (1987) theorizes that concepts are categories composed of radial networks. His analysis of category structure finds that categories do not form hierarchical structures with a limited number of essential attributes, as in classical studies, but rather a radial structure learned through social conventions. Category structure is a complicated network of resemblances rather than defined similarities.

Developing meaningful dialogue is about creating conceptual fields that deepen or shift thinking. When group members become excited about the emerging relevance of the conversation, the group self-organizes around the emerging concepts. Together groups negotiate meaning and labor toward new understanding. Instead of trying to control through telling, leaders must create spirals of meaning by expanding and clarifying the common conceptual fields. Asking questions and rephrasing ideas helps others create common maps from which to act. Stacey (1992) states that managing ambiguity and the unknowable are necessary skills for the postmodern world. We maintain that employing linguistic moves that enable is one of the most powerful ways to manage the unknowable.

ENABLING STRUCTURES FOR DISCOURSE

In many conversations one person's words can escalate into a massive issue for a group, while others' words go unnoticed. By employing a simple paraphrase, for instance, a leader can deemphasize one voice and amplify the other and thereby enrich the field. It is paradoxical that a linguistic move can serve both functions. The paraphrase communicates "I understand" to the loud voice and reduces the need for unnecessary repetition; it amplifies the quiet voice so that the group members hear it. Linguistic moves create simple rules that change the jumble of sentences into meaning-making contexts. The simplest analogy comes from fractal geometry, in which simple iterating equations create wild and complex visual experiences on the computer screen not unlike the way a compelling question generates a wide variety of possibilities, all relevant to the conversational field. It is important here to note that each of these linguistic moves creates a reciprocal relationship in which the language of the group iterates, or repeats itself, to form feedback spirals that define the field.

The way groups act in the linguistic fields distinguishes a meaning-making community from communities of advocacy. Senge (1990) states that in most organizations, group meetings tend to be places where individuals articulate their own views but learn little from one another. From our perspective, these are not meaning-making communities. Senge goes on to suggest that a learning community must actively pursue a balance between advocacy and inquiry. He states that the goal in balancing inquiry and advocacy is to "find the best argument" (p. 199). From the constructivist perspective we would state: The goal is to find the best understandings through a balance of paraphrasing, inquiring, and articulating ideas.

The purposeful application of the linguistics of leadership requires a commitment to public discourse that produces a reciprocal relationship that enables adults to construct meaning and knowledge together. As we have noted in our earlier discussions of "breaking set with old assumptions," instead of ignoring the uncomfortable topic or assuming that no news is good news, leaders and group participants must be tenacious in uncovering the unspeakable and, in so doing, living with discomfort for a period of time. Kegan (1994) describes these conversations as having tremendous potential if only one would take the time to talk. He states: "Potentially they amount to a fascinating lived conversation between equally respectable parties who care deeply about the outcome of philosophical conflict because it has real implications for their own lives and the lives of their students" (p. 48). We have discussed different forms of enabling structures in previous chapters and will present additional examples in Chapter 7.

In the remainder of this chapter, we outline some ways of defining structure, moves, and choices that are needed to foster the linguistics of leadership. These approaches enable us to facilitate dialogic, inquiring, sustaining, and partnering conversations.

For instance, when working in a dyadic relationship, structural guides may come from taxonomies of questions designed for planning and reflection conferences. (Reflection conferences are any conversation in which a person reflects on his or her past practice in a structured way. In Cognitive Coaching the speaker evaluates success, compares intended and actual outcomes, recalls data to support conclusions, projects to future applications, and reflects on the process and the ways that these conversations enhance professional growth.) For personal construction of meaning, Schön's (1983) work on the reflective practitioner provides a structure. For the purposes of our work here in linguistics, we propose an additional set of structures that are helpful when working with large groups and that enable and inform the meaning-making process. The structures can be as simple as paying attention to initiating, constructing, and closing activities. In fact, the structure must not intrude on the meaning-making process; instead it must enable it. We have found that as individuals gain an understanding of constructivism, the need for structures lessens as people become interested in what others have to say.

Initiating activities foster a spirit of inquiry. They help participants come together to begin to bridge the meaning-making from their personal experience to a shared understanding in the group. For structures to be enabling, participants need to believe in the meaning-making process. A group might start with metaphors or stories, or with an interesting question to reflect on in journals—a task that is meaningful to the context and fosters engagement (see Chapter 6). Initially the inquiries are both individual and collegial, as they evoke potential in individuals. As they evolve, initiating activities set tone and purpose for the work the group will do together. Questions become an important part of the framing process in that they crate the need to find meaning.

As the conversations take shape and begin to ebb and flow, leaders concern themselves with issues of sustenance. More than ever before, mutual respect becomes essential. As the ideas gain momentum, differences will occur and conflict may arise. The conversation processes enable groups to learn to respect these differences and to listen and paraphrase as a way of seeking to understand. Diverse viewpoints and multiple responses help to break set with their ideas and entertain new ways of thinking and acting. At this stage group members view their role as building patterns of relationships that are respectful of one another and the group as a whole. When such respect exists, group members persist through the rough waters and emerge with a heightened sense of their own professional efficacy.

Constructing also means that participants learn to live with a certain amount of ambiguity and uncertainty and that out of this chaos comes a more complex understanding of how to work together. Questioning assumptions, values, and beliefs takes the process to another level of understanding and is a necessary part of any meaning-making activity. It is appropriate to reflect on how the espoused theories formed collectively in a group will be acted on by the participants. Questions about what data will inform their decisions and how the group will check for congruence between thought and action are also important elements in maintaining and sustaining the meaning-making process.

Finally, *closing* activities can create communities of memory and commitment. Lively discussions can produce information overload that easily leads to forgetting. Taking time to summarize, finding patterns that connect, creating metaphors, generating new questions, and committing to action are necessary for closure. Honoring a lack of consensus and agreeing to continue the process are equally important. In leave taking, participants need to be able to shift from group meanings back to personal meaning, which is essential to the establishment of commitment. When group members take time to personalize the meaning, they are able to use the new knowledge to inform practice. For instance, a group of faculty have verified for themselves that children learn better and more consistently when parents are involved with their learning. Before leaving the discussion, each teacher grounded this knowledge by thinking about how it applies specifically to two children in his or her classroom.

Closing rituals ought to be reflective as well. Valuing activities provide a structure for evaluating and improving the group work. Did the group produce new insights together? Did the participants discover some new ideas? Will this discussion make a difference? How were the members renewed by the synergy of the group? These are but a few of the many questions that might be asked to help a group become more aware or metacognitive about themselves as a group. An example of the use of this enabling structure follows:

Initiating: A group of teachers, administrators, and parents, 55 in all, have come together to develop a common vision for a new school that has been open for a year. Before the meeting, the members were asked to begin to shape their own personal vision by collecting compelling words. After introductory activities, they reflect on past experiences in which they learned something that they considered significant. Together they make linkages between their compelling words and these experiences. These ideas will be used to construct the common vision for the group.

Constructing: Posted on the wall around the room are excerpts from a lengthy mission statement that was developed the previous year. Key elements of the mission statement are read to the group. They are asked to write their compelling words on index cards and to join together in groups near the part of the mission that makes most sense for their words. If none of these make sense, they will cluster and self-organize into categories that do make sense. For the next hour these groups work together to make sense of the mission statement and their collection of words. Their task is to craft a vision for themselves based on the meaning they are making. Words are bartered, discarded, and embellished to craft a statement that implies action. Because this group has had no formal mediating training, several people have been designated as mediators to help the groups that get stuck and to foster and encourage the search for meaning. The vision statements might appear simple or self-evident, such as "to encourage the students' respect for learning." The important part of the process is the precision embodied in each carefully chosen word and how each member of the group is able to articulate what that vision means for him or her as a teacher, parent, or administrator.

Once the visions have been generated, the group members mill around the room and learn about the rest of the community. Are there any common threads? Are there other visions that are compelling and make sense? What do the other visions really mean? The participants are then asked to choose their top three or four favorites. All of the statements will be saved for future reference. The highest-ranked ones will be used for further conversations. The meaning-making process has just begun. The real work will be in helping a larger community of students, parents, and other staff members to make sense of these vision statements.

Closing: To close the day's work, the participants are organized into new clusters in which they focus on summarizing what has happened for them during this day. They commit to paper their ideas for next steps. Together they reflect on the process, think about some next steps, and create a metaphor to describe how the school is evolving. Before leaving, each group shares their metaphor.

THREE LINGUISTICS MOVES

The Similarities Between the Question and the Paraphrase

When used as meaning-making moves, questioning and paraphrasing share common characteristics. First, both the paraphrase and the question are reciprocal, as they are dependent on the conversation for their focus. They draw their potency from the field of meaning, not from autobiographical thoughts. To further the meaning-making process, these moves must be used with the desire to understand or deepen the conceptual field. This distinction is important. If one only asks questions from his or her own perspective or only makes comments that represent opinions, the conceptual field slips into advocacy. As stated previously, communities of advocacy do not construct meaning in the way described in this chapter. In Chapter 4, Lambert defined these common elements of a conversation in the section "A Taxonomy of Conversations."

Second, the paraphrase and the question are selective tools because they establish the focus. For example, a friend might complain that his district office was not supporting the schools and that this was a hindrance to the implementation of the shared decision-making process. The listener could select the focus by suggesting that "the lack of support is frustrating," or that "the district office does seem to be the hindrance," or "shared decision-making is not so easy." Each one establishes a different focus for the conversation. Later in this chapter we describe how conceptual frameworks aid in this selective process and enable groups to break set with old assumptions.

Linguistic Moves—The Question

As language develops, the ability to pose questions is acquired naturally. However, the art of asking open-ended questions that mediate meaning must be learned, practiced, and refined. The way that leaders frame questions can limit or enhance others' ability to construct meaning and act in context with others. A broad question such as "How can we use student writing samples to inform our teaching?" requires teachers to spend time talking. Framing questions that are too narrow fragments the group into positions. For example, "Should we teach quotation marks in 3rd or 4th grade?" detracts from the larger idea of teaching grammar in the context of writing. Failing to frame meaningful questions confuses the process. For instance, a group member strays from the topic by asking, "What color ink should we use to correct errors?" On the other hand, when a question is meaningful, probes the unknown, and cannot be immediately answered, it stays with the person until it is answered. It is not uncommon for group members to report that they continue to think about questions long after the conversation.

The Rhetorical Question. In English a rhetorical question is based on the desired response. When a speaker does not expect an answer or has a predetermined answer, the question becomes rhetorical. Questions that do not require an answer do not open up meaning-making. In fact, when leaders ask questions with embedded commands, such as "Don't you think we should _____?," they cause groups to adopt defensive postures.

When a group member wants to generate a little humor, the rhetorical question can have a place. Often the extended probing required for meaning-making can be taxing, and poking fun at the process of question-asking can lighten the tone. Recently a friend teased the group, "Who would ever do that?" We all laughed because we knew we were guilty of the implied offense, and we moved on without ever answering the question.

The Categorical Question. A second type of question is one that limits the range of responses to specific categories. We call this type of question the categorical question because a "what" question asks for a label, a "where" question asks for a place, and a "why" question asks for a justification. Often these questions can be answered with one word or a short phrase. In English some "wh-" questions and the yes/no question would be of this type.

If a member wants some specific data, desires clarity, or wants to know more about someone's knowledge, this type of question is useful within a meaning-making context. However, because the categories are self-contained and have a limited range of interpretation, they are only a small part of the processes of conversation.

The Cross-Categorical Question. A third form of question searches for meaning by generating new contexts or reframing the group focus (Costa & Garmston, 1994; Laborde, 1988). Questions that open up possibilities and do not restrict answers to narrow categories also focus thinking in a much broader way. They elicit a broad range of possible answers in that they cross categorical boundaries. For our purposes here, we have labeled this type of question the cross-categorical question. Here are a few examples: What kinds of vacations do you enjoy most (places, activities, types of travel)? How did you come to that conclusion (data, hunches, decisions, plans)? These kinds of questions create positive feedback systems in which they *amplify the meaning* that has been created by the group, allowing it to ebb and flow in many directions. Questions that amplify feedback are essential tools for building constructivist conversations.

It is important for group members to learn how to ask questions that do not have answers embedded in them. In early stages of group work, it is not uncommon to have members ask questions with embedded opinions, such as "Don't you think that we should be using authentic assessment tasks?" A more open-ended question might ask for values, such as "In what ways would authentic assessment enhance this unit?" When groups understand the power of an unanswered question, they begin to self-regulate and frame more open-ended questions. They begin to monitor their own and one another's linguistic behavior.

A new teacher recently returned from a workshop on thinking. When asked what she had enjoyed the most, she told her principal, "I learned how to ask the kinds of thoughtful questions you ask of us. I learned that the powerful questions are ones in which no one really knows the answer. I realized that you ask those kinds of questions all the time." When the answer is not known, the members in the group must negotiate to find answers that satisfy the group. This becomes a meaning-making activity at its finest, as the elements of surprise and discovery are fostered. We believe that it is essential for communities of learners to spend time learning about how to ask questions that further the meaning-making process. Exploring the contexts and boundaries of a concept through questioning and paraphrasing is one aspect; an equally important aspect is how to summarize and inquire in order to create personal meaning.

Linguistic Moves—The Paraphrase

The word *paraphrase* is derived from the Greek "para" (through or beyond) and "phrazein" (to point out or to speak). Most dictionaries define it as a restatement in another form. From a constructivist viewpoint we would define the paraphrase as the way we communicate understanding through speaking. We would also suggest that the paraphrase often points the way in a conversation and that it moves groups beyond their current thinking. Used in this way it becomes a powerful move that enables groups to break set with old assumptions.

In its simplest form the paraphrase is a restatement in the listener's own words of what was said. If the paraphrase captures the essence of the message, it acknowledges; if it misses the mark, it clarifies. The act of acknowledging actually serves as a reinforcer, encouraging the speaker to go deeper or extend his or her thinking. The act of clarifying communicates "I am listening; tell me if I understand."

The paraphrase summarizes meaning and selectively guides the conversation. What is paraphrased becomes the selective focus for the conversation. For example, a leader can summarize behavioral aspects of a proposed solution by saying, "The suggestion is that all teachers impose 3 minutes of silent clean-up at the end of each day." When members of the group disagree on the method and the group begins to debate the merits of "silent clean-up routines," a leader can shift the focus with a new summary statement, such as "The suggestion is that we consider ways for students to demonstrate responsibility for property." This paraphrase shifts the focus away from a debate on method and toward a conversation about assumptions and beliefs. It fosters a shared purpose within the group. Later in this chapter, a framework for advanced paraphrasing is explored as a way of summarizing, constructing, and expanding meaning.

All members of a conversation should take responsibility for paraphrasing for at least part of the time. We find that most adults can generate a paraphrase; however, the paraphrase is often underused in conversations. When this simple rule is in place, groups report higher trust levels and a climate of professional respect. Raising group consciousness is a starting place. Taking time-outs for reflection and to have each member generate a summary statement helps groups refine the skill. Learning how to use paraphrasing to shift focus is a highly refined skill.

The Advanced Paraphrase. A framework that can be useful in interpreting and understanding the foci of paraphrasing is the advanced paraphrase developed by Costa and Garmston (1992). They suggest the use of this framework to extend thinking in the coaching relationship. We have adapted this model and propose it as a framework for deepening thinking in constructivist conversations. In keeping with the original model, we propose four logical levels organized from global to specific: At the core is the level of content. At this level the paraphrase is a simple restatement of *content* or *emotion.* As noted earlier, this type of paraphrase acknowledges and clarifies. The next level shifts to a broader conceptual label. We can suggest new meaning with a *broad concept label,* or a statement of an *inferred goal,* or a statement of an *inferred value.* The broadest level shifts the focus to a contextual level, enabling one to think in a context beyond the current field of meaning. We can suggest new meaning by *juxtaposing context,* or inferring *long-range intention,* or creating a *metaphor.* These two levels help groups break set and consider meaning-making fields that are broader and more inclusive. The final level drops the logical level and serves to clarify or produce specificity. We can build clarity through a *counterexample,* through an *example,* or by *clarifying emotion.* See Figure 5.1 for a listing and examples of paraphrases made in a conversation about authentic assessment.

Our experience with conversations in which group members regularly paraphrase is that many of these types of paraphrases occur spontaneously. The model provides a reminder to groups that paraphrases often extend and refine meaning. Each member can be responsible for generating one type of paraphrase, or the entire group can use this model as a starting place for generating summary statements about the topic.

Linguistic Moves—The Reflective Pause

By some purists, the reflective pause may not be considered a linguistic convention at all. We would like to suggest otherwise. It is the pauses in our speech that give it its cadence and the shape. The pauses give us fractions of seconds to think about what we are saying. Here we are suggesting that groups consciously pay attention to the cadence of a group and impose some quiet time for reflection when needed. Again, this becomes a reciprocal process because it is the meaning-making activity that suggests when reflection time may be useful.

Metacognition, the ability to think about our own thinking, is increased with focused quiet reflection time. Groups need to explore comfortable ways of working with silence. Some have found journal-writing appropriate; others have left it more informal. As mentioned previously, calling time-outs and asking the group to reflect using a framework for interpretation of their language are powerful ways to help groups find new avenues for action. In Chapter 6, Cooper describes the use of narrative in schools as a process of reflection and meaning construction.

These are but a few of the linguistic conventions used in conversations.

Figure 5.1. Advanced Paraphrasing

Juxtapose Context
"We want to have the students helping to design the rubrics."

Long-Range Intention
"Our intention is to have students self-evaluate as they work."

Metaphor
"Teaching kids to self-evaluate is like building a skyscraper; the rubrics are the structure and the students fill in the space."

Broad Concept Label
"Benchmarks will help us develop rubrics."

Inferred Goal
"We want students to judge their own work."

Inferred Values
"We value having the students involved in the assessment."

Summarize
"We have been considering different strategies for using authentic assessment; we have analyzed several strategies to determine key aspects."

Empathic
"We are arguing over details and it is starting to make us feel frustrated."

Counterexample
"Having students also assign letter grades would be counter productive."

Example
"The district writing rubric is another example to consider."

Clarify Emotion
"Trying to figure it out for ourselves can be tedious."

Adapted from a figure designed for the Institute for Intelligent Behavior by Costa and Garmston (1992).

These are chosen here for their value in creating a further context for recipro-cal processes and patterns of relationships that can evolve within a school community.

LINGUISTIC FRAMEWORKS

B. Bloom, Engelhart, Furst, Hill, and Krathwohl (1956), Taba (1957), and Costa (1989) have suggested hierarchies for framing questions that ex-tend student thinking. We refer readers to these frameworks as alternative ways of framing questions not reviewed here. Here we explore ways in which cross-categorical questions expand and extend the field of meaning. At the simplest level, these frameworks provide a scaffold for question-asking that enables members to ask questions that expand perceptions and create rich fields for meaning-making. We do not recommend using all of these frames; they are offered as examples to be used purposefully to broaden perspectives and to shift or break set with old assumptions.

The Logical-Level Framework

One way to begin to frame cross-categorical questions is to frame them using a system of "logical" levels. Bateson (1972) first proposed logical levels as a way of studying systems and schizophrenia. In an extension of Bateson's work, Dilts (1992) has identified five different levels or categories in which the brain processes information:

(1) The basic level is your *environment,* your external constraints. (2) You operate on that environment through your *behavior.* (3) Your behavior is guided by your mental maps (schema) and your strategies, which define your *capabilities.* (4) These capabilities are organized by *belief systems* . . . and (5) beliefs are orga-nized by *identity.* (p. 1)

In the meaning-making arena these levels can provide a useful tool for probing in a variety of ways. In an earlier visioning activity, we described how a group of people working together to discover common values and beliefs stayed at one logical level for the entire conversation. In later conversa-tions the group would want to explore other levels. A group might explore how they would act (behavioral) on the values and beliefs generated or decide to explore capabilities and examine existing schemas. Environmental issues might be studied to discover ways the system supports or hinders the values and beliefs. Or the group might engage in a conversation about what they are becoming (identity) as a result of the process.

Although they do not explicitly state it in this way, both Schön (1983) and Senge (1990) make cases for the power of thinking across logical levels. Schön describes how professionals reflect on their practices (behaviors) in relation to their espoused *beliefs*. Senge identifies the exploration of mental models (capability) in relation to defensive *behaviors* as one of the five disciplines for a learning community.

Often groups find that questioning across logical levels produces shifts in thinking and enables groups to reframe their ideas. For example, the group that was exploring authentic assessment started out their conversation talking about the authentic tasks they had been asking students to perform (behavorial). Some shared strategies they had learned in a workshop (capability). These two kernels established the field of dialogue. In reflection afterwards, the group realized that the question that shifted the logical level had generated the most insight. The question had been, "So, if these are the tasks we are asking kids to perform, what are our deepest beliefs and assumptions about these tasks?" It was this probing that caused the group members to carefully examine what they meant by the word "authentic." It was the examination of values in relation to behaviors and capabilities that brought clarity to the group about authentic tasks. They decided they were not satisfied with their mental maps (capabilities; in this case, old assumptions) for assessment and left the meeting with an agreement that they were going to seek out other strategies and begin to develop some other approaches about how to plan for authentic assessment. The next conversation started where they left off.

There is a growing body of literature about first- and second-order change. Cuban (1988) describes first-order change as making what exists more efficient and second-order change as seeking to alter the fundamental ways in which organizations are put together. In the above example, the group started off operating at the level of first-order change. They were talking about what they were doing and how it could be made more efficient. It was the questions at the level of belief that caused them to shift, to reflect on their own assumptions, and begin to make some new connections. Stated another way, when groups reflect on their "rules" (mental maps/schemas), roles (beliefs and identity), and responsibilities (values and capabilities), their conversations become rich in meaning-making. These are the kinds of conversation that lead to second-order change.

The States-of-Mind Framework

Costa and Garmston, together with a group of colleagues including Lambert and Zimmerman, identified five states of mind that are useful for mediating teacher thinking. In *Cognitive Coaching* (1994), Costa and Garmston describe ways in which these concepts can be used to frame questions during coaching. We have found this framework useful in our conversations.

The states of mind were identified through the categorization of specific linguistic moves that are useful for shifting thinking. We identified five states of mind. (1) The way of searching for inner resources and determining who has the locus of control determines the level of *efficacy*. (2) What one is aware of and not aware of establishes the level of *consciousness*. (3) How to consider options determines *flexibility*. (4) How to think about perfecting a craft develops an ethic of *craftsmanship*. (5) How to think about building relationships establishes the level of *interdependence*.

In coaching, we envision these five as desired states of mind and use them to design questions that shift thought. For example, to cause a person to think in terms of efficacy, we might ask "What resources can you bring to bear on this problem?" or "What elements of the problem are within your control?" Figure 5.2 provides a framework, developed by colleagues Bill Baker and Stan Shalit (1992), that enables groups to ask questions in order to develop these states of mind in their conversations. We have found that asking questions from one state of mind often generates responses from other states of mind. These states are not discrete categories; they are overlapping fields of meaning.

A conversation in which the members use these states of mind as an inquiry map might be as follows: A staff had been working on building respect in the student body. They were working together in a staff meeting trying to define what they mean by respect. The first question that was raised by the group was "To whom or to what should students show respect?" (interdependence). In exploring this question, the teachers started to question their own assumptions regarding respect. Some were more concerned with the teacher–student relationship; others were more concerned about student–student relationship. Another person brought up the issue of respect toward property. The group consensus was that all levels of respect are important. When one member suggested that respect really needs to start at the teacher–teacher level, a shift occurred in the conversation. Later several staff members began to inquire, "What are we learning? What are we becoming more aware of?" (consciousness). Someone else asked, "Where does the responsibility lie?" (efficacy). Again a shift occurred; this time the group had different opinions. Initially one teacher felt that it was the parents who should be responsible; another teacher challenged this assumption since parent responsibility was not within her control. The conversation was lively, with many different viewpoints finding voice. Finally, the focus shifted to conversations about how to build respect (craftsmanship). By this time, there was a high degree of consensus within the group.

Metacognitive capabilities can be enhanced through the application of

Figure 5.2. A Framework for Meaning-Making

**Consciousness–
Expanding Knowledge
and Becoming Aware
of Group's Thinking**

Anticipate • Name • Designate
Order • Explicate • Identify
Monitor time • Match • Scan
Observe • Seek • Outline
Retrieve • Repeat • Define
Search • Select
Sequence
Recall • List

**Interdependence–
Building Relationships**

Affirm • Value • Love • Connect
Coherence • Associate
Compare • Relate • Trust • Care
Express feeling • Appreciate
Empathize • Have esteem
Contectualize • Egocentric
Allocentric • Macrocentric

**Efficacy–
Producing An Effect**

Apply • Construct
Design • Effect
Plan • Commit • Choose
Expedite • Select
Be competent
Be confident
Act on

**Craftsmanship–
Analyzing Meaning**

Group • Categorize • Classify
Contrast • Organize • Sort
Analyze • Evaluate • Explain
Justify • Conclude • Summarize
Formulate • Generalize • If/then
Predict • Distinguish
State cause

**Flexibility–
Breaking Set**

Diverge • Extrapolate
Forecast • Hypothesize
Infer • Suppose
Make analogies
Novel connections
Create • Experiment • Explore
Generate • Brainstorm
Speculate • Envision • Idealize
Imagine • Inspire

Adapted from a figure designed for the Institute for Intelligent Behavior by Baker and Shalit (1992).

states of mind to a conversation. A person proficient in doing this can switch between listening for understanding and contributing to content, or analyzing and inquiring from the states-of-mind framework. A metacognitive conversation might go as follows:

> "It does seem like we are coming to consensus about appropriate strategies. Is there a state of mind that has not been represented? I notice that we have left few options for the students." I ask, "I wonder what options we want students to have in this process." Another person comments, "This is pretty tight on the kids." Again the conversation is off and running in a new direction. We are now exploring ways to expand the options for students.

The advance-paraphrase, logical-levels, and states-of-mind frameworks are complex communication approaches. Since they are advanced ways of examining our linguistics dynamics, their uses may evolve as conversations become practiced and constructivist in nature. These frames provide some additional perspectives for a group of professionals who are intrigued by the meaning of their own engagements in the conversational processes.

LANGUAGE CHOICES FOR A POSTMODERN WORLD

Undoubtedly, the planks of a paradigm are constructed with language; beliefs, assumptions, and therefore actions emerge from that language. In our daily work in schools and in our personal lives, we make language choices that carry with them multiple assumptions. It can be enticing to consider and observe differences that emerge from different words used routinely over time. Lambert and Gardner (1993), in their inquiries into transformative leadership, developed a lens for considering language that is primarily reductionist and language that tends to be transformative or constructivist in nature.

By "reductionist," they mean language that carries assumptions that are mechanistic, static, exclusive, hierarchical, manipulative, directional, and/or predictable. "Transformative" or constructivist language tends to imply assumptions that are dynamic, engaging, inclusive, participatory, open, reciprocal, and/or unpredictable. For instance, reductionist words might include such common words or phrases as *impact, mechanisms, objectives, alignment, deal with,* and *getting results through people.* When replaced by *influence, approaches, outcomes, integration, work with,* and *working with people,* the same ideas become transformative in nature.

As staff develop their professional language (which all communities do), it can be interesting to discuss words and the meanings they carry for others, especially students and parents.

CONCLUSION

The ideas in this chapter are complex and raise the need for a few caveats or questions, primary among them are: How can teachers find the time to learn such complex language patterns? And, if they do not, don't such practices tend to keep power and leadership in the hands of the "expert"? It is essential that the language moves described in this chapter be undertaken with a "talk-aloud metacognitive" approach; that is, that uses of such moves be made explicitly part of the dialogue. If we were to choose a professional development focus from the ideas in this chapter, it would be that of teaching groups about the various linguistic frameworks through direct instruction paired with guided practice. Carryover of these approaches requires that these frameworks be applied to the conversations that take place about professional practices. Asking groups to set goals and choose which part of a framework to focus on simplifies the task and reminds them to share responsibility for generating the linguistic moves. We have found that conversations that are focused in this way produce quality work in shorter periods of time. We present these ideas as a rich repertoire of linguistic moves that will have different meanings for different people.

In the next chapter, Cooper looks inside the lives of educators in narrative schools—schools that engage the power of narrative to reflect on practice and construct meaning and knowledge together.

CHAPTER 6

The Role of Narrative and Dialogue in Constructivist Leadership

Joanne E. Cooper

> Human beings think, perceive, imagine, and make moral
> choices according to narrative structures.
>
> Theodore Sarbin
> *Narrative Psychology* (1986, p. 8)

The study of narrative and the use of stories in the work of educators is a growing phenomenon (Carter, 1993; Jalongo, 1992; Witherell & Noddings, 1991). Narratives or stories are central to our lives in that "the stories we hear and the stories we tell shape the meaning and texture of our lives at every stage and juncture" (Witherell & Noddings, 1991, p. 1). Think back on your own life. Do you have stories of experiences that embody much of what you have come to understand about your life and its meaning? I know I do. Stories about the time I paddled 75 miles down the Salmon River in Idaho in an inflatable kayak embody what I learned about facing my own fears and learning to "paddle like hell" straight into my problems. Stories about my daughter saving a man who had been stabbed in the park embody all the love and pride I feel in the process of parenting. Stories about my mother beating cancer speak of my heritage, the strength and courage that have been passed on to me. Stories I tell myself in my journal help me to sort out who I am and what I believe and care about in this world. All these stories speak of the power of narrative in human lives, its capacity to help define us, to help us grow, and to help us form visions of our future.

The fluid character of narrative or stories encompasses a capacity for reinterpretation and change. Stories can be retold, reframed, reinterpreted. Because they are fluid, open for retelling and ultimately reliving, they are the repositories of hope. As one of my students put it, after having told the story of her life on paper:

> Today I am not really certain where I am heading but am very hopeful
> that since I now have the map, perhaps I can follow it correctly and
> finally emerge a better person.

Stories are a powerful tool for understanding our own lives, for organizing that understanding just as one would draw a map to organize information about a place, and for using that map to begin to move in a desired direction. This is true for individuals and for organizations. Stories provide a vision and a desired direction for adults working in schools—both administrators and teachers. Stories embody the hopes of these adults on both an individual and an organizational basis.

Narratives or stories are easier to remember than lists or disconnected facts (Jalongo, 1992):

> If you doubt this is true, attend an all-day workshop and consider what you recall in any great detail by the end of the day or much later. Chances are, it is a personal anecdote shared by a workshop leader or participant. (p. 68)

Anecdotes are easier to remember because they carry more information in them than the average set of facts or research findings. They carry with them powerful emotions, an understanding of what it is to be human, a sense of connection. They also carry within them tacit knowledge, knowledge gained through experience that is difficult to explain but communicated and understood through the narrative mode. Narratives or stories are little packages of understanding that not only support the process of constructivism but are essential to it.

How is narrative essential to constructivism? First, recall constructivism's major assertions: (1) Human being is meaning-making. In other words, people all construct their own reality or make meaning, often with little awareness as to the exact shape of their own reality-constituting. (2) These meaning systems shape and give rise to behavior (Kegan & Lahey, 1984). Thus it is not the events and particulars of people's lives that are of greatest importance, but how they privately compose or make meaning of what happens to them. In this way, people do not act irrationally, but rather in a coherent manner that is consistent with their construction of reality. However, the construction of that reality must be shared through narrative and dialogue if leaders are to create communities in which they can construct meanings that lead toward a common purpose for teaching and learning. In addition, narrative and dialogue help to create school cultures rich in leadership connections, cultures in which all organizational members can become fully functioning professional leaders (see Chapter 2).

When applied to the understanding and leading of organizations, constructivism stands in sharp contrast to the objectivist philosophy that has been the basis for past organizational theory. Educational administration in the past has relied on the understanding of organizational theory as a set of truths that can be used to properly lead organizational members. Recent theorists have begun to recognize that organizations, such as schools, are merely constructed realities, created through the collected understandings of organizational members. Given the theoretical move to constructivism, questions arise about how leaders, both principals and teachers, can begin to understand their own behavior and that of other teachers and staff. How might leaders begin to change the constructed realities of schools to form new and more powerful understandings of organizational events?

Narrative and dialogue can become powerful tools in the construction of meaning by educators. Because, as Sarbin (1986) claims, human beings think in narrative structures, they make meaning through the use of narrative structures. Stories are a way for school leaders to capture understandings that others might not be able to articulate. By listening to and fostering dialogue and narrative construction, school leaders are better able to understand and to manage meaning systems with others. In addition, narrative and dialogue provide the reciprocal processes essential to constructivist leadership. Carter (1993) claims that narratives or stories are a way of capturing the complexity, specificity, and interconnectedness of life. Often a sense of trust and reciprocity is evoked as each organizational member tells his or her own story. Thus stories are a powerful tool in the constructivist work of schools.

Stories not only support meaning-making of present events; they help form visions of the future. Witherell and Noddings (1991) have underscored the power of narrative truth as a means of envisioning possibility in one's life. In the case of professional educators working together in a single school, it is a means of envisioning possibility at both the individual and the organizational level. Clandinin and Connelly (1991) have described this complex process as "growth toward an imagined future" that involves "restorying and attempts at reliving" (p. 265). (See Ford Slack's restorying in Chapter 8.) For the members of a particular school, it means not only retelling and reliving at the individual level, but also collaborative retelling and reliving at the organizational level. One elementary school experienced enormous change and growth when teachers and administrators began meeting regularly to retell and then relive the story of their math curriculum. Teachers told stories about math in their classrooms: what worked, what didn't; how children were learning; what it felt like to teach math in the ways it was being taught. The stories gave rise to insights about all aspects of teaching and learning and initiated a journey that culminated in whole-school change. As their math curriculum changed, teachers and administrators grew, bringing about more open and collaborative multiage classrooms, team teaching, fundamental changes in curriculum and instruction, and a more collegial school culture.

Narratives and stories not only support constructivism; they are essential to it. First, they provide structure for the ways in which human beings think, perceive, imagine, and make moral choices (Brody & Witherell, with

Donald & Lundblad, 1991). Second, narratives elicit and clarify tacit knowledge (Jalongo, 1992). Third, stories create connection and community and
vision. In this way they guard against one of today's great dangers, professional detachment (Brody et al., 1991):

> One of the greatest challenges for professionals today is to guard against their
> own detachment—from themselves, from their community, and from those with
> whom they form particular relationships. (p. 258)

Western cultures tend to overvalue individualism, autonomy, and competition, values that have structured our social relations, guided our professional
lives, and deeply defined the character of our educational institutions.

Sometimes it takes a major event to awaken us to the debilitating power
of detachment, and what often awakens us is a story. Here is one such story
a student wrote in our class journal. It is a reminder of the power and importance of stories:

> I experienced the death of one of our teachers this year. He went on
> leave before Christmas, letting only the SASA [school secretary] know.
> A month later his family wrote saying he had passed away. . . . We
> never had a chance to say goodbye. Slowly over the past few years he
> had withdrawn from his peers. . . . New teachers never knew him be-
> yond the hello in the hallway, and so he evolved into an odd character
> on campus.
>
> After his death many stories emerged that shed light on him as a
> person as well as a teacher. Particularly insightful were the students'
> stories and perceptions. He touched the lives of more students than he
> was given credit for. I realize the loss of never having shared his stories
> with him. Moral: Don't wait to share stories. Also, teachers share (ei-
> ther purposely or inadvertently) their lives and stories with their stu-
> dents: Ask them.

This principal realized the power of stories to create community only after it
was too late. Through sharing stories, we create healing communities and
guard against the kind of detachment that allows people to slip away unnoticed.

PROVIDING A STRUCTURE FOR THINKING, IMAGINING, AND MAKING MORAL CHOICES

Narratives or stories, both read or experienced and told, can become
powerful guides in helping us make moral choices. These stories reach across

time and cultural boundaries to remind us of who we are and how we want to live. They can be stories read in adolescence, such as J. D. Salinger's *The Catcher in the Rye,* and remembered for the critical understanding they carry, or stories of experience that gain power when they are shared with others.

The following stories are of two men, both elementary principals, one from Hawaii and one from American Samoa, who have each found narrative useful in the construction of their meaning-making systems. They both struggle with one of life's central questions: how to be human from a male perspective.

Our first principal recalls the story of Holden Caulfield in *The Catcher in the Rye* (1951), which he read as an adolescent and which became a powerful guiding force in his life, both when he first read it and now, in his work in education:

> I approached the reading of the book with a typical high school know-it-all disdain, thinking this was about baseball or something equally dumb. . . . What a revelation the book turned out to be. . . . (One) incident that stood out was Holden's encounter with a psychologist friend whom he confided in. After listening to Holden's troubles, the psychologist gave him a piece of advice. He said, "The mark of an immature man is that he die nobly for a cause; the mark of a mature man is that he live humbly for one." I never forgot that piece of advice. It took some of the wind out of my sails. I felt as if the psychologist was speaking to me. . . . Here I was full of idealism and fervor, only to be told I was being immature. Of course I quickly rejected the implication at that time and believed what I wanted to (youth is quick to recover). In retrospect, I knew I secretly took that advice to heart. Today, as a principal, when I have a choice of dying nobly or living humbly in a tense political situation, I remind myself of my responsibility to children and my ultimate effectiveness—in the long run.

This story embodies much of what it is to be a mature man. It helped this principal to confront and make difficult decisions in uncertain times. The story serves as a reminder to live humbly even when there is pressure to do otherwise. This wise advice for leaders was first encountered at a young age, and yet it has remained an important guiding force in the making of moral choices for this principal. That the story has remained with this principal for so long reminds us of the power of stories to teach and guide us long after they have been heard and sometimes supposedly forgotten. Thus stories like this provide a structure for thinking, imagining, and making moral choices. This is true for organizations as well as for individuals. Stories of the struggles of one elementary school to mainstream and care for their special education students help to remind them that all students can learn. Their motto for the year was, "I care. You matter," and their efforts made them a national blue ribbon award–winning school. This story carries with it powerful institutional memories of the school's core values.

Our second principal tells the story of the death of his father and a lesson he learned from his small son at the time. Here the issue is one of how to deal with one's humanity and still live by the dictates of society regarding what it is to be a male in that society. This story gained power and meaning in the retelling to classmates in a graduate course on critical reflection:

> The week after my father's funeral . . . my son was crying in his bed. . . . As I walked into his room and kneeled beside him, I asked him what was wrong. . . . I felt his little arms tightening around my neck . . . I remember telling him how bad it was for a strong boy like him to cry and immediately, his crying was reduced to whispering sobs. Then I heard him whisper between sobs, "Grandpa, Grandpa!" I heard myself repeat, "You miss Grandpa?" Then my son . . . asked me if we could go to Grandpa's grave and ask him if he needed a blanket. . . . Finally, still sobbing, he fell asleep. . . . As I sat there going over events that had occurred earlier in the evening, I realized . . . that despite all [my son's] pain, his love for his Grandpa meant even more. . . . Such love, unselfishness, and caring could only come truly from the heart of an innocent child.
>
> As I kept thinking about my son's request that fateful night many years ago, I realized that my perception of men not being supposed to cry was so distorted and powerful that I was consumed and blinded by my own pride and arrogance, and I was . . . unaware of my being judgmental and critical of my brother and father, distancing myself from them emotionally. I was so concerned and afraid of what people would say or how they would feel if they saw me crying. . . . All that time I thought I was doing something good for the family; as it turned out, I was only concerned with myself. . . . My son's unselfish request helped trigger my selfishness. . . . Eventually . . . I just broke down and cried, and cried, and cried. . . . Throughout my whole life I believed that if a man shows emotion by crying, he was inferior, yet as I was crying that night, finally able to mourn my father, I never felt more complete.

Here is an illustration of a primary dilemma in this man's life: how to share his deepest feelings with his family when sharing those feelings conflicts with his own socially constructed definition of proper male behavior. Through the retelling of his story on paper and to his classmates, this principal was able to break free of a constricting moral sanction and begin to be more fully human. He reports that most important to him was the experience of sharing his story: "This sharing with others has provided me with more confidence . . . [and a] new perspective . . . about men, because I realized that there were others who felt the same way, and that I was not alone." He then extends the moral dilemma he faced to his professional behavior in schools: "I believe that if critical reflection is implemented and nurtured properly in the schools . . . the end result would be that of a work force who are . . . more understanding, less threatening, and more sensitive to each others' problems and needs." Schools, too, must grapple with outdated values and practices, continually questioning their purpose and the core values that drive that purpose.

Granted, simply retelling one's story is not a panacea, suddenly transforming all "the meaning and pain of past experiences" (Dominice in Mezirow et al., 1990, p. 209). Yet reflecting on the meaning of past experiences together helps school faculty and staff to form powerful "communities of memory," which remind everyone that "it does make a difference who we are and how we treat one another" (Bellah, Madsen, Sullivan, Sidler, & Tipton, 1985, p. 282).

The above principal believes narrative and critical reflection in professional education, while not providing "the answer to all our problems," at least "gives all those involved the opportunity to identify the itinerary by which they have become who they are, and to reconstruct the process through which they have learned what constitutes their knowledge." He states, "I am glad that the change began with me because as Mezirow and colleagues (1990, p. 363) state, 'We must begin with individual perspective transformations before social transformations can succeed.' . . . As educators it is important that change begin with ourselves . . . *until we have come to grips with our true selves, we cannot take on the responsibility of changing our students.*"

It is clear that this man has experienced a transformation, a point that was clarified for him in the retelling of his own story. Sharing this story not only strengthened his conviction, but helped him to know that he was not alone. Narratives of experience provide an opportunity to reflect on the meaning of events in our lives and help us to establish connections with others, connections that sustain us and guide our future moral choices. Future decisions about how to deal with his faculty, staff, and students may be guided by this experience, providing both this principal and the members of his elementary school with a wider and more compassionate range of acceptable emotional responses. His experience underscores Witherell and Noddings' (1991) claim that "Understanding the narrative and contextual dimensions of human actors can lead to new insights, compassionate judgment, and the creation of shared knowledge and meanings that can inform professional practice" (p. 8).

ELICITING AND CLARIFYING TACIT KNOWLEDGE

Both writing and sharing our stories help to clarify what we know and believe. Often our understanding of complex tasks such as teaching or leading is so deeply buried in our everyday experience and grounded in our intuitive sense of how best to perform our jobs that we are unable to readily articulate what we know. Schön (1987) calls this kind of intuitive knowledge "artistry" and asserts that it is elicited through reflection both in and on our actions. Here an elementary principal writes about his own misconceptions of reflection and the power of reflective writing to reveal tacit knowledge—thoughts that lie buried and unexamined:

> I always envisioned reflection to be a Buddhist monk sitting lotus fashion in hushed silence, a pebble rippling a still forest pond, or a wizened holy man sitting atop a Himalayan peak. I never envisioned that reflection could occur through a simple act of writing, especially amidst the hustle and bustle of daily living. But it can, it has, and hopefully will continue to be. . . . To think it was possible only for a holy man to reflect was a falsehood. Luckily it is available to ordinary persons caught up in the throes of daily living through the process of reflective writing. Therein lies the hope for us all.

It is only through reflection on our actions that we are able to clarify and articulate what we know. If, as constructivism suggests, we are continually reframing and reinterpreting our experience in the face of new information, school personnel must first be able to articulate what they already know. Much of that information is buried in stories of practice. The elementary school staff mentioned earlier who transformed their school through stories of their math curriculum and teachers' individual efforts to improve their own teaching and learning is an excellent example.

One way to elicit tacit knowledge is through metaphor. Metaphors are like ministories that carry much information in condensed form. Metaphors provide us with a "felt sense" of ourselves and our schools, while pushing us to think more creatively. One elementary school staff created metaphors for their school, first individually and then in collaborative groups. The school was described by one participant as a prison in which each teacher stays confined to a cell and the prisoners are dying to communicate with one another. Others described it as:

> "a huge ship adrift on a calm sea. We're on it and just floating around with no sense of direction. Even the captain doesn't know where we're headed."

"a cushion being squeezed from all directions. There is the administration pushing down from the top and the teachers trying to push up from the bottom. The students and parents are pushing in from one side and the DOE [Department of Education], board of education, and district office are pushing in from the other side."

"an untamed animal preserve with cages and gates where zoo keepers and animal tamers work daily to herd animals to their sprawling assigned stalls for daily animal behavior response training sessions."

These metaphors communicate the sense of frustration and isolation, as well as lack of direction some teachers felt about the school. This in itself is tacit knowledge that school personnel often prefer to leave unarticulated. Yet only through facing the truth of our feelings can we move on to make needed changes. In a meeting of teachers and administrators, one teacher, after hearing each teacher's metaphor for the school, expressed the sudden realization that much of the school's frustration was blamed on the students:

Each metaphor talked about the low morale and the divisions within the faculty and the lack of direction/leadership that really seem to be the trouble. I guess when morale is low, and there seems to be little support coming our way, we find outlets for our frustration. The kids seem to get the brunt of it—yet when you come down to it—kids are kids.

Here the articulation of tacit knowledge about school morale allowed the teachers first to acknowledge their frustration and then to reach the insight that students were receiving the brunt of their frustrations. Only by acknowledging this fact, by breaking with old assumptions, can teachers and administrators take the needed steps to change it. This teacher's final statement was to question how helpful this knowledge would be unless administrators were involved in the work of reflection and dialogue. This seems to be an essential component. School leaders may not like what they hear when teachers and staff begin to reflect on their organizational life, but only by acknowledging what is and beginning to work together to construct a new organizational reality can schools change.

In addition, without really being able to articulate what they know, educators are left "voiceless," unable to confirm their own worth, knowledge, and ability and thus unable to connect what they already know to new information. By eliciting tacit knowledge through reflective writing, narrative, and dialogue, school leaders can support the constructivist work of all adults in schools. If this work is done collectively, teachers reach insights about their own work as they listen to others struggle to articulate what they know through story and dialogue.

One teacher in an elementary school wrote in her journal about the powerful effect of articulating and sharing stories of her practice:

> At times I've had difficulty expressing myself, communicating, and then I find I've almost withdrawn and let the "squeaky wheels" take charge. Perhaps the way I was brought up and instances along the journey made me resistant to conflict, attack. Then, I was left with the emotional war of *needing* to speak up but not doing so for fear of being verbally attacked. My writing and thinking and talks in class have helped me find some courage, some listeners and others who share many of the same feelings.

Thus constructivist work in schools can provide teachers with the supportive audience they need and the courage to speak up rather than to remain mute, leaving valuable stories of experience unarticulated. Constructivist leaders need to be alert to all voices in schools, not just those heard on a regular basis.

CREATING CONNECTION, COMMUNITY, AND VISION

Sharing past critical incidents and other narratives of our professional lives not only provides a structure for thinking, elicits tacit knowledge, and gives voice to school personnel; it also begins the important work of creating community. Shared stories help build trust and understanding as well as a common set of values and a common vision for organizations.

One principal, as he kept a journal that contained stories of critical incidents in his professional life, commented on how the process began to clarify his own understanding and vision:

> Somehow the process of writing and reflecting is comforting and clarifying. I feel a sense of breaking away from rigid expectations and exploring thought pathways that I never went down. I guess I am talking about freedom. I never thought journal-writing could be so liberating. I always thought it was what elementary teachers did to help kids learn to write better. I know now that I should reevaluate my thinking.

In addition, school principals can often feel isolated and unappreciated. In reevaluating his thinking, this principal began to see his journal as a place to value himself:

> I liked the notion that journal-writing becomes a way to value oneself more and to value one's own growth process. This idea appeals to me because so often the stresses of being a principal tend to be destructive and demoralizing. At the end of a day you are left in little pieces that someone sweeps up and empties into the trash. You don't get the feeling that your efforts were valued and appreciated.

He then went on to write about the power of collaborative reflection:

> In your class, despite the fact that I don't know my group intimately, I feel I can share more than I can share with my staff at school. I wonder why?

The life of administrators and teachers in schools is often lived at a frantic pace. There is seldom the time for educators to come together, reflect on their professional lives, and share stories through writing and dialogue. Hence this principal felt closer to people in his class whom he had known a few short weeks than to those with whom he had been working for years. Without the value of narrative and dialogue to help us form community, connection, and collective vision, we are left in little pieces to be swept into the trash. In essence, without a chance to share thoughts and stories, we remain disconnected from ourselves as well as others. When we remember and share stories of educational practice, we are literally "re-membering" the pieces of professional life.

As teachers and administrators "re-member" together, they are able to build trusting relationships, which are the backbone of community-building in schools. By making meaning together, both individual and organizational growth are fostered. Here, a teacher reflects on the impact of this process in her school:

> How nice it is to see how our "coming together" is evolving. The trust is building and it becomes easier to share, the longer the time we're together. It's nice to see this—everyone wanting to hear each other's thoughts and appreciating ideas, uniqueness. I think I'm feeling more positive about our school now than I had been feeling. I can see how we are really able to work together.

For school leaders, this sense of trust and the appreciation of individual ideas and uniqueness are fertile soil in which to begin the important work of organizational development. Through reflection on individual lives and shared dialogue, teachers and administrators can begin to construct new organizational realities that allow all members to grow and work more productively together. This might be accomplished in a variety of ways, such as specific programs of staff development, grade-level meetings aimed at improving the curriculum, or the work of a leadership team searching for alternative forms of assessment.

CONCLUSION

For me, the words of my students are powerful testimonies to the transformation possibilities of sharing our stories. I believe that through the use of journal-writing and the creation of shared histories, organizational members are able to reflect on the meaning and direction of both their individual professional lives and the life of the school in which they live and work. Writing and discussion, as forms of critical reflection, are powerful components of this meaning-making process.

Throughout their lives adults engage continually in the construction of meaning from the events of their lives. Narrative or story is a central tool in that process. Stories have the power to help define who we are, to foster growth and development, and to help us envision our possible futures. School leaders need to provide opportunities for educators to engage continually in the process of retelling and reliving the stories of their lives, both individually and organizationally.

Narratives or stories provide a structure for thinking, imagining, and making moral choices. Whether these stories are read and carried with us through the years, such as *The Catcher in the Rye,* or are stories of our own life experience, such as the principal who learned an important lesson from his son at the time of his father's death, stories can act as guides to our daily living. In addition, narratives elicit and clarify tacit knowledge. Through devices such as metaphor, a kind of condensed narrative, we are able to elicit both thought and feeling, to tap our own intuitive knowledge, to find our own voices, and to gain helpful insights about ourselves and our organizations. Finally, narratives provide connection, community, and vision. Reflection in writing and in dialogue can help us pick up the pieces of our lives and deposit them not in the trash, but in a community of understanding colleagues. It is through dialogue that we begin to form trusting professional bonds that can sustain us individually while they move us organizationally to new insights and visions. In the most powerful sense, narratives help all of us to begin to "re-member" who we are as educators and who we are as communities of professionals engaged in the construction of meaning about our lives and our work.

In Chapter 7 we are reminded that the communities of professionals provide a broader context than that of individual schools. M. Lambert and Gardner describe the district as an interdependent community in which the structures, policies, and practices encourage and sustain constructivist learning and leading.

The School District as Interdependent Learning Community

Morgan Dale Lambert and Mary E. Gardner

"Why doesn't the district move out of our way so we can get on with our restructuring work?"

"They block everything we try to do . . . because it might rock the boat for other schools"

"We feel like we'd like to build a moat around our school!"

"We need their help!"
> feedback comments by participants in a statewide symposium for restructuring school teams, Anaheim, California, May, 1994

"The main challenge of our time is to create and nurture sustainable communities."
> Fritjof Capra
> "From the parts to the whole: Systems thinking in ecology and education" (1994, p. 31)

"You think because you understand one, you understand two, because one and one makes two. But you must also understand 'and.'"
> Ancient Sufi teaching quoted in Margaret Wheatley
> *Leadership and the New Science* (1992, p. 7)

For very good reasons, most recent waves of educational reform have crashed on local school shores, with the principal and teachers at the heart of the rescue operation. Consistent with this "local school site as the locus of change" orientation, the message in most of the other chapters in this book is directed mainly toward school-level people—principals, teacher leaders, and other change agents who are engaged in the vital work of constructing learning communities in their schools. The emphasis is appropriate, but it has become increasingly apparent that even the most dynamic constructivist school culture can wither if it attempts to function for too long in isolation or in a larger district or community environment that is alien, unsupportive, perhaps even hostile.

The quotes from California restructurers that introduce this chapter illustrate the frustration being felt by local school change activists as they interact with their districts—"Help us or get out of the way!" In response, leaders in the school restructuring program in that state launched a major initiative to study how districts can best provide support as well as guidance for the school-restructuring efforts. Reform programs in a growing number of states have broadened their scope to focus on both schools and school districts. And the new Goals 2000 federal program design recognizes the need for genuinely systemic reform that promotes whole-school change and coherent partnerships among schools, districts, and regional support providers.

THE SCHOOL DISTRICT AS ECOSYSTEM

Recognition of the importance of district support linkages and the systemic nature of school change is an important strategic insight, but it is also essential that the context for local school renewal be made even broader and deeper and that the linkages be seen as reciprocal. The focus in this chapter shifts to that larger context of the school district and its environment, and we develop the thesis that the fully functioning school district must become a learning community in the same sense that each school must form its own learning community culture. The district is a larger entity (ecosystem) than the individual schools, but it is also interconnected in that same "web of relationships in which all life processes depend on one another" (Capra, 1993, p. 24). And that web includes each of the individual schools and school communities in the district—all connected and interdependent.

It is intriguing and exciting to reflect on how naturally the ecological principles enunciated by Capra (described and expanded in more detail in Chapter 2) can be adapted to virtually all forms of collaborative learning group interaction—cooperative learning teams, collaborative teaching groups, schools and school districts as congruent learning communities. Rephrased to fit the school district when it is viewed as a constructivist learning community, Capra's principles might look like this:

Members of a dynamic school district are interconnected in a web of relationships in which all interactive processes depend on one another. The success of the whole school district depends on the success of its individual schools and participants, while the success of each individual person and unit depends on the success of the community (district) as a whole. Individuals and groups, schools and the district environment in which they operate adapt to one another—they coevolve.

From this perspective, schools are not seen so much as dependent on benevolent district support but as interconnected in a web of reciprocally supportive relationships with not only the district but also with other schools, networks, the community, and so forth. The web has an intriguingly fractal character, with the relationships among student learners, adult learners, school communities, and district communities all sharing many qualities. And those qualities bear a very close resemblance to the principles of ecology—interdependence, network patterns, feedback loops, cooperation, partnerships, flexibility.

As this ecological and contextual orientation to school change grows in its influence on practitioners, it will become increasingly clear that the status and function of the school district also must change in congruent ways. Site-based management, shared leadership, teacher empowerment, and the evolving commitment to whole-school change—all of these promising innovations make urgent the need to rethink the traditional hierarchical organization structure. It is our hope that constructivist leadership principles will inform the new possibilities—that the old hierarchies will be replaced by more flexible structures, by interdependent networks, by enabling processes.

THE TRADITIONAL PARADIGM

Before starting construction of a new set of approaches, it will be helpful to remind ourselves of traditional school district structures and operations. Most district functions are currently drawn from the managerial and bureaucratic domains—allocation and management of resources (money, materials, and personnel); collection and dissemination of information; monitoring, evaluation, and accountability; strategic planning; development of policies and regulations; coordination of departments, sites, and programs (viewed primarily as discrete components, all arrayed in boxes in a vertically aligned "table of organization"). In many enlightened districts, there may be substantive provision for community and school involvement in the strategic planning and decision-making functions, but the participant role is still seen as that of contributor rather than reciprocal partner in a collaborative endeavor. Even in districts in which the "decentralized decision-making, site-based management" model has been embraced, there is the tendency to assign functions to discrete elements—textbook budgets to schools, monitoring and accounting to district departments, goal-setting and policy-making to school boards. School boards may suggest in their superintendent search brochures that they are looking for an "instruction-oriented systemic change agent," but résumés that boast of business management experience, fiscal skills, and a commitment to tough-minded accountability still float to the top.

In contrast, let's now envision what roles, structures, and processes would look like in a community that is animated by constructivist thinking.

THE SUPERINTENDENT AS CONSTRUCTIVIST LEADER

When asked who the school district's "leader" is, most people would identify the superintendent, even in a constructivist district. But they would probably add caveats about the role being shared and might submit descriptors to clarify the role. In addition to the usual managerial leadership functions, the shrewd observer might stress these five functions (the first three taken from Senge's *The Fifth Discipline,* 1990):

Steward of the vision, values, and purpose of the district. This requires that the superintendent be focused, curious, and courageous. He or she is continually ready to ask the essential questions and to resist political agendas that would divert attention from teaching and learning.

Designer of the enabling structures and processes that support dialogic, inquiring, sustaining, and partnering conversations.

Teacher of the board, community, district staff, principals, and leadership teams about teaching and learning and dimensions of community.

Learner with the board, community, district staff, and students. He or she listens, converses, reflects, and makes sense of the world in interaction with new ideas, information, and other people.

Participant in the array of reciprocal processes that give texture to the culture of collaborative inquiry that is growing in the school, district, and community. He or she recognizes that roles such as steward, designer, and teacher are shared by many co-leaders and that they are multidimensional.

The new roles expected of superintendents are complex and challenging, and they will not necessarily be embraced by incumbents who are comfortable in an older hierarchical tradition. Murphy (1994) studied the reactions of Kentucky superintendents who had a decentralized school-restructuring program imposed on them by state law. Most felt that authority had been removed from their office but that responsibility and accountability were left behind. Even those who supported the changes reported that much more systematic support and a longer time-line of preparation were needed.

It is imperative that the district's superintendent believe in, promote, and model the reciprocal processes that are at the core of constructivism. But it is equally clear that the role changes may come slowly and encounter resistance, that these changes will evolve within the context of shared participation with other constructivist leaders.

THE DISTRICT AS INTERDEPENDENT COMMUNITY

The basic characteristics of participantship and leadership described in Chapters 2 and 3 in reference to schools apply as well to the whole set of people who provide district office services, not just the superintendent. Miller (1988) provides vivid examples of what the instructional administrator(s) can do to create the enabling structures for a professional district culture—opportunities to write curricula in teams, organize and conduct their own staff development, engage in substantive action research, become consultants as well as coaches to one another, and serve in a myriad of leadership roles—frequently in collaboration with district office staff. Bringing school people into the policy-making process and involving them in budget-building and other business decision-making are other examples.

Following a study of "The Role of the School District in School Improvement," Louis (1989) identified two correlates of productive support—"high engagement" (frequent interaction and communication, mutual coordination and influence, and some shared goals and objectives) and "low bureaucratization" (absence of extensive rules and regulations governing the relationship).

In order to achieve that kind of supportive relationship, it is our thesis that the district organization must be redesigned to become the same kind of self-organizing, self-renewing system that is being proposed for schools, one that imports free energy from the environment and exports entropy, providing both "positive feedback and disequilibrium" (Wheatley, 1992, p. 78). Its primary function would be to support the needs of schools and the formation of connections among schools and with the community, providing whatever guidance, resources, and expertise it can to meet those needs—with both the needs and the strategies to meet them being collaboratively determined and carried out by collegial partners. The district must assist in facilitating the appropriate mix of freedom, dissonance, guidance, resources, opportunity, and support needed by schools to grow and evolve. And the support must be delivered in the spirit of reciprocity, for the schools and district are co-evolving. The Jefferson Union High School District story below provides an example in which the district/school board developed a policy and some guidelines concerning school restructuring, provided a large measure of autonomy, supported the engagement in networking, and made clear their readiness to change their own way of doing business.

In describing traditional district functions and structures above, we identified accountability as a high-priority function—one about which schools sometimes feel anxiety and resentment. Paradoxically, the commitment to a particular form of "accountability" could possibly provide a thread that can help to pull together the traditional and the constructivist patterns of successful school districts. But it would not be the old model of centralized and standardized bean-counting. Accountability in the constructivist glossary has much more to do with responsibility, self-monitoring, critical reflection on data (especially dissonant data), dialogue with "critical friends," collaborative action research, and the internalization of evaluative criteria—the kinds of processes that sustain a healthy, self-renewing organization.

In an article appropriately entitled "Reframing the School Reform Agenda: Developing Capacity for School Transformation," Darling-Hammond (1993) declares:

> The foundation of genuine accountability . . . is the capacity of individual schools: (1) to organize themselves to prevent students from falling through the cracks; (2) to create means for continual collegial inquiry (in which hard questions are posed regarding what needs to change in order for individuals and groups of students to succeed); (3) to use authority responsibly to make the changes necessary. . . . It will occur only if we build an inquiry ethic, a community of discourse in the school that is focused on students and their needs rather than on the implementation of rules and procedures. (p. 760)

The responsibility for building that kind of capacity for self-monitoring and an ethic of student-centered inquiry represents perhaps the most challenging function of school districts today. Capacity-building and accountability are not exclusive school or district functions. They are significant examples of roles and responsibilities that must be "owned" fully but also shared at each level of the school/district learning community—in each classroom and school, at the district office, and in the spaces in between individuals and units in this complex and interconnected web of reciprocal relationships in which all interactive processes depend on one another. Only then will the "system" become adaptive, responsive, and capable of renewal—organically accountable.

As we sketch an outline for a constructivist district, it will become increasingly apparent that the discrete function boxes no longer sit, passive and discrete, on the organizational table. Responsibility for functions is shared, and much of the most important work gets done in the "spaces" in between schools, district office, and community. These spaces and connection points do not usually get much attention in the traditional school district, but they are significant—they are the kind of "and" to which the Sufi teaching quoted at the beginning of this chapter refers.

Making connections, forming relationships, sharing responsibilities as colleagues—these are complex interactions that are negotiated through the kinds of conversations and stories that are described in previous chapters. Accordingly, some actual stories may help to form the foundation for the constructivist approaches we are in the process of building.

STORIES AND EXAMPLES

The Saratoga School District Story
(by Mary Gardner, Superintendent)

Saratoga is a small (2,000 students) suburban school district, serving a predominantly upper-middle-class population. The community is becoming increasingly diverse, with 34% of students of Asian heritage. Some of the roles and strategies I report will not fit the circumstances faced by large-district superintendents. But those collaborative, co-learner interactions can and should be engaged in by some staff member (perhaps by an assistant superintendent or coordinator) if the district office is to play an authentically constructive role.

It was in the second year of my superintendency that I experienced what it would really mean for teachers to be in a reciprocal relationship with the administration and to be involved in shared constructivist leadership. The district curriculum committee had decided that one of its major tasks would be to work on studying and "improving" our K–8 science program. In playing the scribe, listener, and facilitator roles that I had decided to assume, I started our conversation by asking them to recall a time when they had learned something scientific, when they had suddenly known they understood something in science that they had not understood before. They were to describe it as vividly as they could. Where were they? Were they with someone? How did they learn? How did they feel? Out of this reflection and subsequent sharing and discussion, we defined how we wanted kids to participate in science and what we wanted them to experience—nourished by the memory of our own moments of discovery, connected to powerful experiences.

As the facilitator, I also became the scribe for the ideas being discussed.

It was clear in this meeting that they had the information and were invested in being certain that their experiences as learners and as teachers were recorded. All 15 participants were actively engaged. The meeting was alive with reflective and creative energy. My role was to write as fast as I could, to clarify, and to be certain that what I recorded was what someone meant to say. Occasionally, I also connected thoughts together when I could see a pattern. If I misinterpreted or did not give the proper emphasis to particular words, participants would correct me and expand their ideas or rephrase.

That meeting signaled a shift in the control of information in the district. Now we all had a collective experience demonstrating how meetings could be different from the typical information-giving structure. That meeting was the beginning of teachers having more to say and opening up to involved conversations. I am now a listener to their ideas and discussions that come back from grade-level and team meetings. Although meetings are not always as full of energy or connectedness, we as a group are different. The teachers have become the primary leaders.

After 6 months of collegial curriculum development, a different group formed around a common purpose and decided to apply for a technology grant. The group was comprised of a science resource teacher, a second-grade teacher, a parent, the principal of each school, a board member who sometimes writes grant proposals for the district, and the superintendent. A meeting was held to decide whether we should apply for the grant as a consortium of schools or whether individual schools should apply. We concluded that if we applied for a district grant, we could begin to connect all of the schools in a meaningful project.

This was a very busy time of year; everyone was tired, overworked, and ready to "wind things down." As we established the criteria for the project, identified a natural study focus, and created teams and time-lines to ensure completion of a proposal, we all became energized. Within an hour and a half, we had not only made the decision to apply for a districtwide grant but had agreed on design principles.

When we began the meeting, none of us anticipated the connectedness that would come out of the process. Because of the energy created by an open discussion about possibilities, all participants were ready to take on responsibilities, to find others to help, and to begin the work. The parent and board member agreed to do the writing, while the teachers and administrators would provide the structure and content information. The enterprise was affectionately named "The Saratoga Creek Project." Through the collaborative writing process, an exciting curriculum was initiated, with potential partnerships with local and county government, with the community college in Saratoga, with businesses, and with the local high school. The magic of this synergistic event and collaboration continues to create resources and to draw additional teachers into the constructivist experience. Five months later, we received the grant and the "construction" moved into a new phase.

Stories from Practice: A 30-Year Perspective
(by Morgan Dale Lambert)

My first major experience as a change agent was 25 years ago as principal of an innovative high school in which many of the currently popular reform strategies were being pioneered—modular/flexible scheduling, collaborative planning and team teaching, self-directed (independent) study, small-group instruction, and community-based learning. Exciting successes were experienced, many of them foreshadowing the cooperative learning and collaborative teaching practices currently in vogue. But the negative lessons were just as instructive—and more relevant to the theme of this chapter.

District office involvement and support were conspicuously and painfully absent, and this proved to be the fatal flaw that led to the eventual abandonment of the modular/flexible scheduling program. The maverick school was isolated and suffered particularly from an absence of articulation ties with feeder schools; students arrived with no real preparation for the responsibilities entailed in self-directed study.

We learned two other important lessons. First, the developmental needs of *all* students must be kept as a central focus for instructional change initiatives—not just those who respond eagerly and responsibly to new and exciting learning opportunities. Second, parents must be involved as fully participating and informed partners; and the involvement must come early, be continuous, and be perceived as substantive and respectful. The minority of parents whose children were floundering ultimately sealed the fate of this noble early experiment in "restructuring" (M. Lambert, 1993).

Lack of district office support was key to the failure to reach potential at our innovative high school. Curiously, my second story reveals the other side of that same coin—and also has both positive and negative lessons from which to learn. Later in my career, I responded to a job announcement that used the title "Assistant Superintendent for Instruction and School Improvement." Recognizing a school district that would support innovation and change, I leapt at the chance. Again, many satisfying ventures and successes grew out of this opportunity to function as school-oriented district office change agent, and I still heartily endorse this posture. But my experiences revealed also the power of what has been called "systemic inertia" (Szabo, 1995) and the limitations on the effectiveness of a central office change agent (particularly an outsider brought in to "reform" schools), especially when the school board is in a hurry to get the job done quickly and massively. In spite of the press for quick change, perhaps even because of it, I learned to value complex collaborative processes that build respectfully on local school strengths and on relationships that strengthen over time. These insights were of great value when I later became superintendent of a school district that was already highly innovative and where the culture supported collaborative leadership among teachers and parents. In that setting, the superintendent's roles were largely those of facilitative leader and mediator among empowered initiators.

In my current role as consultant, facilitator, and school coach for the California Center for School Restructuring (CCSR), I have a rare opportunity to use the lessons learned in these earlier positions and in many other change agent roles. As in my own personal early experience as high school principal, California's restructuring program began with a heavy emphasis on local school initiation and only token regard for district involvement. Entering its third year in 1994, much more interest developed around the broader context, particularly in the strategies for engaging the district office as collaborative partner. And the statewide leaders are fully aware of the need to build cultures of inquiry and reflective learning communities—in each school but also in the district and broader community as well.

The orientation of CCSR leaders and the design of the state restructuring program itself are distinctly constructivist in character, especially in the commitment to plan and implement programs collaboratively, to focus on student learner outcomes, and to learn by reflecting on authentic experience and engaging in carefully designed "cycles of inquiry" (Shawn, 1994). The design of a research and development initiative on the district office role in facilitating school restructuring was formed largely by this kind of reflection on experience and promising practices. An early lesson in the CCSR initiative was that there must be an underlying support system that has two interrelated dimensions—one that provides for monitoring and public accounting and a second that emphasizes the collective organizational learning that sustains systemic change. The Accountability/Learning Support System (A/LSS, CCSR, 1993) that resulted was designed and constructed by the actual participants—a set of teachers and administrators working collaboratively with CCSR staff. Participant reflection and feedback after a year's experience with A/LSS produced a new understanding—that the support network must include the district office as a fully participating partner. Accordingly, the new CCSR format calls for district representatives to join school teams in certain network functions.

Many of the 147 schools and districts in the CCSR network are not yet functioning as constructivist learning organizations. But some districts are increasingly using the collaborative processes and enabling structures that can move the culture in that direction. The Jefferson District story that follows will illustrate. Other stories will be embedded in the section on "Guidelines and Recommendations" that appears later in this chapter.

The Jefferson Union High School District Story
San Mateo County, California

This low-wealth suburban district borders urban San Francisco and serves a diverse community. It was once almost paralyzed by a labor dispute but has now placed teachers in key leadership positions and negotiated significant decision-making roles for teacher groups at individual schools and in the districtwide organization. The school board has adopted policies aimed at promoting teacher-designed restructuring in each of the five high schools in the district, and two of the five are deeply engaged in comprehensive restructuring. Academic councils, comprised of teacher leaders, have assumed very heavy responsibility for program and personnel decisions.

The superintendent has encouraged participation by restructuring schools in a variety of regional and national networks—notably the Coalition of Essential Schools, CCSR, and California's Second to None High School Network. All of these initiatives share some common values and practices, such as an emphasis on student outcomes, integrated curriculum, performance-based assessment, and collaboration among teacher leaders. The district office is supporting cross-school communication and cooperation and is crafting new channels for sharing learning and problem-solving among all district schools.

Major responsibility for promoting, guiding, and supporting restructuring initiatives is carried by a council comprised by representatives from each school's academic council. Significantly, a teacher who was a leader in the earlier labor dispute is now principal of one of the restructuring schools.

ENABLING DISTRICT STRUCTURES AND STRATEGIES

The stories and vignettes throughout this chapter and book that depict changing schools and school districts portray many of the elements of constructivist organizations. Patterns and themes begin to emerge in those stories—policies that encourage and support innovation in schools, acts of collaborative behavior by superintendents that promote the shift from authoritative to facilitative leadership, district office modeling of team-building behaviors and strategies. These process patterns and structural themes rather naturally form design features for use in constructing a set of approaches for a constructivist school district. These approaches address the criteria of constructivist learning and leading that are essential to the creation of constructivist districts:

- Framing the processes within which a common purpose can be constructed
- Seeking to equalize power relationships through the replacement of hierarchies with collaborative networks
- Creating a culture of inquiry in which information forms feedback spirals and self-renewing organizations
- Developing communities of learning as a medium for human growth and development
- Forming enabling structures that enhance human interaction
- Selecting and developing constructivist leaders

In a culture that reflects constructivist principles, the responsibility for co-leading the change process is shared at all levels, but the district has a pivotal guiding and facilitating role, with the superintendent bearing ultimate responsibility.

Whether the district office is a barrier or a facilitator for change efforts of schools depends on its own development as a learning organization. If the support it offers is to have the ring of authenticity, it too must be engaged in discovery, redefining and reorganizing its roles, interactions, and structures to make them truly functional. The critical test will be: Are they enablers?

While seeking its own change, stability, and renewal, the district office must maintain "global stability in the presence of many fluctuations and instabilities occurring at the local level throughout the system" (Wheatley, 1992, p. 94). In the final analysis, a district that is constructivist in nature would be open to change and be involved with school partners in designing the processes that build resiliency into a system.

"Resiliency" . . . "interactive processes" . . . "web of reciprocal relationships" . . . "culture of inquiry" . . . "capacity building" . . . "enabling structures"—these are all noble concepts and goals, but how can they be realized in the tough, real world of schools and school districts? The stories of school/district change are encouraging, but practitioners need to see a more comprehensive set of guidelines and recommendations. Those guidelines must in themselves be "enablers" in the sense described in Chapter 2—facilitating the reciprocal processes that evoke potential, construct meaning, reconstruct assumptions, and frame actions. The last part of this chapter suggests such a framework of guidelines (see Figure 7.1).

GUIDELINES AND RECOMMENDATIONS

Districts have a special role to play in identifying common values and creating compelling visions, mission statements, and unifying purposes. The processes that produce such statements must be inclusive and collaborative and

Figure 7.1. Guidelines and Recommendations for Creating Constructivist School Districts

---

- Districts have a special role to play in identifying common values and creating compelling visions, mission statements, and unifying purposes.
- There needs to be large-scale but carefully crafted devolution of authority, resources, and responsibility.
- District policies and procedures, processes and structures must be redesigned to pass the "enabler test."
- Personnel policies and practices must be developed that nurture the continuous development of all staff members.
- An information-gathering and -processing system will be needed that supports but is not dominated by administrative and accountability functions.
- District staff will need to model and support efforts to make assessment programs more authentic.
- Promotion of and support for collegial and collaborative strategies are essential at all levels.
- The district must assign high priority to the promotion of the strategies and processes that create professionalism in a culture of inquiry.
- In its relationships with unions and associations, the district must move beyond condescension and confrontation toward interest-based collaboration.
- The district must work proactively to enrich and cultivate the "spaces" among schools and between schools and the community.
- Schools need support and direct assistance in solving the perennial problems of time and resources.
- More effective strategies must be developed for recruiting, inducting, and supporting the continuing development of leaders at all levels (including teacher leaders).
- School board roles must be redesigned to ensure that they are supportive of the learning organization.
- Above all else, the district must promote and model the participation and informed decision-making processes that contribute to preparing students and adults to participate effectively in a democracy.

---

must take place in individual school communities as well as the district. The special district responsibilities are to assist in finding time and resources for this time-consuming process, to monitor for congruence among the many visions, and to ensure that data reflecting the needs of students and expectations of the broader community are accessible and are used in the vision-building process. The superintendent should be centrally involved (as "steward of the vision, values, and purpose of the district"), but it must be a shared stewardship to have sustainable impact.

Alameda Unified School District, in a diverse community next door to urban Oakland, California, took imaginative advantage of business and community partnerships in developing strategic plans for the whole district, for each school, and for the community itself. The visioning exercises asked all participants to reexamine paradigms in their thinking and to reflect on powerful learning outcomes for students who will be living and working in the twenty-first century. The whole process was inclusive and collaborative in character, with more than 2,000 people directly involved (teachers, parents, students, businesspeople, and civic officials). The student outcomes that emerged are at the core of school restructuring initiatives, and the linkages and processes are still being used as the district and community struggle with a new crisis—the impact of closure of a major U.S. Navy base.

There needs to be large-scale but carefully crafted devolution of authority, resources, and responsibility. This devolution affects classrooms, teams of teachers, schools, and school clusters—and it must occur in a systemic way that also provides for capacity-building and accountability.

The decentralization show has played to mixed reviews in a number of large urban districts over the past decade (New York and Chicago are two notable examples), but it has not often been accompanied by the needed staff development and other systemic supports. There is the danger that the locus of coercive or authoritative power may simply move from the center to neighborhoods unless a culture that supports facilitative leadership is carefully nurtured.

In the Jefferson Union High School District story, the script is different. An enabling structure for collaborative decision-making has moved to the school sites, along with authority and control over resources. Academic councils are operating under a policy incentive to restructure, but they have the power to design their own system. And a cross-school communication system is evolving that should facilitate congruence.

Other districts are working for community by clustering schools and bringing principals and teacher leaders together for planning, problem-solving, team development, professional development, and collegial interaction. Tim Cuneo, Superintendent of the Oak Grove School District, located on the edge of urban San Jose, California, describes the district's plans to cluster schools into "learning communities." These communities will combine intermediate and elementary schools into a single school with satellite campuses. The governance structure will include teacher leaders as co-directors of each community (T. Cuneo, personal communication, August 1994).

District policies and procedures, processes and structures must be redesigned to pass the "enabler test." This redesign must support the decentralization essential to a system of interdependent learning communities. Policies can be designed to satisfy legislative or school board intent without getting in the way of new ideas and well-planned change initiatives. The policies and practices must be made consistent with a commitment to informed innovation, risk-taking, continuous growth, and change. Involvement of school representatives at the developmental stage is an obvious first step on this path. Readiness to revise policies and procedures, negotiate waivers and exemptions, decentralize budget and personnel decisions, seek changes in laws—these are signs that the system is becoming responsive in the policy arena. A few enlightened districts are auditing old policies to make sure they are congruent with current decentralization and school-restructuring goals. Clearly, skill and sensitivity will be required in balancing the paradoxical district roles of creating dissonance and providing support.

Personnel policies and practices must be developed that nurture the continuous development of all staff members. Because of their critical importance, some of the recommended personnel policies and practices that contrast with those in more traditional school district cultures are highlighted separately in Figure 7.2.

Personnel selection and induction practices will become more collaborative, systematic, and school-based. More natural and functional strategies will be used (realistic simulations in selection, mentoring during induction). A much more comprehensive professional development program will start with selection and incorporate staff development, supervision, and evaluation in a seamless process. Activities and strategies will have a more collegial feel, but they will also promote self-analysis and self-direction with the flavor of autonomy. Policies relating to contracts and administrative regulations will be less legalistic and more flexible; negotiations will move from confrontational toward interest-based approaches. These qualities are portrayed more clearly in Figure 7.2.

An information-gathering and -processing system will be needed that supports but is not dominated by administrative and accountability functions. Many school districts are taking the lead in developing comprehensive technology/information systems, usually with a primary emphasis on business, administrative, and accountability (reporting) functions. In second- and third-priority position are usually found pupil personnel services and direct instructional applications. Seldom is much attention given to the vital dimension of communication networking among teachers, teams of teachers, principals and other school leaders, and school networks. The district must reorder priorities to make certain that the information system serves effectively to support informed decision-making, to build a culture of inquiry that is informed by data as well as driven by values. The self-organizing system that we are advocating requires/demands a continuing inflow of information—freshening, renewing, reinventing the way things are perceived, the way things are done.

If teachers are to become full participants in the culture of inquiry, along with their school and district administrator colleagues, they must have easy

Figure 7.2. School District Personnel Practices and Policies

TRADITIONAL/HIERARCHICAL/ CENTRALIZED	COLLABORATIVE/CONSTRUCTIVIST/ DECENTRALIZED
Selection of Personnel	
Paper screening followed by broad-based interview panel; occasional teaching/supervision sample or observed performance; site visitations for administrative positions; final selection by central authority.	Augmented by mini-assessment center featuring authentic simulations, interactive role-playing, problem-solving exercises, personal valuing of dilemmas (with teachers trained to serve as assessors); major authority for selection at the site, with broad-based participation in the process.
Induction of New Personnel	
Formal orientation activities, followed by standardized staff development programs; may include access to a mentor; usually self- contained and not sustained.	Orientation and enculturation processes for both teachers and administrators include formal and informal activities that are part of a complex professional development program. Strong links with local universities, regional and county offices, other districts, professional networks. Professional practice schools as exemplary model.
Professional Development	
Emphasis on skill development, knowledge acquisition, training by prescription; delivery through formal workshops, courses.	Emphasis on professional development as multiple learning opportunities embedded in authentic tasks such as collaborative action research, study groups, participation in decision-making, co- planning, mentoring of new educators.
Individual professional development plans, where they exist, are objective-based in relation to teacher evaluation criteria and are determined by evaluator	Professional development plans are personalized, collegial, and school-based, with room for choice, sustained commitment, and multiple forms of learning.
Majority of professional development days are scheduled and structured by the district and/or board	Majority of professional development days are designed by local staff who are also involved in determining district priorities that shape the common days and programs. Programs feature work in reciprocal processes, action research, teaching and learning from student work, leadership team development, protocols, reciprocal team coaching, collaborative planning.
District goals dominate the design of local school improvement plans. School plans are viewed primarily as instrumental in moving towards district goals.	Local school improvement plans have ongoing professional development at the center. School plans inform as well as are informed by district goals.

Figure 7.2. (*continued*)

TRADITIONAL/HIERARCHICAL/ CENTRALIZED	COLLABORATIVE/CONSTRUCTIVIST/ DECENTRALIZED

Reassignment and Transfer

Contract provisions and the "needs of the district" control matters of assignment and transfer. Often, poorly performing staff are transferred from school to school.

Reassignment is requested by an educator attracted to the program and philosophy of another school; educator is invited to another school because of needed skills and perspective.

Supervision and Evaluation

Supervision is performed by administrators and quasi-administrators, such as department chairs. Peer coaching and informal supervision may be encouraged, but the enabling structures for sustained collegial work do not exist.

Critical self-analysis, peer observation and feedback, cognitive coaching, critical friendship, engagement in collaborative action research. These norms constitue the core of collegial "supervision" and evaluation practice.

Evaluation is performed only by administrators and in strict compliance with contract and district effectiveness criteria. Number of allowable observations often limited by contract.

Administrators participate in evaluation (especially with new teachers and those experiencing difficulty), but their assessments simply add to a performance portfolio which also includes self- and peer assessment reports, student and parent feedback, research findings, and other performance artifacts.

Contracts, Regulations, and Waivers

Adversarial contract negotiations and centrally designed policies and regulations.

Nonconfrontational, interest-based bargaining produces contracts that are congruent with flexible district policies.

Emphasis is placed on developing clear, detailed, and replicable clauses, regulations, and procedures for compliance.

Policies and procedures parameters serve emerging goals; flexible policies grow out of change efforts and respond to needs identified by school-site leadership teams.

Exemptions and waiver procedures may be made available but they are viewed as evidences of weakness or failure.

Waivers to state department and legal regulations are framed and supported by district as such waivers respond to local changes.

and direct access to the channels and tools of communication. In today's school, that means access not just to a telephone, but to a fax machine, modem, E-mail, electronic bulletin board, and so forth. And the content that goes through those channels will be varied—ideas, questions, suggestions, critiques, feedback, of course, but also data. Schools, districts, networks, counties, universities, and other service providers—all need to be linked by technology that makes accessible multiple forms of data about students (attendance, test scores, performances), family, graduates, the community, and business needs and requirements.

While technology is an increasingly vital information vehicle, the most significant communication channels in a constructivist culture will be personal and relational—conversations, peer coaching, study groups, protocol sessions, reciprocal team coaching. The inquiring school will take nourishment out of a rich stream of data and other forms of information.

It is a shared school and district responsibility to generate and discover information and then to use it to make connections, to find and analyze problems, to disclose and process dissonant information, to link information and evidence to action-oriented decision-making. One of the most promising strategies for achieving the desired critical discourse and inquiry ethic is through engagement in collaborative action research, which has been described in Chapters 3 and 4—much of it at the school level but some in cross-school and district inquiry teams.

District staff will need to model and support efforts to make assessment programs more authentic. Data should be produced for the dual purposes of forming decisions and informing stakeholders. Standards of authenticity need to be applied not just to student learning but also to teacher self-assessment and evaluation, peer supervision, and program evaluation. The portfolio approach to assessment of student learning (described in Chapters 1 and 9), for example, can be adapted to the parallel functions of assessing/evaluating teacher performance and program progress. When the assessment and evaluation functions are seen primarily as dynamic dimensions of a multifaceted learning and feedback system, the gathering and analysis of student, teacher, and program performance data become congruent processes that reinforce and inform each other. When these data become a part of the information system described above, and the responsibility for sharing information with all stakeholders is taken seriously, the assessment function will become an enabling structure for the district.

While most assessment activity will remain focused on classroom and school levels, the district has enabling functions that are vital. Among those functions are those of catalyst, contract negotiator, policy-maker, and key participant in efforts to keep community stakeholders reciprocally informed and engaged. Because of the potentially controversial nature of some forms of alternative assessment, another district function is to act as buffer, defender, and interpreter, especially during the early stages of innovative assessment initiatives.

Promotion of and support for collegial and collaborative strategies are essential at all levels. The district staff must model this stance in their own interactions. Cooperative learning, collaborative planning and teaching, peer coaching, collegial observation and feedback, study teams, reciprocal team coaching, leadership teams, interest-based bargaining—these are all mutually reinforcing fractals of the same generative and collaborative processes that sustain a constructivist culture. The district must use the same processes in forming and facilitating its own committees and activities and in creating a climate of expectancy that will be used in school communities. District staff must "walk the talk" of democratic collaboration. The Saratoga School District story revealed many of these processes.

In addition to helping to provide time and resources, skillful personnel from the district or other support providers may be needed in the early stages of learning how to surface assumptions, formulate critical questions, and engage in inquiring conversations. District staff may also play a key role in balancing the press by the community and the board for quick accomplishment with the need to build the relationships that are essential in making sustainable systemic change.

Another remarkable district, Ross Valley in Marin County, California, is half-way through a 5-year project aimed at building "collaborative learning communities." The project's formative evaluation design is itself a nice example of constructivist accountability, being developed and implemented collaboratively by (district) project and school staff and an outside evaluator. One of the functions and structures being tracked in this evaluation is the extent to which "the schedules, procedures, and physical structures of this school are set up to facilitate collaboration." They report as one of their early lessons learned about change that "flexibility in how schools achieve agreed-upon district goals promotes a sense of ownership and personal commitment to the changes" (Thompson, 1994, p. 4).

The district must assign high priority to the promotion of the strategies and processes that create professionalism in a culture of inquiry. Attaching substantial resources to professional development undertakings and moving major decision-making authority concerning activities and programs to the school-site level are significant enabling strategies. So too are the modeling and promotion of dialogic, inquiring, sustaining, and partnering conversations; reflective journals; narrative and stories, protocols, rituals and ceremonies that promote and celebrate collegiality and professionalism.

Sharing authority for professional development with schools in no way implies abdication of district responsibility in this vital area. Ensuring that schools have access to coherent and substantive programs for team development and for sharpening the skills that are essential to reciprocal and general communication processes, problem analysis, rapport and trust-building, mediation and conflict resolution is a function for which the district should retain major, albeit not exclusive, responsibility. District participation has an important role also in ensuring that student needs are kept at the center of focus in all instructional programs. Another function is to facilitate the kinds of cross-school and networking experiences that provide the rich bed that nourishes professional growth (collaborative action research and reciprocal team coaching are two examples—see below for more on this).

Modeling a commitment to build a culture of inquiry and readiness to participate actively in that effort is an important act of leadership for a district. In their study of how districts can best support local school restructuring, the CCSR invited school districts around the state to volunteer to engage in a collaborative inquiry process—sharing and reflecting on their own promising practices, seeking critique/feedback from critical friends, participating openly as learners in a journey of discovery designed to identify new strategies. It is this kind of inquiry/action research and modeling that will promote the evolution of a multilayered learning community—in classes, schools, and the district as a whole.

In its relationships with unions and associations, the district must move beyond condescension and confrontation toward interest-based collaboration. A culture of collaboration, reciprocity, and critical friendship will not survive long if administrator and teacher colleagues routinely abandon these relationships to engage in adversarial bargaining. A growing number of California school districts are moving toward quite a different approach, toward negotiations that emphasize beginning with the identification of common or overlapping interests and then engaging in joint problem-solving, working hard to build and maintain trust and mutual respect (Butler, 1995).

Beyond negotiations, the deeper relationships with unions in many school districts need serious attention. A number of restructuring schools in California complain that it is more difficult to secure contract waivers from unions than it is to modify district policies and practices. But others report some successes in building partnerships and involving union personnel in co-leadership roles. The Jefferson Union High School district story describes a paradigm shift into collaborative relationships. The San Francisco Unified School District has taken a somewhat similar approach, giving union representatives major responsibility for promoting and implementing a sophisticated three-phased restructuring program. A teacher selected by the union heads the program in this complex urban district. Structural strategies such as this may help, but the subtler relational and cultural changes will take much longer.

The district must work proactively to enrich and cultivate the "spaces" among schools and between schools and the community. Vibrant school communities are stretching into these spaces, and the district has a key role in facilitating the process, making the web of relationships that connects individuals and groups strong and supportive. The artificial lines that traditionally separate schools are being erased or at least made permeable; the border areas are becoming the context for cross-school dialogue, for the exchange of energy between subsystems in a larger ecosystem.

A growing practice among CCSR network schools is to engage in a form of collegial observation and feedback, with teams exchanging visits over a period of a year or more. Modeled after an innovation in the Coalition of Essential Schools, this reciprocal form of team coaching entails identification of essential questions, systematic observation by the visiting team, and critical dialogue among the combined teams of "critical friends." The term "reciprocal team coaching" (M. Lambert, 1995) has been coined to stress the reciprocal nature of this form of coaching: Each team coaches the other; all participants exchange observations and suggestions as critical friends. The critical dialogue is structured in part by using a modified form of the protocol, an inquiry tool developed by schools in the CCSR network.

Districts are finding that reciprocal team coaching and the protocol are both useful strategies for constructing a new norm for sharing insights and understandings across school lines, for moving toward a new culture of inquiry in the entire district community.

Another area in which districts can function as enabler is in supporting school leadership team development—by offering staff development directly, by facilitating linkage with other agencies that provide this service, and by simply encouraging and providing resources to schools that are interested in making such a connection on their own. In addition to assisting in local school team development, some districts are scheduling sessions in which school leadership partners (the principal and a designated teacher leader) from clusters of schools come together for collaborative planning, decision-making, and skill development. Oak Grove School District furnishes one example of this strategy; other districts are extending the strategy to include high schools in a "vertical slice" structuring of collaboration.

The Peer-Assisted Leadership Program from the Far West Laboratories (Lee, 1991) teams principals in year-long peer observation and reflective interviewing partnerships that focus on understanding the relationships among the beliefs, values, knowledge, and actions of the principals. Principals report significant insights and shifts in perception and style; and there is a subtle but significant impact on the district culture, an opening of the system, a broadening and deepening of the cycle of inquiry.

Schools need support and direct assistance in solving the perennial prob-

lems of time and resources. Moving major authority for scheduling and conducting staff development activities to the school level and encouraging weekly late-start or early-dismissal days (by lengthening the other days) are two rather simple tactics, but more substantive adjustments are frequently needed. Block scheduling and other strategies for making schedules more flexible are coming back into vogue because they allow schools to better adapt to variable learning approaches—including greater depth and better integration of curriculum, increased options for project-based learning, and extended opportunities for interaction and sustaining relationships. One of the more popular and promising schedule variations entails assigning a large block of time to an interdisciplinary team of teachers, giving them great authority to use that time in flexible and creative ways. A parallel practice is to incorporate community-based learning time into the school week, and to use part of that time when students are off campus for curriculum and professional development. These promising practices are "pushing the envelope" in ways that could arouse faculty resistance and community opposition, and the need for district involvement in developing and interpreting them should be obvious. They are intriguingly reminiscent of the features in the flexibly scheduled school story described above—a story that ended disappointingly, at least in part because of the lack of proactive district involvement/support.

A pragmatic district function is to help schools secure waivers (from state or district time requirements and from contract provisions) when it is established that those hurdles are getting in the way of achieving school program goals. District support of this kind may well need to be contingent on the school's readiness to assume increasing levels of the kind of responsible accountability described above.

Districts also need to take an aggressive leadership role in seeking the additional funding that will be needed to support fundamental redesign of school schedules, including the incorporation of planning, collaboration, and staff development time in an extended work year. The traditional 9 ½-month contract year will probably continue to be an attraction for some, but most full-time professional teachers should expect to have significantly longer contracts, with substantial time for curriculum and professional development built into the calendar.

More effective strategies must be developed for recruiting, inducting, and supporting the continuing development of leaders at all levels (including teacher leaders). A rich array of teacher leadership roles is developing as schools restructure—mentors, teachers on special assignments, lead teachers, consulting teachers, teacher researchers, information/media specialists, adjunct professors (in so-called professional practice schools, for example). For these and for the more traditional administrative positions such as superintendent and principal, new selection tools are needed. In addition to screening for the usual managerial skills, districts must use strategies that can help to identify constructivist leaders, those who have the qualities of leadership described in Chapters 2 and 4. Such leaders are value-driven and purposeful, collaborative, flexible, and responsive and have a sense of agency. Their group process, communication, and information-processing skills must be sharp. They must be engaged and able to engage others in striving for continuous growth, a culture of inquiry, and a learning community for all children and adults.

The traditional paper-screening and interview processes are clearly not adequate to assess the presence and potential for development of these complex leadership qualities. A well-designed assessment center (see Figure 7.2) will help substantially—one that features simulations, role-playing in realistic situations, interactive group issue analysis and problem-solving—all observed systematically by skillful colleagues who are functioning as assessors. But a sophisticated selection process is only one dimension. It must be preceded by early identification and support for potential leaders, especially among underrepresented groups, and should move through a seamless induction/enculturation process and ongoing professional development program.

A number of progressive districts now encourage each teacher and administrator to create and maintain a professional portfolio, which contains products and artifacts that sketch a profile of professional development, and universities are beginning to incorporate this strategy into their leadership preparation programs (see Chapter 9). Chapter 4 describes some other promising practices that entail district collaboration with universities, county offices, and other support providers.

School board roles must be redesigned to ensure that they are supportive of the learning organization. As with other participants in a constructivist enterprise, school boards and board members need to be continuously reexamining and reflecting on their roles to ensure that they are congruent with those of other district leaders and with the collaborative cultures that are needed in schools. Their most appropriate focus should be on policy formation, articulation of vision and goal statements, reciprocal communication with the community, the facilitation of partnerships and collaborative network linkages, and interaction with the broader contexts of regions/states/ the nation. Board members may also design or seek out roles that entail participation in such emerging activities as authentic forms of program evaluation, the assessment of student progress (e.g., senior "exhibitions"), and the celebration of individual and group achievement. When board members become involved in micromanagement activities, their individual voices and perceived authority disrupt the reciprocity of a learning community.

District office staff and principals will be forgiven if they feel some skepticism as they read the above paragraph. It does sound idealistic, perhaps even naive, but most critics would agree that the proposed direction of change is "devoutly to be wished"—especially if the broadly based construc- tivist ethos is to thrive.

The question "How?" can be answered best by emphasizing the highly significant enabling functions that would still be assumed by governing boards and their district office colleagues. Resisting the temptation to micro- manage would give board members time and energy to invest in much more important (and appropriate) tasks, such as developing flexible policy sets that respect both the need for an increased sense of school autonomy and power and the need for coherence in the total district system. With the superinten- dent playing the roles described above (steward, designer, teacher, partici- pant), we believe that this goal is achievable. Some districts are already func- tioning in this manner, and many others have started the journey. The study of district office engagement that the CCSR is currently conducting will pro- vide more examples.

The political nature of school boards represents both a value, in terms of keeping schools grounded in the processes of representative democracy, and a weakness and danger. Every board election is a potential "fluctuation" that can challenge the capacities of a self-renewing system—a shift in policy- making power that could be most disruptive. Various radical proposals for dealing with this "problem" are getting an unusual amount of attention at this time—ranging from abolition of school boards to curtailment of district powers and the formation of regional boards with most operational power devolved to vertical clusters of K–12 schools. Less dramatic but more hopeful strategies would be to strengthen significantly the educational and encultura- tion processes for board members (especially those newly elected) and to develop the whole ecosystem so that it can learn to accommodate this and other kinds of fluctuations in its co-evolution.

Above all else, the district must promote and model the participation and informed decision-making processes that contribute to preparing students and adults to participate effectively in a democracy. A major theme throughout this book has been the renewing of the mission of public schools in this country to prepare learners for life in a democracy. Every district policy and process needs to pass the test of contributing to the accomplishment of that mission—directly and by serving as catalyst, model, promoter, and account- ability partner. It is our contention that the constructivist processes espoused here will enable the district to pass that authentic performance test—the pro- cesses that engage both adults and students in problem-analysis and problem-solving, in interactive and reciprocal processes that facilitate growth and development, in the informed and responsible decision-making that is at the heart of democracy.

CONCLUSION

A school district that restructures itself to function as a constructivist learning community will look and act very differently from a traditional district. In this chapter, we have attempted to make some of the design principles clear. It is vital that school districts become collaborative places of learning in which adults as well as students are continuously engaged in inquiring, reflecting, conversing, changing, growing. Some of the learning will occur in individuals who are building an increasing sense of efficacy or agency; and most of it will grow out of reciprocal relationships in interactive learning groups. Many of the adult learning groups (study teams, curriculum development councils, collaborative action research teams) will cross school lines; those lines among schools and between schools and the district will become more permeable; and the spaces will become more like synapses that connect than voids that separate.

With the increase in the amount of autonomy and authority assumed by schools, clusters of schools, and cross-school teams and committees, the district roles will become more complex yet equally significant. They will emphasize capacity-building, creating enabling structures and processes, co-ordinating school and district initiatives and services, facilitating reciprocal relationships, and ensuring coherence in the whole system. They will attend carefully to the admonition in the Sufi teaching, "But you must also understand 'and'" as they nourish the connections in their increasingly interdependent learning community.

While the design principles for building a constructivist school district culture are getting somewhat clearer, there remain some profound issues and questions:

- Are most school boards and district offices so comfortable in their hierarchical ivory towers that it is hopeless, that it would be better to abandon the structures altogether?
- Can any but small suburban school districts create community?
- What is the role in constructivist leadership for charismatic style or the capable hierarchical thinker?
- Will universities be able to play their part in preparing constructivist leaders?

The answers to these questions is, of course, "in construction"—being explored as pioneers blaze the trail and reflect on the obstacles they encounter. In Chapter 9, Walker responds to that last question by describing three universities in the throes of constructivist work and proposing an innovative framework for preparing constructivist leaders.

CHAPTER 8

Reflections on Community: Understanding the Familiar in the Heart of the Stranger

P. J. Ford Slack

You ask me about how I understand the word *community*. I think you are ready to hear my answer. Communities are not what you think. If you take time to watch nature, you will understand community. The moose up the road lives in community with the wolf; and the eagle is in community with the fish—but they do not always agree, and sometimes one sustains the other by feeding their young. People are no different—we just have two legs. Our brain sometimes misinforms us—we think *we* are the community instead of understanding our part in the many communities. *Webs*—I've heard you use that word—webs are communities serving spiders, flowers, the dew, people, sister wolf, and brother moose. Sometimes we all live together in harmony, sometimes a piece of the web is stretched by disagreement. This is important for you to understand because if a person leaves the community who you do not agree with, chances are a new person will appear that you also will not agree with. Balance and movement—communities are sustained that way— just like nature.

Nadine Chase, Ojibwa elder

Throughout our text the concept of community is central to a definition of constructivist leadership. Schools as communities—spiraling to interlink with other communities require the reciprocal processes that enable participants in community to construct meanings leading toward a common purpose.

Over the past 20 years the discourse of school reform has focused on words and phrases such as *excellence, effectiveness, equity, learning systems,* and now *community.* While the definitions of what community might be are just beginning to appear in airport bookstores and academic publishing firms, the concept has been central and embedded in most of the world's longest-surviving cultural groups. The authors of this text have described the importance of the concept "community" to constructivist educational practice and particularly to constructivist leadership. Many chapters in this book foreground the importance of community in student/adult learning, meaning-making, and school practices.

Historical as well as present textual perspectives on the notion of what community is in the United States tend to focus on essentialized or universalized definitions of the word—that is, a Western, European, or Judeo/Christian framing (A. Bloom, 1987; Cohen, 1994; Etzioni, 1993; Hirsch, 1988). Absent from these theories and practices are the tensions and metaphors that are inherent in our national struggle with the notion of *e pluribus unum,* or plurality in unity (Bowers, 1969, 1991, 1992; Ford Slack, 1994; Takaki, 1993; Trask, 1993). Perhaps nowhere is this struggle more apparent today than in our schools. As diversity (*pluribus*) is recognized and listened to, other voices raise alarm that diversity is destroying community (*unum*).

Perhaps the fear would be lessened if we did not hold fast to a need for one best metaphor that describes what we all should be as a diverse population. Recognition of the value of orality as well as the written text would cause other stories and metaphors of community construction to emerge (Deloria, 1969; N. Chase, personal communication, 1992–94; Irwin, 1990; Trask, 1993). Education texts are beginning to broaden the definition to allow other stories to affect our thinking regarding democracy and community, particularly when speaking about processes in education—teaching, leading, learning, and shared decision-making (Takaki, 1993).

COMMUNITIES OF DIFFERENCE

In this text, the authors have attempted to "cross borders" (Moraga & Anzaldua, 1981; Giroux, 1992; Greene, 1993) through travel and story in order to listen, practice, and converse with educational communities that are familiar by profession and discipline but perhaps strangers by practice. These *communities of difference* are the essence of constructivist communities. *Communities of difference* are relationship-centered. Buildings, roles, work descriptions, culture, and geography do not present barriers to recognizing the interdependence of one community with another. This begins to unbind our notions and rootedness about what a school is or who is related to the education process.

Conversations, reflections, and life experiences often raise questions about the hidden or root metaphors embedded in the word *community* (Bowers, 1993; N. Chase, personal communication, 1993; Cohen, 1994; Ford Slack, 1993; Trask, 1993). Often in uncovering root metaphors we become uneasy with the community-versus-diversity debate. Gregory Bateson's (1972) comments on "common patterns of understanding" couple nicely with Maxine Greene's (1993) writings about the importance of understanding and listening to the "stranger" in ourselves, as well as others, in order to begin constructing conversations about community. These thoughts are central to unbinding our thinking regarding constructing educational communities, understanding diversity's importance to community, and understanding community as a multifaceted concept instead of a homogeneous construct.

Language is often a barrier to having a conversation. We feel it important to provide boundaries for these conversations. Ecology provides phrases and ideas that offer bridges in our discussion. Lambert argued in Chapter 2 that by linking social and biological conceptions of ecology with oral stories, an ecological community of difference is created. Lambert asks us to "imagine leadership transcending role, event, person." This same imagining can create a framework for *communities of difference*. As part of our ongoing imagining, the authors of this text have constructed a *community of difference* themselves and have agreed on the following definition of *community* in their conception of constructivist leadership:

> Community is part of a social ecological construct that might be described as an *interdependent* and complex web of reciprocal relationships *sustained* and informed by their purposeful actions. Complexity is manifested by the *diversity* of the systems; the more diverse, the more rich and complex. Such communities are flexible and open to information provided through feedback *spirals,* as well as unexpected fluctuations and surprises that contain possibilities. The *coevolution,* or shared growth, of the participants in this community is propelled by the joint construction of meaning and knowledge and involves continual creation and adaptation.

Community seen through this lens of ecology offers a beginning language that assists in describing its role in constructivist leadership. Elements of interdependence, sustainability, cycles, energy, partnership, flexibility, diversity, and coevolution provide words that cross the border of the "unfamiliar" when talking about stories of community construction in alternative school settings or cross-cultural settings, for example.

For many cultures the root metaphors of community are not only old but very different from how the Puritan forefathers constructed community (Northrup, 1993; Rosaldo, 1993; Takaki, 1993). Their constructed communities envisioned a moral sameness. Homogeneity of community would be reached through education by certain "church-sanctioned individuals" (Bowers, 1969; Tyack, 1974). Ecological metaphors propose the inclusion of a notion of diversity that is not embedded in colonial root metaphors of community. Instead, these metaphors cause our mind's eye to see the spiraling in nature, and the diversity that is needed to sustain an ecological community (Bateson, 1972; Bowers, 1993; N. Chase, personal communication, 1992). The ecological web illuminates for all of us the interdependence among diverse definitions of community. Difference is not to be feared or made the same, but to be added, mixed, energized, and partnered, in order to better teach all.

Constructivist educational theory and practice offers an opportunity to go beyond the rootedness of the old one-lens metaphors of community of Hirsch (1988) and A. Bloom (1987) and to further expand the notions of responsibility described by Etzioni. The idea of *communities of difference* (N. Chase, personal communication, 1992; Ford Slack, 1993; Takaki, 1993) as defined here focuses first on the infinite number of communities that reside in what appears as one community. Community as many different, interdependently linked communities draws on the ecological metaphors established in Chapter 2 or the story told by Chase at the beginning of this chapter. To maintain themselves, *communities of difference* recognize the central importance of relationship, how interdependence catalyzes action, and how through reflection and meaning-making we begin to link communities across generations. Community, then, is not bounded by time, limited to constructs of responsibility and obligation, about creating moral sameness (morality, however, is important), or about setting a group apart, isolated from others. *Communities of difference* assist us in "imagining" different metaphors for leadership and school.

Cooper's work in Chapter 6 documents the importance of story to meaning-making in the creation of shared histories. Cooper views journal-writing as a narrative form of problem-solving and reflection that illuminates life histories merging with other life histories to form a reflection of meaning in an educational community. In this chapter storytelling is rooted in oral traditions as well as histories of East and West. The storyteller in Ojibwa communities as well as other cultures throughout the world is a person who creates an *environment for wisdom to emerge* (Aitken, 1992; Chase, personal communication, 1992; Rosaldo, 1993; Scheiner & Bell, 1990). In this chapter I act as storyteller, hoping to establish an environment in which the reader will listen to the familiar stories of community construction from the hearts of educational communities that may be strangers. Case stories differ from case studies (Merriam, 1988; Stake, 1978) in the following ways. They are bounded stories of practice in education that are practitioner-generated and controlled rather than researcher-generated (Ford Slack, 1994). Case stories in education and in this chapter focus on meaning-making, culture/diversity, relationship, community, and world. Case stories honor the orality of our day-to-day lives by honoring the interdependence of the personal, professional, and community threads that so often weave together to inform our understandings and decisions. Not all case stories have endings, but rather tend to recognize the evolving and spiraling nature of educating.

CASE STORIES FROM COMMUNITIES OF DIFFERENCE

This first case story is about a growing partnership between two distant educational communities (a U.S. tribal school and primary and Kohanga Reo school in New Zealand) and a few of the reflective pieces of their acknowledged interdependence. What the story seeks to do is to point out the diversity within one reservation, how diversity is extremely important, and how it focuses educators and community members not just on this generation of children but on educating across generations. The second case story describes the partnerships and action that emerge from the construction of community. This case story is student-driven—students becoming the authors constructing meaning. In the restorying I describe how the students of a newly formed chartered school described the creation of an educational community and articulated relationships. The last case story places the author as the stranger in an educational teaching community in northeastern China. This restorying from China is about teachers in community with teachers. It illustrates the strength of the community, partnership, and cooperation inherent in the teaching in China and how a non-Chinese teacher was taught how to belong to this teaching community. Again, the Chinese story emphasizes that in constructing a teaching community the focus is on multigenerational teaching—not just on teaching the present students. The story also suggests that lack of diversity and flexibility might become problematic in U.S. constructions of community. All of the schools in the stories have people in traditional school leadership roles as well as in less traditional roles. What makes all of these schools' actions and problem-solving a "reimagining of leadership" has to do with the ebb and flow of who decides what, when, and how. Students, teachers, community members, staff, and administrators all lead at various times—they exemplify the phrase, "leading from a network of relationships." The educational communities described here are variations of schooling in the United States and so become the strangers in this chapter. Listen for the familiar in the telling. It is hoped that the stories will assist in understanding how diverse our public education system is and how that diversity continues to offer us energy needed to sustain and change our educational communities.

Case Story One: Learning from Two Worlds

The Bug O Nay Ge Shig School is a grant-operated Bureau of Indian Affairs (BIA) Tribal School on Leech Lake Reservation in Minnesota. This federally funded school represents a form of public education available to tribal communities as set forth in the federal constitution (Weatherford, 1991). The Ojibwa tribal community is old and has a rich and sometimes difficult history in relation to arrangements for formalized schooling. Traditional U.S. public education has held little but sorrow for most tribal members. Many parents of today's Bug O Nay Ge Shig students can still recount stories of boarding schools or relocations to other areas. Loss of language, loss of identity, loss of family are the stories that challenge the current educational community. The reservation is located in an area of Minnesota with one of the highest levels of unemployment in the state, which is another challenge for this school.

The school is less than 20 years old and began when an Anglo teacher and over 30 students walked out of the local public school (Ford Slack & Cornelius, 1993). Issues related to the walk-out (lack of cultural focus, lack of Ojibwa representation in clubs and sports, lack of cultural understanding) as well as various visions from many community partners (public schools, BIA, Minnesota education consultants, tribal village needs, parent advisory committee, various universities, reservation tribal council, etc.) challenge and invigorate this evolving educational community. The Bug O Nay Ge Shig school exists today due to the many concerns family members have regarding educating their children; for example, families want a more traditional education focusing on culture, families want their children to be prepared to enter the job market, families want children to help change the reservation, and families want children to move off the reservation. The student population is not homogeneous and is currently comprised of students who have lived off the reservation, students from other tribes, Anglo students, interracial students, students from traditional homes, students who are court-enrolled (tribal and nontribal), and students who move with family members between the rural and urban contexts due to shifts in employment.

It is at the tribal school that I start my restorying. The graduation banquet had begun. Juniors served students, family members, and guests. Three bears were rummaging around the back of the school, giving all at the banquet a sense of their part in nature's cycle. An Ojibwa educator spoke about the cycles and community of which these students were a part, as well as the larger community where they might chose to move. A New Zealand educator was present at the banquet. She crossed the cultures and languages of both Maori and Pakeha (the white descendants of British and other European colonists, Middleton, 1992). When she stood to address the graduates, she offered greetings and a blessing in Maori: "I want to extend greetings to you from the people of New Zealand (Aoteroa). I acknowledge the goodness of our ancestors and honor your ancestors. Our communities are linked and our children are those communities. May you find happiness in your future."

Later, a number of community members asked her about the Maori language and talked about the loss of much of the Ojibwa language. She spoke of the importance of holding on to their Ojibwa language and culture, as that would sustain them in other communities. She talked about the Kohanga Reo movement in New Zealand and invited members to consider visiting to see if this experience might be helpful for the school (Irwin, 1990; Sharples, 1993).

This visit encouraged a number of school members to talk about the possibility of observing this Kohanga Reo movement. The secretary for the elementary principal, an elementary teacher, the educational consultant for the tribe, the superintendent, and others started planning a fact-finding trip to New Zealand. The New Zealand educator's monthly faxes suggested attendance at the World Indigenous Conference, which could afford an opportunity to visit Maori Kohanga Reo schools. There they would be able to talk with other Maori educational communities about what they had felt was important when constructing their educational communities for their students. There was an energy and focus and outreach that fall that brought communication from places where communication had been cut off. Nevertheless, after much discussion and visits with elders, six educators, at their own expense, decided to make a 2-week trip to New Zealand.

Meaning-making, as described by Lambert, "is born of negotiating experiences together, evolves us, gives force and purposeful direction to community." Large change has not occurred overnight at the school, but small changes have taken place. New Zealanders continue to visit the school once a year, working with teachers, talking to community members, interacting with students. There is a hope that the principal of the Kohanga Reo school (a Maori immersion school that starts children at 6 months of age learning Maori) and some of their community members will visit the tribal school and will go to each village and talk to community members about the importance of language. New Zealand visits, faxes, and stories from the traveling team have maintained an energy flow at the school. The energy flow has assisted in broadening the meaning of community from the local site to the Leech Lake geographic area and to educational communities of another tribal group in another part of the world. Students have requested their own educational trips and are beginning to see themselves as active participants in creating what this school will be. Communication with the public school from which the students walked out years ago is seen as building a larger educational community. Teachers from the public school have requested information about what was learned about the New Zealand Kohanga Reo movement and what that means for students in their classes. The educational community was flexible and open to learning from other communities. The Ojibwa valuing of diversity allows for the growing reciprocity that is occurring because of the continued interaction with New Zealand educational communities.

Case Story Two: We Are Always with You

City Academy is a Minnesota chartered school whose mission is to construct a high school learning community with students who are no longer in the public school system since having dropped out or been expelled. The state legislature in 1991 attempted to construct other ways to educate by designing a policy that allowed people who were interested in trying innovative methods of improving teaching to construct their own schools. Stringent guidelines needed to be followed in order to procure state funding. Many learned that while it is easy to talk about changing teaching and schools, it is more difficult to step out on the end of the branch and put forth a plan. Energy, an ability to sustain personal financial upheaval, the belief and fortitude to argue for your school vision, and the desire to energize others about your idea are all essential. City Academy is part of the vision of two teachers who believed in their ability to construct an education community. They demonstrated a determination to start a school regardless of loss of financial and positional security, and they convinced many nay-sayers of their belief in teaching students to love learning. Teachers started this school, and students, teachers, and community continue to cause the school to evolve together. The school's sustainability depends on community involvement, so teachers partner with others in an attempt to not only bring resources to the school but to create constant reflection about current processes. On a cold evening in November, a group of seven high school-aged students visited a graduate principalship class at the local university to explain to these educators different ways "to do school." These students crossed culture, gender, and class borders. That night it was clear from the beginning that they entered the room as teachers.

The stage was set for the students—chairs, an overhead projector, and an assortment of food awaited their arrival. Adults in the class were a bit nervous about what these students would say. Would they be angry, accusatory, or perhaps embody why we should not allow "this kind of school" to exist. The class of future administrators had heard of chartered schools and were very concerned that these schools would syphon off precious state education dollars from their future jobs. They also wondered if a viable school could be created by teachers with a student population of "students off the street."

One of the teachers who started the school accompanied the students. The students made it clear that they would teach us about their school. As introductions proceeded, going from the students to the graduate students, a little cough stopped the process. The graduate student introduced herself and said, "I think I was your teacher in third grade." The student nodded. "But you were such a good student then; what happened?" The student said, "Life. But I am a good student, because this school gave me another chance." Other students acknowledged teachers they recognized. Before the descriptions of City Academy even began, the interdependence across educational communities had been established. As one female student said, "We are members of the community and we are always with you; we are not just students that go to 'that school.' We were *your* students and still are."

The students established what this new school was about—relationship and sustained community. The connected students were able to describe how the public or parochial system had helped or hindered their education. In describing how the school was started, one student said, "They [the teachers] are always there for us; they don't accuse us but constantly ask about what we need to be here, learning. I even have their home phone numbers." The graduate students asked questions related to discipline, gangs, curriculum, jobs, and classroom appearance. The students, not the teacher/administrator present, answered the questions. For the future administrators in that class, it was an eye opener. Many of the graduate students thought they knew why and when these students had lost interest. "Oh, it must be the junior high's fault," or "If the middle school or elementary school would just prepare them to read," or "Well, I think it is the family—you know those one-parent families don't supervise as they should." They were surprised when they found that each student had a different reason and different story for how he or she had come to be out of school and on the street. The discussion regarding gangs, what the symbols meant, and how they (the students) decided on discipline at the school had everyone on the edge of their chairs. As one student pointed out, "All of you in this room are part of my educational community. You can be part of the problem or work with me on a solution." Another student added, "I can't be seen as your neighbor now, but I am your neighbor."

City Academy will have many more challenges to face as it constructs one of the different ways of perceiving an educational community. The school's staff and students are not only flexible in entertaining ideas of what a school might be, but they also take risks in trying participantship with other communities, allowing students to author their educational meaning and looking for ways to add to their diversity. As one graduate student later reflected, "They [the students] are all so diverse; the teachers are from all over, and yet they talk and demonstrate that they are a learning community, they are constructing educational meaning together. I wish our high school looked like that."

Case Story Three: A Stranger Learns the Teaching of Goodness

Over hundreds of centuries, the Chinese have focused on creating a moral order on earth (Spence, 1978; Wood, 1991). Michael Wood (1991) talks about the Chinese people as being able to withstand anything as long as their leaders are good. This belief in goodness in leadership led to a belief by the teachers that teaching students is about preparing a multitude of leaders who might lead in any profession, but always in service to their community, to their country. As Lao Jing (1990) once said, "Leaders are not born good—goodness needs to be taught. No matter what subject we are teaching we are also teaching goodness, connection to community, and that success is not for the individual but for our country" (p. 56). This is one of the ways that I was introduced to the importance of my position as a teacher in Shenyang, China. Primarily I taught upper-division students at the university, but in the afternoons I would teach at a middle school (high school in the United States). Lotus Lao-shi, of number 120 middle school, was my teacher, friend, and enculturator.

Teaching was not just about communicating and evaluating learning, but also about being in community with other teachers. My background in teaching included cooperative and team-teaching techniques, but teaching with other teachers in Shenyang was beyond teaming; it was community. We ate together, shared notes, swept snow, drank tea, and even fished together. As they included me in their lives, they were teaching me not only what it meant to teach together in Shenyang but the responsibility of teaching their children.

Teaching was a moral commitment. While the profession had suffered during the Cultural Revolution, it was clear that to be a teacher was a moral responsibility. Teaching was seen as a way to help China, as a way of life. The teachers I worked with taught me that how I interacted and what modeling I gave served to reinforce the social structure of China. Lotus, along with my teaching community, instructed me not only about what I was teaching but also about what I was *really* teaching. Although I was teaching English, a bit of science, and some U.S. literature and sociology, what I was really teaching was how to compete and honor the local community and country. As Jing says, I was teaching goodness.

REVISITING THE FAMILIAR WE LEARNED FROM THE STORIES OF THE STRANGER

These case stories provided a structure for thinking and imagining other constructions of community. From a tribal school that is learning from another educational community 10,000 miles away, to a chartered school founded by teachers and demonstrating a partnership in educational meaning-making with its students, to the historically community-rooted teaching methods of Chinese teachers in preparing students to give to their country, these restoryings all suggest the importance of relationship in education. These educational communities also acknowledge meaning-making as difficult, challenging, evolving, and sustainable. It is slow, and the results might not be observable for many years. In China change is measured in terms of a hundred- or thousand-year period, a perspective that parallels the importance the Ojibwa attribute to intergenerational learning.

Meaning can sustain a community (Chinese teaching) or spiral the community into new directions (Bug O Nay Ge Shig school); and it is built out of the energy emanating from the stories of the community (founding of the chartered school). Diversity in a community is key for the stability as well as the growth (coevolution) of members. When a community begins to see its interdependence, to spiral, to story itself, partnerships grow in unusual places.

At the Bug O Nay Ge Shig school the choice is always to help the student, because the student is the link to the generations yet to come. This belief was also part of the educational community of the chartered school and part of the philosophy of teaching in China. The first two case stories were examples of *communities of difference* where the schools valued listening to the stranger in order to learn and move their own educational community forward. In China, they too listened to the stranger but would not talk about wanting differences or diversity. Diversity seen in the West was often seen as out of harmony and leading to chaos (Jing, 1990). *Sustainability* was a goal of all the educational communities. Meaning-making through relationship was seen as one way to plant a seed in order to guarantee that the community would grow. Stories added sustenance to meaning and allowed for supported community flexibility and change. Stories were the ways in which Lotus Laoshi and other teachers described how they were taught to be teachers. New Zealand stories were what captured the imagination of the Leech Lake educational community, catalyzing members of the community to go to listen to other tribal educators. So, too, the students of City Academy teach about their school with stories; this sustains a newly constructed educational community by establishing a community memory as well as serving as a way to enculturate new students to the school. Leaders in the traditional sense were present in all three schools, yet their leading was through and with a network of relationships. While their title was "leader," it was clear that students, elders, and teachers were all leaders at one time and during various stories. Stories at each school were used to move the community forward or to allow a time of reflection. Each person in the community might tell and restory the piece to clarify its meaning. This developed an *interdependence* within and across communities. Interdependence is important not only to open global awareness but because students in Western societies, particularly the United States, are mobile, causing one educational community to impact another as a student moves. Therefore it is important to think of partnership as well as participantship. As one student stated, "We were *your* students and still are."

Constructing community is not easy. As we listen to the stranger in these stories of communities of difference, it is important to realize some of the tensions. In both the tribal and charter schools, politics has become part of the very fabric of each school. Political processes and hierarchical authority can threaten these community fabrics.

The shared perception that change happens over generations enables members to work through tensions over long periods of time, attending to life and work and relationships. China's teachers do not talk about personal accomplishments, but rather about how their grandchildren may complete what they initiate. In the United States, intergenerational thought seems to have been lost with our ancestors. Fortunately, ecologists such as Bowers, Capra, and Roszak are invoking intergenerational thinking as a significant part of community and systems change.

Understanding and working with the richness of diversity is important to communities in the United States. While China's history has much to teach us, their constructions of community may not serve our people well. Their focus on homogeneity and sameness could lead us back to our need for one best metaphor.

Our *communities of difference* present many journeys for our children and for our evolving democracy. Perhaps "it is our journey in educating for the next seven generations that assists in creating the lived educational experience of our country" (Jing, 1990).

CHAPTER 9

The Preparation of Constructivist Leaders

Deborah Walker

The preceding chapters offered a new theoretical construct for thinking about leadership. While the first chapter presented an evolutionary view of leadership theory, in fact constructivist leadership represents a leap in conceptions of who leads and how that leadership is manifested. Leadership is described as a set of reciprocal processes shared by many, rather than a set of behaviors invested in one person. It is not role-specific but derives from a mutuality of purpose, shared values, and communities of memory (Bellah, Madsen, Sullivan, Sidler, & Tipton, 1985) that connect teachers and administrators who work in the same school and are engaged in common efforts to create professional knowledge and grow together.

What most separates the theory of constructivist leadership from other theories is the emphasis on the professional growth of the faculty. Barth's (1992) metaphor of a community of learners is a powerful one that has reshaped thinking about school norms and refocused attention on the development of the adults who work in schools. The goal of leadership, then, is to enhance not only student learning but also the learning of teachers and administrators, based on principles of constructivism. These principles suggest the following:

1. Learning is an active rather than a passive process.
2. Learning is by nature social and is most likely to occur when learners share ideas, inquire, and problem-solve together.
3. Learners, to go beyond rote learning, must have opportunities to make sense of new knowledge and create meaning for themselves based on individual and shared experiences.
4. Reflection and metacognition contribute to the construction of knowledge and the process of sense-making.
5. New learning is mediated by prior experience, values, and beliefs.

The principles of constructivism, applied to the leadership of schools, call forth vivid images that challenge existing views of leadership. Earlier chapters in this book developed these images in depth. The notion of a community designed to promote individual and collective growth has been advanced throughout this book and given life through the narrative about Evergreen Middle School, through examples of numerous other schools and districts, and through the retelling of Native American stories. The metaphor of a sea change was extended to describe deep, fundamental change that alters the ecology of the school and the patterns of relationships among those who work in the school. The use of a typology of conversations—dialogic, partnering, inquiring, and sustaining—to further the reciprocal processes of leadership moved the discussion of constructivist leadership from the theoretical to the application stage. New understandings about leadership were gained not only from the discussion of types and purposes of conversations in schools, but also from the chapters that illustrated the power of language to effect change and the use of narrative, story, and personal metaphor to promote adult development. The chapter on the role of the district office stressed the importance of acquiring skill in creating enabling structures that support constructivism.

This chapter builds on these previous images and offers some new images related to the preparation of constructivist leaders in university graduate programs. The chapter presents a design for leadership preparation based on the principles of constructivism and the theory of leadership advanced in this book. It also provides examples of constructivist approaches at three universities around the country and suggests some promising directions for the development of constructivist leadership.

NEW IMAGES FOR LEADERSHIP PREPARATION

The following images are grounded in reality and derive from some pioneering work at California State University at Hayward, initiated in the 1992–93 academic year and continuing to the present. This work shifted the focus from the technical preparation of school administrators to developing constructivist leadership understandings for those in formal and informal leadership roles (Walker, 1994).

Image 1: Collaboration and Community Building

Students work together as members of a learning community. They belong to a standing support group of classmates who share in their thinking and respond to their work over the course of the year. In any given class session, they can be observed giving feedback to one another in writing-response groups on their action research proposals and reports; or sharing, in a fishbowl setting, their successes and problems encountered in conducting action research; or doing reflective writing and sharing their written thoughts. Each of these activities requires students to establish new patterns of relationships that run counter to the kind of isolation and independent work characteristic of teachers in our schools. Because the university class-room can be structured as a safe environment, these new patterns of relation-ships are perhaps easier to nurture there than in a real school setting. The challenge, of course, is to help students transfer these patterns to their own workplace and thus to have an effect on the cultures of their schools.

As the year progresses and the sense of community evolves, these adult students exhibit a high degree of trust in their colleagues and the interdepen-dency that characterizes a true learning community. During inquiring conver-sations regarding the conduct of their action research, they ask one another probing questions, laugh together over their initial naiveté in attempting to promote change among their faculty, and offer thoughtful suggestions to one another about how to proceed. They also tackle issues that are rarely ad-dressed with any comfort or depth in schools—issues of race, of authority deriving from expertise rather than position, and of individual struggles to improve practice and become more reflective. These conversations are pos-sible because of shared intentions, beliefs, and experiences, and because of mutual reflection and revealing of self—the common elements of conversa-tions described in Chapter 4 of this book.

Image 2: Portfolios

Students design and compile a portfolio portraying their sense of them-selves as leaders. They select samples of their work and themes to highlight and tie them together by means of narrative. Each portfolio is unique, re-flecting the individuality of the candidate and the many possible approaches to leadership. The commonality among the portfolios derives from the shared experiences and communities of memory of the class members. Students share their portfolios-in-progress, reading the narratives, stories, and poems written for inclusion in the portfolios. In one session a student who vowed that he could not write well read a poem he had written and illustrated that portrayed his Hispanic/Indian roots and moved the class with its simplicity and power. The poem and drawings served as an organizing device for his portfolio and captured his growing identity as a leader.

While one possible model for portfolio development was offered, stu-dents were encouraged to experiment with the portfolio format and to share their individual models of organization, entries, and narratives with the class. The process proceeded slowly, with students initially hesitant to offer original ideas. The students had to develop their own norms for encouraging one another, such as literally applauding one another's efforts, offering positive remarks about what they liked about one another's work, listening well, and finding value in different approaches.

Image 3: Exit Interviews

Through a performance task, students demonstrate their ability to synthesize their beliefs, values, and knowledge into a unified portrait of themselves as leaders. The interviews, conducted by faculty-practitioner committees, organize students into groups of three and use conversations rather than a question-and-answer format. This format allows students to take control of their own assessment and to shape the outcomes. In advance of the interviews, faculty-practitioner committees review the portfolios of the students they are about to meet.

Prior to the interviews, students expressed anxiety that they were really participating in oral exams, having been socialized to expect a testing culture in university programs. Despite a year of working together to establish new norms and patterns of interaction, their trust was still easily shaken. They arrived at the interviews dressed in their finest clothes and visibly nervous. They finished their interviews elated, energized, and proud of themselves and the colleagues they had worked with throughout the year. They stayed nearly an hour after the first interviews had ended, wanting to share their excitement and sense of accomplishment and to affirm that the interviews had really allowed for a professional dialogue among colleagues. This was constructivist leadership applied to a real-world setting beyond the college classroom. They understood in a visceral way what it was like to be a member of a learning community and to engage in a sustaining conversation. The interviews allowed for new paradigms of leadership to emerge and for authentic assessment of skills and knowledge to take place.

Image 4: Use of Stories and Metaphor

Students develop a personal leadership story based on real experience that reflects their own characteristics and their beliefs about leadership. The story can take place within or outside of the educational setting but must illustrate a time when they assumed leadership. In remembering the story, they must not only relate the actual events but frame them in such a way that they reveal leadership understandings, beliefs, and values. To illustrate the process, the instructor reads her own leadership story to the class, then interacts with a small group of students to analyze the story and what it says about leadership. Other members of class can join in analyzing the story, asking questions that prompt reflection and making their own interpretations. The story the instructor shared conveys a sense of the complexity of leadership decisions, showing that risk-taking can lead to successes as well as problems.

Students then write their own stories and share them with members of their standing support group for deeper analysis and implications. Their written reflections incorporate their own understandings and those new insights gained from interpreting the story to and with class members. The story reinforces desired leadership attitudes and values; it also points out areas for growth and deepening of understanding. The story is refined over time through further reflection and revision.

Using their story, students formulate a personal leadership metaphor that becomes an organizing device for their portfolio and also a way of giving them insight into their leadership style. This metaphor, developed early in the third quarter of the year, provides students with a personal reference point from which to question their assumptions about leadership and gain a sense about themselves as leaders of a learning community. Notions of shared leadership, reciprocal processes, and mutual growth influence the conceptualization of the metaphor. The metaphors students select and refine are varied, and they shape the development of their portfolios in different ways. Some are visual in nature, such as a learning tree that bears fruit as the leader promotes self-growth and growth for the faculty. Some take the form of an extended metaphor, such as leadership as a symphony, with *overture, movement, score,* and other musical terms defining leadership functions and introducing each section of the student's portfolio and work samples. In each case, however, the metaphor causes new learning to occur, making more visible and real the student's development as a constructivist leader.

These images are, of course, a work in progress. Both the instructor and students learn a great deal about leadership development during the course of the year. They also work in concert with a second cohort operating simultaneously, with which there are shared learning experiences. These lessons learned have contributed to the refinement of the master's program and the credential programs offered at California State University at Hayward.

NEW IMAGES AND THE DESIGN OF LEADERSHIP PREPARATION PROGRAMS

The new images for leadership preparation suggest a restructuring of existing preparation programs. These images are supported by literature on professional preparation (Murphy, 1990, 1992) and by experimental practice, such as E. M. Bridges' work with problem-based learning at Stanford University (1992). The literature suggests a more thematic approach to leadership preparation that produces broad understandings and the ability to see connections among various leadership functions. It also recommends that the curriculum reflect issues and problems in educational practice and that the structure of the programs allow for cohort groups to work collaboratively over time, weaving together theory and practical application. Figure 9.1 contrasts traditional approaches to administrator preparation, Murphy's recommendations for a restructured approach, and the steps toward restructuring taken by the educational leadership program at California State University at Hayward (CSUH).

Problem-based learning, as developed by Bridges and implemented at Stanford University, borrows heavily from the medical model for training professionals in which the curriculum derives from actual problems encountered by medical practitioners. As applied to the educational setting, leadership students study problems of practice, and through the process of developing solutions they pull together the various disciplines that constitute most administrator preparation programs, namely, finance, law, management, leadership, instructional improvement, and group process. Rather than studying these disciplines in isolation, students use them as parameters for addressing pressing issues in education.

These two examples from CSUH and Stanford representing new thinking about leadership preparation are offered as an anchor to the images presented in the previous section and to the following program conception, which is rooted in the theory of constructivist leadership. This program conception does not describe an existing program. Instead, it offers some principles or guidelines for program planning that support constructivist leadership. As defined in Figure 9.2, students are adult learners enrolled in graduate programs for leadership preparation; examples are meant to be illustrative, not comprehensive.

This conception of leadership preparation includes some basic assumptions that should be made explicit:

1. Adult learners must be able to draw on their experiences, knowledge, and values if learning is to have meaning for them and if they are to experience constructivist learning as a basis for constructivist leading.
2. Students play a key role in the design, operation, and evaluation of university preparation programs and at the same time experience firsthand the reciprocal processes that are central to constructivist leadership.
3. Successful experiences with change can begin in the university classroom and then be applied to real school situations.
4. Content is embedded in the processes that exemplify constructivist learning and leading.

Figure 9.1. Conceptions of Administrator Preparation Programs: A Comparison of Three Approaches

TRADITIONAL PROGRAM	CSUH	RESTRUCTURED PROGRAM
Curriculum		
Content-secific courses– law, finance, administrative theory	Content-specific courses designed around core values	Significant educational problems related to practice rather than particular disciplines
Role-specific courses– principalship, superintendency	Role-specific courses designed around core values with emphasis on instructional leadership	Discipline-based knowledge brought to bear on problems of practice
Mastery of essential blocks of knowledge	Synthesis of major concepts and relation to values	Employment of solution strategies to deal with future problems
Organization		
Self-paced program within guidelines	Cohort groups	Cohort groups
Individual instructors responsible for course content	Team planning, individual and team teaching	Core team of instructors working collaboratively to shape, facilitate, and evaluate program
School administrative department, sometimes in collaboration with business, policy, or statistics	Administrative deptartment made up exclusively of practitioners-turned-professors who are still active in the field	Interdisciplinary or interprofessional, using practitioners from the field
Linear sequence, with theory-building first	Developmental sequence moving toward dialectic	Dialectic sequence, tight weaving of theory and practice
Textbook based	Limited use of texts; professional publications, original source knowledge	Original source knowledge
Pedagogy		
Professor centered	Balance between professor- and learner-centered	Learner-centered–student as worker
Lecture-discussion model	Various teaching strategies from four families of teaching models	Cooperative/collegial model; balance of instructional approaches
Delivery Structure		
Certification-, calendar-, and discipline-based	Meets Commission on Teacher Credentialing standards and is based on adult learning theory	Learning theory–based; outcome-based, with emphasis on centrality of human relations
Instruction based on conformity, compromises. and trade-offs	Principles of adult cognition, problem-solving, use of craft knowledge	Principles of adult cognition, problem-solving, use of craft knowledge

Source: Walker, 1991.

Figure 9.2. Program Conception for Constructivist Leadership

GUIDELINE	EXAMPLE
Program Structure	
1. Mirrors the processes a faculty uses or undergoes to create a sense of community and opportunities for growth.	Group goal-setting and work teams organized to accomplish course goals. Weekend retreats for synthesis of learning and for emergence of student leadership.
2. Allows for problem identification, inquiry, and collaborative planning.	Students identify and study issues and problems at their sites, through collaborative action research and fieldwork.
3. Encourages construction of knowledge and meaning-making, and an effort to connect theory with application.	Students use case studies, simulations, and scenarios to induce theoretical principles, understand issues and problems, and test solutions; also, collaborative and team learning.
4. Provides time together to allow patterns of relationships and norms for constructivist leadership to evolve.	Cohort structure whereby students are together for an academic year of core coursework. Establishment of standing support groups that allow students to develop a trusting relationship, to share their ideas and work, and to obtain helpful feedback.
Program Content	
1. Applies learning theory to student and adult learners, including implications for curriculum and instructional methods.	Lessons from cognitive psychology on how students learn; demonstration and sample lessons so adult learners experience this learning firsthand. Opportunities to view student and adult learning theory in the context of staff development and teacher supervision.
2. Examines evolution of leadership theory, including its historical contexts and relationship to the understanding of learning; encourages development of a leadership identity, values, and understandings.	Review of literature and case studies of real leaders as a source of content. Use of narrative, story, and metaphor.

Figure 9.2. (*continued*)

GUIDELINE	EXAMPLE
3. Examines processes that build school culture, facitlitate participation and decision making, develop the capacity for growth and change, and create a learning community with a common sense of purpose.	Course simultions in which faclty groups work on planning tasks, desigin and facilitate professional development activities, and develop both an individual and a collective vision of schooling. Use of analogy and Synectics to break set with old ways of thinking and to foster creativity.
4. Examines processes that facilitate individual and collective growth and development of ethical principles.	Use of action research, reflective writing and discussion, and authentic means of performance assessment, such as portfolios and performance events. Study of ethics and experience with solving ethical conflicts.
5. Examines issues in educational leadership examined within the context of real school problems. Management functions such as personnel, finance, law, and collective bargaining are taught in relation to these issues, not as separate disciplines.	Desegregation, for example, studied for its implications for student achievement and also as it relates to other disciplines, e.g., legal requirements, funding, magnet and choice programs, and staffing patterns.

While no two preparation programs can or should look alike, the kinds of understandings and sensitivities they develop in their students can contribute to creating a new generation of leaders for our schools.

CURRENT UNIVERSITY PRACTICE AND CONSTRUCTIVIST LEADERSHIP

Constructivist learning has received a good deal of attention recently, if book titles and journal articles are an indication of interest. The impact of constructivist approaches can be seen most clearly in K–12 education, professional literature, state curriculum frameworks, and school reform provisions. At the university level, interest in constructivist learning and leading appears to be in the infancy stage; that is, professors of educational leadership are aware of the theory, may see its promise, but have yet to introduce constructivist approaches in any systematic way across university programs.

As always, there are outliers who are experimenting with constructivist approaches and documenting their experiences in the professional literature. Three such efforts are described here as illustrative of a broader range of university innovation in leadership preparation. The exemplars are the Department of Educational Leadership at California State University at Hayward; the Department of Educational Administration at the University of Hawaii; and the Department of Educational Administration, Wichita State University, Kansas. All have made significant changes to their programs and teaching practices to incorporate theories of constructivist learning and leading into their preparation of school leaders. Information about the programs comes from responses to a survey regarding constructivist approaches to leadership preparation, papers and monographs describing these innovative efforts, and, in the case of California State University at Hayward, the first-hand experience of the author.

California State University at Hayward

Several years ago the faculty of the Department of Educational Leadership made a decision to redesign its preliminary- and professional-level credential programs and its master's program to reflect constructivist approaches. The decision was partly a response to an ongoing process of visioning and goal-setting, of reading and discussing current literature, and partly a response to national calls for the reform of administrator preparation programs. The implications of the decision meant involving students more fully in the design of curriculum, in structuring the classroom around generative models of teaching and learning, and in exploring alternatives to student assessment. Several structural and content changes emerged that further the development of constructivist leaders. These include the following:

- *A cohort structure for all programs in which students spend a minimum of three quarters together in core coursework:* The structure allows for the integration of curriculum and for more thematic teaching to occur. It also allows for norms of trust, collegiality, and mutual support to emerge as students work together over the course of a year.
- *Assessment that applies theoretical learnings to real school situations:* Assessment is viewed as integral and connected to instruction, so that instead of taking tests, students help design performance activities that synthesize learning and mirror the growth processes in which school faculty engage. For example, professional credential students end their cohort year by designing a "faculty" retreat. They develop the topics and learning activities, make all the arrangements, and spend a weekend together planning how to apply new learnings to the improvement of teaching and learning.

Students also play a key role in assessing their own performance and growth through both formative and summative assessments.

- *Student participation in the design of curriculum and in the creation of professional knowledge:* Preliminary credential students in the Diversity in Leadership intern program identify issues and learning activities for their Saturday seminars as well as their twice-monthly, day-long courses. The program structure allows for extended periods of time together during which students can explore in depth issues that have meaning for them and can create new knowledge together. Professional-level credential students conduct collaborative action research to test out new solutions to school problems they identify.

- *Processes that stimulate individual and collective growth and that draw on prior experience, values, and beliefs:* Students in credential and master's programs use reflective writing and discussion, journals, narrative, story and metaphor, Grand Conversations, and other generative learning processes to make sense of new knowledge based on what they bring to the learning. (A Grand Conversation is a teaching approach where, after an initial question, students carry the discussion regarding some reading they have done or ideas they have encountered, with their own insights guiding the direction of the discussion, and their previous knowledge and experience contributing to their new understandings.) Forms of cooperative learning, including group investigation, are prevalent.

- *Redesign of the master's program to emphasize the development of constructivist leadership:* Faculty agreed to eliminate the thesis and instead focus on action research based on real school problems that graduate students were experiencing. The idea was to help students become scholar-practitioners who could use and conduct research for the purpose of improving teaching and learning at their site. Action research, portfolio development, use of exit interviews to synthesize learning, and student self-assessment were program features designed and piloted to prepare constructivist leaders.

The program at California State University at Hayward forms part of a continuum from traditional programs to restructured ones. Figure 9.1 provides program descriptions along this continuum.

University of Hawaii

The Hawaii Task Force on Educational Leaders for Hawaii's Schools, formed with representatives of school, university, and community in response to national reform reports, explored the possibility of initiating an administrator preparation program that had both the university and public schools as partners and major players. The task force's 1988 report contained recommendations to guide the development of school leadership necessary for the twenty-first century (Araki, 1992). The recommendations resulted in the design of the Cohort School Leadership Program (CSLP), a joint venture of the university's Department of Educational Administration and the State Department of Education. The CSLP was created to address these themes in school reform: (1) adaptation of leadership to the local context; (2) shared decision-making; (3) school renewal; and (4) use of knowledge, in particular, reflective inquiry. These themes resulted in changes to the structure and content of administrator preparation efforts, specifically the following:

- *Emphasis on participatory management:* The CSLP substituted a new set of leader behaviors to enable school administrators to invite participation and build a sense of community with faculty and parents. These behaviors are: "ability to unify staff and build sense of commitment to high performance goals; commitment to school-community based improvement and team building; achievement-oriented and supportive leadership and relationships; and management of the full scope of administrative responsibilities and facilitation of work" (Araki, 1992, p. 5).
- *Learning process principles:* The new program was structured around a set of principles to shape the design of learning activities, such as the study of cases, participation in simulations, problem-solving, and clinical work. These principles are: (1) Professional learning should take place in the context of thinking and acting as a principal; (2) administrative interns should be involved in and responsible for their own learning; (3) interns should learn about leadership and administration collaboratively and with practicing professionals; and (4) interns should routinely evaluate and be evaluated for their own learning in order to develop as thoughtful and self-critical practitioners.
- *Thematic teaching built around principal domains:* CSLP reordered the 21 leadership domains identified by the National Commission for the Principalship into four areas that "define the scope of responsibility faced by the principals and the knowledge required to accomplish the tasks of the job" (Araki, 1992, p. 7). These domains include the *functional,* such as leadership information collection and problem analysis; the *programmatic,* such as instructional programs, curriculum design, and staff development; the *interpersonal,* such as motivating others, sensitivity, and written and verbal skills; and the *contextual,* such as philosophical and cultural values, policy, and political influences. The domains form the basis of thematic teaching, using a problem-based learning approach and tying the domains closely to field experiences.
- *Reflective inquiry seminars:* During the year the students are engaged together in the study of school administration; they participate in ten

full-day Saturday seminars, led by a cadre of practicing principals. The seminars focus on real-world issues of schooling drawn from the areas of curriculum theory and practice, staff development, school–community relations, and school finance. The seminars encourage students to create meaning through the use of "themes and metaphors so that the unfamiliar becomes familiar" (Araki, 1992, p. 12). Students keep journals, drawing on past knowledge and experience to make sense of new learning and to develop the ability to be effective (Cooper, 1995). Both the act of writing and the sharing of thoughts and experiences support the construction of knowledge and the making of individual and shared meaning.

Wichita State University, Kansas

Two years ago the university initiated a new doctoral program in educational administration, partly in response to national reform reports on administrator preparation programs. The goal of the new program was to prepare "school administrators to use applied inquiry for the purpose of school improvement" (W. Furtwengler, 1994, p. 3). Participating students were released one day a week for 2 years to participate in day-long classes or seminars. In return, the students and their professors conducted action research in those districts, designed around district-identified needs. Both the structure and the content of the program are unique and at the same time supportive of developing constructivist leadership in its candidates. Not only do students play new roles in the program, as partners in action research along with their professors, but the faculty also assume new roles and responsibilities, including team planning and functioning as assistants and learners in classes their colleagues are teaching. Program features supportive of constructivist leadership include the following:

- *Cohort structure in which students are together for 2 years of coursework and field-based inquiry:* A team of professors and visiting practitioners work with cohorts of students to complete their coursework during the first 2 years and their dissertation during the third year. The cohort structure enables students to develop collegial relationships with one another and with their professors as well as mentoring relationships with students in the second year of the cohort. Students and faculty learn their own strengths and how to work together to accomplish tasks based on individual and group expertise.
- *Opportunities to create new norms and build a more supportive and growth-oriented culture:* Students and faculty together experience the stresses and exhilaration of creating new rules, roles, and relationships. A culture emerged after 2 years of program operation that supported flexible roles,

open debate and the challenging of ideas, rotating and shared leadership. All participants, even faculty, were learning and growing from their experience in the program (C. Furtwengler, 1994; Hurst, 1994).

- *Community building as both a structural component and a learning outcome of the program:* Students learn to collaborate rather than compete with one another and to function as part of a team. Thus the reciprocal and collaborative culture students and faculty build as they implement the new program is analogous to the process of culture-building in schools, giving leadership candidates firsthand experience with one of the more critical pieces of their job. Students learn to function as part of a learning community, an essential and foundational step in becoming a constructivist leader.

- *A curriculum that integrates content with field inquiry and program goals with student learning goals:* Some assumptions were tested with the implementation of this program. Course content became secondary to field inquiry for three reasons: (1) The action research that comprised the field inquiry took longer to design, conduct, and analyze than anticipated; (2) students needed skills that would help them conceptualize the research, collect data, and interpret the results; and (3) students demonstrated an ability to access the readings and knowledge gained in relation to the action research more readily than that gained as a result of content instruction. Moreover, classes were designed to respond to student needs and questions, so that the "planned curriculum" was often postponed or incorporated into field inquiry. Thus students helped shape the curriculum to a large extent.

- *Generative learning processes that connect prior knowledge and experience to new knowledge and application to real-world issues and problems of practice:* Action research conducted by teams of students and professors, in response to requests from superintendents, constitute the most visible real-world learning, but other activities based on the principles of constructivism characterize the program as well. Students use case study techniques to "examine ethical and leadership issues, articulate their own values and styles, discern those of others, and analyze conflicts among them" (Owens, 1994, p. 1). They maintain reflective logs or journals that chart their progress and describe their feelings, insights, and emerging understandings. During the second year of the cohort, they assume the lead in designing and conducting action research and in deriving meaning from the results of their inquiry.

These three programs at three different universities represent attempts to rethink the shape and texture of professional preparation. Because the theory of constructivist leadership is still emergent and is being defined by these early innovations, the programs are varied. There are, however, common elements among them that provide signposts for other institutions desiring to reform their approaches so as to incorporate constructivism into their conception of leadership. These elements include the following:

1. *Program restructuring based in part on calls for reform:* Reports recommending significant changes in the form and content of administrator preparation programs include the 1987 report of the National Commission on Excellence in Education and the 1989 report of the National Policy Board for Educational Administration (in Araki, 1992; Vaughn, Furtwengler, & Furtwengler, 1994). All three universities cited these reports as responsible for or at least influential in their decisions to restructure.

2. *The use of cohorts to integrate the curriculum and to build among students a sense of collegiality and collaboration:* The cohort structure allows classes to function as a school faculty and to engage in goal-setting, team planning, shared learning, and community building. Trust develops over time as knowledge, experience, values, and aspirations are shared.

3. *Pedagogy that emphasizes generative forms of instruction:* These include team learning, shared inquiry, action research, reflective writing and discussion, and use of narrative, story, and metaphor. Generative forms of instruction enable students to construct knowledge based on their prior experience, beliefs, and values and to make meaning together.

4. *Experience in changing cultural norms and fostering growth:* Because all three programs represented departures from traditional preparation programs, students and their professors assumed new roles and responsibilities. Students took a more active role in their own learning and in shaping the outcomes of the classes. Professors shifted from center stage to a facilitation role, helping students to create meaning and apply new knowledge. One student in the Wichita State University program commented that the program changes forced students to act differently in the field, explaining "You can do a traditional program without making major changes in life," but that this program caused changes in real school behavior as well as in the university classroom (Holcomb, 1994, p. 8).

The above program descriptions and synthesis of common elements provide only a snapshot of how constructivist approaches shape the structure and content of leadership preparation programs. They do, however, reveal what is possible when constructivist theory informs the design of leadership programs. They also provide a bridge from what is to what can be.

PROMISING DIRECTIONS

Models for reform of leadership preparation programs come from inside and outside of the university. Since notions of constructivist learning and leading have originated largely from elementary and secondary school settings, these settings hold promise for further development of constructivist leadership and suggest that partnerships between universities and school districts can lead to new conceptions and practices in the preparation of school leaders. Such partnerships can facilitate the blending of theory and practice, providing opportunities for leadership candidates to experience the community, reciprocal processes, visioning, and mutual growth that are characteristic of constructivist leadership.

Other players may emerge to stimulate thinking and experimentation regarding the preparation of school leaders and to expand the role-group definition of who, in fact, leads. Chapters 1 and 2 made a case for leadership as shared among faculty members who function as a learning community. In this conception of leadership, teachers share responsibility for decision-making, goal-setting, identifying core values, and developing processes that spur the growth of teachers and students alike. Leadership development efforts originating outside of the school or university, but conducted in concert with these two institutions, can enrich efforts to prepare leaders from multiple role groups who can model and encourage constructivist leadership.

Two examples of promising directions for the development of constructivist leadership that represent partnerships among schools, universities, and other agencies merit attention here. While both examples are in the planning stages, they give an indication of what is possible when those interested and invested in education develop a deeper understanding of the complexity of school leadership and the relationship between theory and practice. Both examples are taking place in states engaged in systemic reform of public schooling—California and Kentucky. These two states have enacted legislation to reform K–12 education as well as the professional preparation programs and requirements for teachers and administrators. They have made substantial commitment to the training of practicing educators, and in the case of California, to the induction of new teachers. The leadership work in progress in these two regions can provide lessons to practitioners, university faculty, and others in how to prepare constructivist leaders.

California Administrator Induction Program

Research results from the California New Teacher Project led to increased and ongoing state support for district teacher induction initiatives. At the time these results were made public, the state was also engaged in studying its two-tier administrator credential program in order to determine whether the program met its legislative intents as administered by the public and private universities of California. The study, conducted by the Commission on Teacher Credentialing, led to several changes in credentialing, such as new standards, stronger assessment, a formal role for nonuniversity agencies, and induction of new administrators.

The induction component of administrator preparation is important for several reasons. First, it recognizes that novice administrators, like novice teachers, need mentoring and support if they are to be successful in their new roles. Second, it takes into account the time needed to make sense of new roles, responsibilities, and relationships. The induction period allows the beginning administrator time to develop leadership understandings and facility with the mechanics of the job before entering the second tier of the credential program. It also provides for ongoing professional development and mentoring meant to meet the needs of the individual novice administrator.

The state legislature, in enacting into law the commission's recommendations for changes in credentialing requirements, asked local universities to develop induction plans with cooperating school districts and to explore ways to include other professional development agencies. This interagency cooperation has led to the formulation of a set of planning principles for administrator induction, principles that take into account the developmental nature of induction and growth as a leader and that include opportunities for extended learning, reflection, collegial conversations, choices and options regarding career and professional paths, and planning for lifelong learning. Universities and districts, with assistance from leadership institutes and academies, are in the process of designing induction plans that incorporate many of the constructivist principles discussed in this chapter and book. While still in the planning stage, the emphasis on induction and school district–university collaboration can shift the focus of preparation efforts from the technical to the generative, allowing for the development and encouragement of constructivist leadership.

Jefferson County Public Schools Leadership Development Center

Jefferson County Public Schools (JCPS), a district that encompasses Louisville and the surrounding area, is the largest district in Kentucky, with more than 93,000 students and 157 schools. The district has a track record of school innovation, made possible in part through a collaborative effort with a private foundation to establish a teacher and administrator training center. Started more than a decade ago with a substantial grant from the Gheens Foundation, the JCPS/Gheens Academy provides professional development to schools in Louisville and across the commonwealth of Kentucky as well as encouragement for experimentation with new practices.

This year the academy has entered into a partnership with the Center

for Leadership in School Reform (CLSR), a national center based in Louisville and headed by Phillip Schlechty, the first executive director of the
Gheens Academy. A major purpose of the partnership is to start a leadership
development center through a grant from the Gheens Foundation and with
the advice and technical assistance of local universities. The center will encourage the development of constructivist leadership among three groups:
practicing principals, potential administrators, and teacher leaders. Design
efforts will be guided by a working advisory group comprised of JCPS administrators and teachers and university faculty involved in leadership preparation. The intent is first to provide a source of renewal and growth for school
leaders in Jefferson County, and eventually a resource for school leadership
across the commonwealth and nation.

JCPS has been interested in leadership development for some time and
last year authorized the creation of a principals' college. The concept of the
college has been expanded to focus on school leadership teams, which is essential in a state that has mandated school-based decision-making and site
councils by 1996. At present only 10% of the district's schools have made the
transition to school-based decision-making. The proposed center can help
develop—among administrators, teachers, and parents serving in school governance capacities—the sense of community, shared goals, reciprocal processes, and commitment to growth that are indicative of constructivist leadership. Moreover, the center can provide the district with a pool of qualified
candidates to assume school leadership positions, which will be a district
need over the next 5 years. These candidates will also obtain Kentucky certi-
fication via a university preparation program, although there has been an
effort by the state Department of Education to shift more of the responsibility for leadership development to the local schools. In any event, it will be
critical for the district to expand its collaboration with CLSR to include key
university players, so that leadership development efforts will be complementary rather than duplicative.

This emphasis on leadership development is especially crucial in a district that has experimented with creating professional development schools
that model the application of research and best practice and that serve as
centers for the induction of new teachers and principals. While teacher training and induction have received a good deal of attention and support over
the years, leadership development has not. It has been an afterthought and
part of the reason that innovative efforts have not been consistently sustained
over time. The leadership development center offers an opportunity for nurturing leadership across role groups, based on the principles that stimulate
both student and adult growth and that build caring cultures in classrooms
and schools.

CONCLUSION

This chapter has presented a series of images intended to make constructivist leadership and its influence on leadership development more real, vivid,
and comprehensible. The images from university classrooms, from innovative
programs, and from newly developing leadership initiatives are all drawn
from the real world. They involve real educators struggling to make sense of
their world of schooling and to make a difference in the lives of the students
and adults who work with them. The chapter does not provide answers so
much as a series of questions university faculty, school practitioners, and
others participating in the professional development of administrators and
teachers can ask themselves. The questions include:

- Can constructivist leaders make a difference in school systems that do
  not have norms for community, collaboration, reciprocal processes,
  and individual and collective growth?
- What kind of knowledge base and understandings are required of
  those who prepare constructivist leaders?
- Can teacher education programs integrate constructivist leadership
  preparation into their work or become active partners in preparing all
  educators as leaders?
- How can we overcome turf issues and competition among universities,
  school districts, and other professional development agencies so that
  new forms of leadership development can emerge?
- How can we begin to document the effects of constructivist leadership
  on student learning and teacher growth?

Such questions can lead us to new insights about the reciprocal processes
that comprise constructivist leadership—and also to a vision of the future of
schooling, as portrayed in the next and final chapter of this book.

CHAPTER 10

Constructing the Future of Schooling

Linda Lambert

> ... Each of us, by the very nature of our consciousness and the
> need of that consciousness to integrate its experience, is a vision-
> ary. . . . Each time a child makes a clay pot or a person makes a
> decision, each in some sense creatively discovers some element
> of the vision that unites us all—our world view.
>
> Danah Zohar
> *The Quantum Self* (1990, p. 231)

We do not propose to predict the future, for the fluctuations of change lead
us into uncharted territory. Stephen Hawking (1993) reminds us of the hum-
bling understanding that scientifically we can predict events no more than 5
days into the future. The now-famous "Tasmanian butterfly" of chaos theory
has become the metaphor for our limitations in prediction. As the story goes,
all of life is so interconnected and sensitive to changes in the environment
that a butterfly flapping its wings in Tasmania will alter the weather patterns
in China. We have only to watch the evening news to note that we cannot
predict the weather more than 5 days in advance. After that, it becomes
guesswork, however educated. The challenge to predictability by chaos theory has given pause to a world of modernity bent on precise measurement,
analysis, and prediction. Prediction and intervention have been equated sim-
plistically with competence, efficiency, and "civilization" itself.

In social systems such as schools and districts, one good conversation
can shift the direction of change forever. For those of us who have tried to
monitor and guide change toward objectives, this phenomenon is abundantly
clear. Since conversations can serve as the context for the construction of
meaning and knowledge, we find ourselves in the throes of invention, of discovery, of possibilities. To attempt to predict this process pulls us back to the
assumptions of behaviorism, assumptions that are being cast aside in our
search for individual autonomy, communal interdependence, and diverse responses to complex encounters.

Intriguingly, however, we can "predict" or add to the multiple interpretations of the past. When Einstein was developing the theory of relativity early
in this century, he incorporated a major faulty assumption into his work: that

the universe is static, fixed. This assumption had remained part of our world views since Copernicus. Einstein was later to remark that this error in thinking was the biggest mistake of his career (Hawking, 1994). We now know that we are part of a dynamic, expanding universe.

The universe was not the only entity presumed to be static. Our root metaphors or paradigms for intelligence, gender roles, ethnicity, race, family, work, career, age, health (as the absence of illness), sexuality, the economic system, cultural practice, organizational structure—all were essentially conceived of as static. Our world views were studded with fixed concepts of the major facets of life. While life was admittedly a physically growing entity, the forces that influenced it were perceived as static. In retrospect, it sounds incredibly implausible.

SCHOOLING IN A POSTMODERN WORLD

We would contend that the major accomplishment of this century has been the alteration of our world views about the static nature of life. Relinquishing static notions of life and the universe for dynamic notions has enabled constructivism to surface as a major interpretation of human growth and development. Epistemologically, constructivism, like meaning, is motion. Constructivism implies development: evolving world views; changing cultural, historical, and personal interpretations; emerging intelligence and interaction patterns. It is not surprising that our static world views had to become altered in order for constructivism to gain momentum and credibility. Constructivism necessitates a dynamic conception of intelligence, learning, and reality.

In only his second book since his inquiry into values in *Zen and the Art of Motorcycle Maintenance* in 1974, Pirsig in *Lila* (1991) undertakes an "inquiry into morals" in which he contrasts static quality and dynamic quality. In this "metaphysics of quality" he contends that "good" is "freedom from domination by any static pattern . . . that quality is moral growth" (1991, pp. 344–345). Perhaps the more interesting perspective for our work is the equation of dynamic quality with growth and development. The metaphysics of quality, argues Pirsig, tells us that the fundamental purpose of knowledge is to dynamically improve and preserve society. Further, world views that hold moral intention envision relationships and human events as possessing dynamic qualities. Pirsig concludes that "good is a noun rather than an adjective" (1991, p. 468). We do not think that this goes far enough, for good is even more appropriately a verb.

Armed with this verb for dynamic quality, "good as growing," we run headlong into conflict with Bowers and Flinders (1990), who challenge progress-oriented Western thought, which tends to equate growth and change with progress. This societal perception of "progress" involves the enchantment with technology and the consequent destruction of the global environment. The ambitious Western agendas of consumerism, capturing and controlling the earth's resources, and establishing a preconceived essential quality of life by the "developed" countries, has modeled for the world a notion of modernity that is being sought by nearly all countries. These countries, too, are buying or borrowing the technological means for environmental exploitation.

Impassioned pursuits of modernity suggest the putting away of the ways of the past—for example, the understandings of native peoples that slow change evolves out of community and respect for the earth (Bowers, 1992; Bowers & Flinders, 1990; Capra, 1993; Roszak, 1992). The non-Western perspective is that change is perhaps a result of living, not a target of living. To accept the Western root metaphor for progress, however, draws us into domination by the same static patterns that have limited our perceptions of community, intelligence, democracy, growth, and leadership. In contrast, progress may be more of a spiraling, paradoxical process than we have understood. Progress can be destructive, but it is also instructive and constructive.

We are persuaded that humans are capable of co-evolving in ways that will broaden our senses of agency and responsibility about the earth and one another. Bowers and Flinders (1990) appropriately argue that we cannot "wait until the political process yields a new consensus of core cultural values and beliefs" (p. 248). They charge the schools with the major responsibility for "contributing to the deepest levels of cultural change when there are no agreed-upon templates" (p. 248). We agree that the schools can be the major context for such change.

We are suggesting that, while the shift from static to dynamic thinking has been the major accomplishment of this century, the next major undertaking will be the reconstruction or reconstrual of root metaphors or paradigms that bind us to the limitations of individualism and circumscribe our potentials for social vision. As noted in earlier chapters, a significant contribution of Lev Vygotsky (1978) was the understanding that we construct intelligence, meaning, and thought in interaction with others and that this construction is also historically cumulative and sociocultural, thereby shaping our relationships over time. To alter the root metaphors, or frames of meaning, will be to alter our cumulative and communal perceptions of the world.

The altered metaphors must transcend the paradigms that separate and create a world view out of static, isolated portions of reality. The new sciences and philosophy have taught us some valuable lessons about the transcendence of paradox (Zohar, 1990), a process that requires complex thinking skills that seem to emerge from opportunities to construct knowledge and meaning by mediating experience, beliefs, identity, and new ideas. Few things are either/or, but are rather a blend of both. Transcendence enables us to forge common values and purposes; transcendence may well form the center of the highest forms of human conversation. It will take transcendent thinking, the letting go of old assumptions, to effectively undertake the challenges described in this text.

We are suggesting that the phenomenon of schooling must provide the context for the reconstruction of the root metaphors that shape our world views. This text provides a perspective that we believe can be the basis for our reinterpretations. As we synthesize those understandings, we offer the following ideas:

1. Schooling as we now know it is becoming obsolete.
2. The relationship among authentic experience, constructivism, and world views provides the *basis* for the reinterpretation of root metaphors.
3. Leadership that engages us in the reciprocal processes that enable participants in an educational community to construct meanings that lead toward a common purpose can provide the *means* for the alteration of our world views.

Schooling Is Becoming Obsolete

Policymakers and the public are alerting us to their lack of confidence in public schooling through measures for parent-choice vouchers, charter schools, private entrepreneurs, limiting resources, and outright abandonment. Although Berliner (1994) refers to the crisis of declining performance as "manufactured," there are numerous indicators that legitimately challenge the efficacy of public schooling. Schools and districts have organized themselves in ways that reinforce a class society, a class society that is becoming more pronounced each year as access to employment, housing, education, political participation, the arts, and information defines the deepening chasm between and among classes. These tragic conditions follow and precipitate poverty like a dark and crippling shadow. And we respond with more prisons and less support for front-end interventions: health care, child care, education. According to Berliner, schools seem to be doing moderately well for about 30% of our children—that is, for those who define "moderately well" as enabling them to pursue their individual ambitions for a college education and a relatively well-paying job. Thus we have a portrait of public institutions that are preparing 30% for life in society as we have known it while disengaging and fragmenting the lives of the other 70% of our children.

A significant debate in a democracy, although not always part of the visible discourse, is whether schooling plays a leadership role, seeking to alter the norms and practices of a society, or a responder role, reinforcing current practice and protecting past norms. We understand that the best that we might hope for would be to transcend this paradox as well, accepting schools as both leaders and responders. In playing a predominantly leadership role, schools must seek to redefine the norms and practices of this society. In Chapter 2, we proposed that the purpose of schooling is to engage children and adults within patterns of relationships in communities that serve as centers for sustained growth and development.

If we are to create schools and districts as communities, we must restructure interaction patterns so that communal relationships can be built and conversations held. We need educational leaders who are prepared differently than those that now inhabit the schools. We need teachers who perceive themselves first and foremost as educational leaders.

These interaction patterns may also require that we alter the role of school boards so that more authority for action can be shifted to the school community; redesign the size, shape, and function of school districts so that interactions can be more free of arthritic bureaucratic constraints; reshape county and regional support structures to support partnerships with common purpose; and reinvent schooling through public charters, educative communities, personalized technology, and district and regional choice for all children. These structural changes can assist in the creation of parameters within which the meaning of education can be reinvented as well.

The Relationship Between Authentic Experience, Constructivism, and World Views

For many generations (and still today in many schools) it was understood that making sense of the world was something that happened to individuals in the "world"—street, family—not in school. At school we tried to remember book learning. Some of the fortunate among us, usually those who had practiced thinking in language early on in their families, were able to bridge the gap. We were able to manufacture a place in our personal schemas for book learning and later use it in college and work. Many were not able to do so.

As we have noted, one of the most promising and revolutionary movements in education is in the area of authentic work, authentic experience, authentic assessment. While we have partially known the importance of authentic work since the progressive era, it was not until it was connected to assessment that it began to gain broad credibility.

Authentic experience creates a common medium through which children can negotiate and create meaning and knowledge together. We now have knowledge about teaching and learning that enables us to bring to bear a common experience base with interpersonal and intrapersonal approaches that enable children to make sense of their lives in "school" settings. Children can experience learning as thick and coherent descriptions; they can develop their natural anthropologist eyes to see underneath, unfold, and make sense of life's mysteries. The child can "make that clay pot or decision, each in some sense creatively discovering some element of the vision that unites us all—our world view" (Zohar, 1990, p. 231).

Since the beginning of the notion of schooling, most forms of education have been disconnected, isolated from the communities in which the schools are located (Clinchy, 1994). According to Clinchy, this separation of formal and practical learning has been the "conscious and deliberate creation of *education ghettos,* secluded enclosures inhabited solely by teachers and students of a certain age, with the rest of the world carefully excluded" (p. 745). Connecting the disconnected is challenging, for these foreign worlds have seldom been one and the same. Again, we are being asked to redefine a vital root metaphor of schooling: the learning place and the relationship to community.

Once we open up the possibilities for learning, real work can be found everywhere: in the community and "urban sanctuaries," in libraries and museums, in businesses and agencies, in hospitals and senior citizen residences, in the neighborhoods and bookstores and coffeehouses, with such public agencies as transportation, parks, and police. The list goes on and on. Problem-based learning and other interdisciplinary approaches to learning set in the community transcend the isolated disciplines and facilitate knowledge construction. Parents can be talented coordinators of such learning opportunities, and faculty positions will need to be reframed to include coteaching with community participants in our new "schools."

Common engagement in authentic experiences enables us to form and re-form world views and personal schemas in concert and conversations with others. This opportunity enables us to move closer together, to construct common purpose, and to redefine root metaphors. Ask a group of children who have experienced constructivist learning all year to define learning. "Learning" as a root metaphor will be thought of as significantly different than it was the year before. How about "community"? and "caring"? As we realize that learning is about the development of schemas, we can think more clearly in terms of the big ideas that give meaning to all our lives and that allow all children to construct worthy futures.

Let's consider a circumstance through which new teachers and mature teachers alike could begin to reconstruct the root metaphor for "teaching." In the fall of 1994, Saratoga (see the description of Saratoga School District in Chapter 7) began its districtwide opening day with an initiation process designed to invite the newly hired teachers into the teaching profession. All teachers had a role to play, with particular roles for three groups: new teachers, mentor teachers, and veteran teachers (up to 30 years in the district). Veteran teachers introduced the new teachers to the gathering; mentor teachers described their work in the district and what it would offer for new teachers; and three veteran teachers told their stories—stories of a lifetime of teaching, what it meant to them, and why they chose to spend it in Saratoga. Three generations of teachers, each declaring the promises and fulfillments of teaching. For each educator in the room, perceptions about teaching were shifting. A new root metaphor was being formed.

Constructivist Leadership

In this text, we have conceptualized a notion of leadership that will engage us in the reciprocal processes that enable participants in an educational community to construct meanings that lead toward a common purpose of schooling. We contend that this conception of leadership will enable us to accomplish goals of schooling that we have thus far been unable to achieve. The perspective in this text envisions:

- Leadership as manifest throughout the community, thereby separating the opportunities for leadership work from role, person, and traditional authority
- The engagement of both children and adults in a common learning community that serves as a context for growth and development
- Constructivism at the heart of the concept of community, establishing meaning as the driving force, as the sun's energy is the driving force in natural ecosystems
- The work of leaders as facilitating the conversations that guide meaning-making toward common purpose
- The preparation of educational leaders who can understand and undertake such challenges because they have been there, because they have experienced the mutual creation of meaning and knowledge in a purposeful community

We are persuaded that our common work in constructivist leadership can reconstruct our most fundamental perceptions of the concepts that define who we are: community, learning, and democracy. We might then anticipate a future in which global citizens come to understand the meaning of interdependence with the earth and one another.

CONCLUSION

The recommendations in this book are difficult to carry out. They require multiple leaders proficient in process skills; they require the patience and engagement of parents and community; they ask teachers to participate in relationships with students and with one another that are not part of the "bargain" when they entered teaching. To undertake these reforms calls for a reinvention of schooling.

Constructing meaning out of our lives and the lives of our children is a complex undertaking. Constructivist leadership responds to the need to "reinvent." Constructing a future of schooling is synonymous with constructing the everyday lives of people living in our institutions. Just as the sea moves in upon itself, feeding life and information continuously into the flow and depth of its own creations, educational leaders and participants must reinvent themselves through continuous reflection on the experiences, beliefs, and values that give daily interpretation and meaning to their lives in schools.

References

Adler, M. (1984). *The paideia program.* New York: Macmillan.

Aitken, L. (1992). Lectures from tribal law and federal government course, University of Minnesota, Duluth.

Araki, C. (1992, Summer). Education of school leaders for the 21st century in Hawaii: A developmental model. *Hawaii School Leadership Academy Monograph.*

Bakan, D. (1966). *The duality of human existence: Isolation and communion in Western man.* Boston: Beacon.

Baker, E., & Popham, J. W. (1973). *Expanding dimensions of instructional objectives.* Englewood Cliffs, NJ: Prentice-Hall.

Baker, W., & Shalit, S. (1992). *Exploring norms and structures that enhance our working together to improve schools—A training syllabus.* Oakland, CA: Group Dynamics Associates.

Barth, R. (1988). School: A community of leaders. In A. Lieberman (Ed.), *Building a professional culture in schools* (pp. 129–147). New York: Teachers College Press.

Barth, R. (1992). *Improving schools from within.* San Francisco: Jossey-Bass.

Bateson, G. (1972). *Steps to an ecology of mind.* San Francisco: Ballantine.

Bellah, R., Madsen, R., Sullivan, W., Sidler, A., & Tipton, S. (1985). *Habits of the heart.* New York: Harper & Row.

Berliner, D. (1994, August). *The manufactured crisis.* Paper presented at the meeting of the National Council of Professors of Educational Administration, Indian Wells, CA.

Bloom, A. (1987). *The closing of the American mind.* New York: Simon & Schuster.

Bloom, B., Engelhart, M., Furst, E., Hill, W., & Krathwohl, D. (1956). *Taxonomy of educational objectives: Handbook I. Cognitive domain.* New York: McKay.

Bowers, C. A. (1969). *The progressive educator and the Depression: The radical years.* New York: Random House.

Bowers, C. A. (1991, April). *The relevance of John Dewey and Gregory Bateson for addressing the ecological crisis.* Paper presented at the annual meeting of the American Educational Research Association, Chicago.

Bowers, C. A. (1992, April). *Double binds in a cultural approach to environmental education.* Paper presented at the annual meeting of the American Educational Research Association, San Francisco.

Bowers, C. A. (1993). *Critical essays on education, modernity, and the recovery of the ecological imperative.* New York: Teachers College Press.

Bowers, C. A., & Flinders, D. (1990). *Responsive teaching: An ecological approach to classroom patterns of language, culture, and thought.* New York: Teachers College Press.

Braddock, J. H., II, & McPartland, J. M. (1990). Alternatives to tracking. *Educational Leadership, 47*(7), pp. 76–79.

Brandt, R. (1985). On teaching and supervising: A conversation with Madeline Hunter. *Educational Leadership, 42*(5), 61–66.

Brandt, R. (1987). On leadership and student achievement: A conversation with Richard Andrews. *Educational Leadership, 45*(1), 9–16.

Brandt, R. (1990). On knowledge and cognitive skills: A conversation with David Perkins. *Educational Leadership, 47*(5), pp. 50–53.

Bransford, J., Goldman, S., & Pellegrino, J. (1992). Some thoughts about constructivism and instructional design. In T. M. Duffy & D. H. Jonassen (eds.), *Constructivism and the technology of instruction: A conversation*. Hillsdale, NJ: Erlbaum.

Bridges, E. M. (1992). *Problem-based learning for administrators*. Eugene: University of Oregon. ERIC document number EA023722.

Bridges, W. (1991). *Managing transitions: Making the most of change*. Reading, MA: Addison-Wesley.

Brody, C., & Witherell, C., with Donald, K., & Lundblad, R. (1991). Story and voice in the education of professionals. In C. Witherell & N. Noddings (Eds.), *Stories lives tell* (pp. 257–278). New York: Teachers College Press.

Brookover, W., Beamer, L., Efthim, H., Hathaway, D., Lezotte, L., Miller, S., Passalacqua, J., & Tornatzky, L. (1982). *Creating effective schools*. Holmes Beach, FL: Learning Publications.

Brooks, J. G., & Brooks, M. G. (1993). *In search of understanding: The case for the constructivist classrooms*. Alexandria, VA: Association for Supervision and Curriculum Development.

Brophy, J., & Good, T. (1986). Teacher behavior and student achievement. In M. Wittrock (Ed.), *Handbook of research on teaching* (pp. 328–375). New York: Macmillan.

Bruner, J. (1966). *Toward a theory of instruction*. New York: Norton.

Bruner, J. (Speaker). (1994). *Four ways to make a meaning* (Cassette Recording No. RA 4–13–54). New Orleans, LA: American Educational Research Association.

Bruner, J., & Haste, H. (Eds.). (1987). *Making sense: The child's construction of the world*. New York: Methuen.

Burns, J. M. (1978). *Leadership*. New York: Harper & Row.

Butler, K. (1995, Feb.). Defining the problem—an essential aspect of successful negotiation. *CFIER Viewpoints, 3*(2), 4–5, 9. Sacramento: California Foundation for Improvement of Employer-Employee Relations.

Capra, F. (1975). *The tao of physics*. Berkeley, CA: Shambhala.

Capra, F. (1982). *The turning point*. New York: Simon & Schuster.

Capra, F. (1993). *Guide to ecoliteracy*. Berkeley, CA: Elmwood Institute.

Capra, F. (1994). From the parts to the whole: Systems thinking in ecology and education. *Elmwood Quarterly, 10*(2).

Carlsen, M. B. (1988). *Meaning-making*. New York: Norton.

Carter, K. (1993). The place of story in the study of teaching and teacher education. *Educational Researcher, 22*(1), 5–12, 18.

Chittenden, E., & Gardner, H. (1991). Authentic evaluation and documentation of student performance. In V. Perrone (Ed.), *Expanding student assessment* (pp. 22–31). Alexandria, VA: Association for Supervision and Curriculum Development.

Clandinin, D. J., & Connelly, M. F. (1991). Narrative and story in practice and research. In D. Schön (Ed.), *The reflective turn: Case studies of reflective practice* (pp. 258–283). New York: Teachers College Press.

Clinchy, E. (1994). Higher education: The albatross around the neck of our public schools. *Phi Delta Kappan, 75,* 745–751.

Cohen, S. (1994, July 31). Community: An impossible dream. *The Washington Post Magazine,* pp. 46.

Coleman, J., Campbell, E., Hobson, C., McPartland, J., Mood, A., Weinfeld, F., & York, R. (1966). *Equality of educational opportunity.* Supplemental Index 9.10. Washington, DC: U.S. Office of Education.

Cooper, J. E. (1995). Digging, daring and discovery: Sifting the soil of professional life through journal writing. In D. Dunlap & P. Schmuck (Eds.), *Ethical and social issues in professional education* (pp. 235–246). Albany: State University of New York Press.

Costa, A. (1989). *The enabling behaviors: A course syllabus.* Sacramento: Search Models Unlimited.

Costa, A., & Garmston, R. (1992). *Cognitive coaching leadership training—A training syllabus.* Berkeley, CA: Institute for Intelligent Behavior.

Costa, A., & Garmston, R. (1994). *Cognitive coaching: A foundation for renaissance schools.* Norwood, MA: Christopher-Gordon.

Costa, A., & Kallick, B. (1993, October). Through the lens of a critical friend. *Educational Leadership, 51,* 49–51.

Costa, A., & Kallick, B. (1995). *The role of assessment in the learning organization: Shifting the paradigm.* Alexandria, VA: Association for Supervision and Curriculum Development.

Covey, S. R. (1991). *Principle-centered leadership.* New York: Simon & Schuster.

Cuban, L. (1988). Fundamental puzzle of school reform. *Phi Delta Kappan, 69,* 341–344.

Darling-Hammond, L. (1993). Reframing the school reform agenda: Developing capacity for school transformation. *Phi Delta Kappan, 74*(10), 752–761.

Deloria, V. (1969). *Custer died for your sins: An Indian manifesto.* New York: Penguin.

De Vries, R., & Kohlberg, L. (1987). *Programs of early education: The constructivist view.* New York: Longman.

De Vries, R., & Kohlberg, L. (1990). *Constructivist early education: Overview and comparison with other programs.* Washington, DC: National Association for the Education of Young Children.

Dewey, J. (1916). *Democracy and education.* New York: Macmillan.

Dewey, J. (1938). *Experience and education.* New York: Macmillan.

Dilts, R. (1992). *Changing belief systems with NLP.* Cupertino, CA: Meta Publications.

Dominice, P. (1990). Composing education biographies: Group reflection through life histories. In J. Mezirow et al. (Eds.), *Fostering critical reflection in adulthood: A guide to transformative and emancipatory learning* (pp. 194–212). San Francisco: Jossey-Bass.

Duffy, T. M., & Jonassen, D. H. (Eds.). (1992). *Constructivism and the technology of instruction: A conversation.* Hillsdale, NJ: Erlbaum.

Dunlap, D. M., & Goldman, P. (1991). Rethinking power in schools. *Educational Administration Quarterly, 27*(1), 5–29.

Edmonds, R. (1979, October). Effective schools for the urban poor. *Educational Leadership, 37*(1), 15–24.

Egan, K. (1979). *Educational development.* New York: Oxford University Press.

Eisner, E. (1988). The ecology of school improvement. In *Educational Leadership, 45,* 24–29.

Etzioni, A. (1993). *The spirit of community.* New York: Crown.

Festinger, L. (1957). *The theory of cognitive dissonance.* Palo Alto, CA: Stanford University Press.

Feuerstein, R. (1990). The theory of structural cognitive modifiability. In B. Z. Presseisen, *Learning and thinking styles: Classroom interaction* (pp. 68–134). Washington, DC: National Education Association.

Feuerstein, R., Klein, P., & Tannenbaum, A. (1991). *Mediated learning experience: Theoretical psychosocial and learning implications.* London: Freund.

Follett, M. P. (1924). *Creative experience.* London: Longmans & Green.

Ford Slack, P. J. (1994, January). *Walking the red road: Other stories of democracy, community, and education in the U.S.* Paper presented at the New Zealand Educational Administration Society Bi-Annual Meeting, Waipuna Lodge, New Zealand.

Ford-Slack, P. J. (1993, November). We hold up half the sky!: Stories from women leaders in China. Presentation at the Research on Women in Education Conference, San Jose, CA.

Ford Slack, P. J., & Cornelius, P. (1993, February). *We are not all the same: A case story about constructing community in a tribal school.* Paper presented at a meeting of the Minnesota Principal's Association, Bloomington, MN.

Fosnot, C. (1992). Constructing constructivism. In T. M. Duffy & D. H. Jonassen (Eds.), *Constructivism and the technology of instruction: A conversation* (pp. 167–176). Hillsdale, NJ: Erlbaum.

Foster, W. F. (1989). Toward a critical practice of leadership. In J. Smyth (Ed.), *Critical perspectives on educational leadership* (pp. 39–62). London: Falmer.

Foster, W. F. (1994, April). *Preparing administrators for ethical practice: State of the art.* Paper presented at the annual meeting of the American Educational Research Association, New Orleans.

Freire, P. (1973). *Education for critical consciousness.* New York: Continuum.

Fullan, M. (1993). *Change forces.* New York: Falmer.

Fullan, M., & Hargreaves, A. (1992). *What's worth fighting for?* Andover, MA: Regional Laboratory for Educational Improvement of the Northeast and Islands.

Furtwengler, C. (1994, February). *Teaching problem-based, field inquiry skills.* Paper presented at the meeting of the American Association of School Administrators, San Francisco.

Furtwengler, W. (1994, February). *Lessons learned about curriculum integration.* Paper presented at the meeting of the American Association of School Administrators, San Francisco.

Gardner, H. (1983). *Frames of mind.* New York: Basic Books.

Gardner, H. (1991). Moving toward more powerful assessment. In Perrone, V. (Ed.), *Expanding student assessment* (pp. 164–166). Alexandria, VA: Association for Supervision and Curriculum Development.

Gardner, J. W. (1990). *On leadership.* New York: Free Press.

Getzels, J. W., & Guba, E. G. (1957). Social behavior and the administrative process. *School Review, 65,* 323–411.

Gilligan, C. (1982). *In a different voice: Psychological theory of women's development.* Cambridge, MA: Harvard University Press.

Giroux, H. (1992, May). Educational leadership and the crisis of democratic government. *Educational Researcher, 21,* 4–11.

Glatthorn, A. (1984). *Differentiated supervision.* Alexandria, VA: Association for Supervision and Curriculum Development.

Glickman, C. (1990). *Supervision of instruction: A developmental approach.* Boston: Allyn & Bacon.

Glickman, C. (1993). *Renewing America's schools: A guide for school-based action.* San Francisco: Jossey-Bass.

Goals 2000: Educate America Act of 1994, P. L. 103–446, H.R. 1804 (1994).

Goldman, P., Dunlap, D. M., & Conley, D. T. (1993). Facilitative power and nonstandardized solutions to school site restructuring. *Educational Administration Quarterly, 29*(1), 69–93.

Goodlad, J. (1979). *What are schools for?* Bloomington, IN: Phi Delta Kappan Education Foundation.

Goodlad, J. (Ed.). (1987). *The ecology of school renewal.* Chicago: National Society for the Study of Education.

Greene, M. (1988). *The dialectic of freedom.* New York: Teachers College Press.

Greene, M. (1993, October). Imagining the familiar in the heart of the stranger. Lecture given at the University of St. Thomas, St. Paul, MN.

Habermas, J. (1973). *Legitimation crisis.* Boston: Beacon.

Hallinger, P., & Murphy, J. (1987). Instructional leadership in the school context. In W. Greenfield (Ed), *Instructional leadership: Concepts, issues and controversies* (pp. 179–203). Boston: Allyn & Bacon.

Hawking, S. (1993). *Black holes and baby universes, and other essays.* Cambridge, England: Cambridge University Press.

Hawking, S. (Speaker). (1994). *Life works: The Cambridge lectures.* (Cassette Recordings No. 80080). Beverly Hills, CA: Dove Audio.

Hershey, P., & Blanchard, K. (1972). *Management of organizational behavior,* 2nd ed. Englewood Cliffs, NJ: Prentice-Hall.

Hirsch, E. D. (1988). *Cultural literacy: What every American needs to know.* NY: Vintage Books.

Hodgkinson, C. (1991). *Educational leadership, the moral art.* Albany: State University of New York Press.

Holcomb, E. (1994, February). *Perceptions of program effectiveness.* Paper presented at the meeting of the American Association of School Administrators, San Francisco.

Hugo, V. (1978). *Notre-Dame of Paris.* New York: Penguin. (Original work published 1831)

Hurst, D. (1994, February). *Barriers to innovation in a new educational administration doctoral program: The view from experience.* Paper presented at the meeting of the American Association of School Administrators, San Francisco.

Irwin, K. (1990). The politics of Kohanga Reo. In S. Middleton, J. Codd, & A. Hones (Eds.), *New Zealand education policy today: Critical perspectives* (p. 33). Wellington, New Zealand: Allen & Unwin/Port Nicholson.

Jalongo, M. R. (1992). Teachers' stories: Our ways of knowing. *Educational Leadership, 49*(2), 68–73.

Jing, L. (1990). *About being a woman leader in China.* Taped interview with P. J. Ford Slack and the Liaoning Women's Leadership Group, Liaoning Province.

Johnson, R., & Johnson, D. (1988). *Circles of learning,* 2nd ed. Alexandria, VA: Association for Supervision and Curriculum Development.

Kegan, R. (1982). *The evolving self: Problems and process in human development.* Cambridge, MA: Harvard University Press.

Kegan, R. (1994). *In over our heads.* Cambridge, MA: Harvard University Press.

Kegan, R., & Lahey, L. (1984). Adult leadership and adult development: A constructivist view. In B. Kellerman (Ed.), *Leadership: Multidisciplinary perspectives* (pp. 199–230). Englewood Cliffs, NJ: Prentice-Hall.

Knowles, M. S. (1970). *The modern practice of adult education, androgogy versus pedagogy.* New York: New York Association Press.

Kohlberg, L. (1976). Moral stages and moralization: The cognitive developmental approach. In T. Lickona (Ed.), *Moral development and behavior* (pp. 31–53). New York: Holt, Rinehart and Winston.

Laborde, G. (1988). *Fine tune your brain.* Palo Alto, CA: Syntony.

Lakoff, G. (1987). *Women, fire, and dangerous things.* Chicago: University of Chicago Press.

Lakoff, G., & Johnson, M. (1980). *Metaphors we live by.* Chicago: University of Chicago Press.

Lambert, L. (1982). Community as cult: A study of Synanon. Unpublished manuscript, University of San Francisco.

Lambert, L. (1986). *Communication patterning.* Training Module. Bay Area Regional Administrative Training Center, Marin County, CA.

Lambert, L. (1988). Staff development redefined. *Phi Delta Kappan, 69,* 665–668.

Lambert, L. (1989). The end of an era of staff development. *Educational Leadership, 7,* 78–83.

Lambert, L., & Gardner, M. (1993, November). Transformative leadership and language. A presentation to the Association of California School Administrators, Burlingame, CA.

Lambert, M. (1993, October). *Back to the future: A retrospective perspective on restructuring.* Paper presented at the annual meeting of the California Association for Supervision and Curriculum, Orinda, CA.

Lambert, M. (1995, February/March). Reciprocal team coaching. *Thrust for Educational Leadership, 24,* 20–23.

Land, G., & Jarman, B. (1992). *Breakpoint and beyond: Mastering the future—today.* New York: Harper Business.

Lee, G. (1991). Peer-assisted development of school leaders. *Journal of Staff Development, 12*(2), 14–18.

Leinhardt, G. (1992, April). What research on learning tells us about teaching. *Educational Leadership, 49*(7), 20–25.

Lieberman, A. (1985, June). *Enhancing school improvement through collaboration.* Paper prepared at the Allerton Symposium on Illinois Educational Improvement, Chicago.

Lieberman, A. (Ed.). (1988). *Building a professional culture in schools.* New York: Teachers College Press.

Lieberman, A. (1992, April). Presidential address, American Educational Research Association, San Francisco.

Lieberman, A. (1994, April). *Women, power, and the politics of educational reform: A conversation about teacher education.* Paper presented at the annual meeting of the American Educational Research Association, New Orleans.

Lieberman, A., & Miller, L. (1981). Synthesis of research on improving schools. *Educational Leadership, 38,* 583–586.

Lightfoot, S. L. (1983). *The good high school.* New York: Basic Books.

Little, J. W. (1982). Norms of collegiality and experimentation: Workplace conditions of school success. *AERA Journal, 19*(3), 325–340.

Little, J. W., & Bird, T. (1987). Instructional leadership: "Close to the classroom" in secondary schools. In W. Greenfield (Ed.), *Instructional leadership: Concepts, issues, and controversies* (pp. 118–138). Boston: Allyn & Bacon.

Loevinger, J. (1976). *Ego development: Conceptions and theories.* San Francisco: Jossey-Bass.

Louis, K. S. (1989). The role of the school district in school improvement. In M. Holmes, K. Leithwood, & D. Musella (Eds.), *Educational policy for effective schools* (pp. 145–167). Toronto: OISE Press.

Mager, R. F. (1962). *Preparing instructional objectives.* Palo Alto, CA: Feron.

Merriam, S. B. (1988). *The case study research in education.* San Francisco: Jossey-Bass.

Mezirow, J. et al. (Eds.). (1990). *Fostering critical reflection in adulthood: A guide to transformative and emancipatory learning.* San Francisco: Jossey-Bass.

Middleton, S. (1992). Equity, equality, and biculturalism in the restructuring of New Zealand schools: A life-history approach. *Harvard Educational Review, 62*(3), 301–324.

Miller, L. (1988). Unlikely beginnings: The district office as a starting point for developing a professional culture for teaching. In A. Lieberman (Ed.), *Building a professional culture in schools* (pp. 167–184). New York: Teachers College Press.

Milstein, M. M., & Belasco, J. A. (1973). *Educational administration and the behavioral sciences: A systems perspective.* Boston: Allyn & Bacon.

Mitchell, D. E., & Tucker, S. (1992, February). Leadership as ways of thinking. *Educational Leadership, 47*(5), 30–35.

Moraga, C., & Anzaldua, G. (1981). *The bridge called my back: Writings by radical women of color.* Watertown, PA: Persephone Press.

More, L. T. (1934). *Isaac Newton: A biography.* New York: Dover.

Murphy, J. (1990). Restructuring the technical core of preparation programs in educational administration. *UCEA Review, 31*(3), 4–5, 10–13.

Murphy, J. (1992). *The landscape of leadership preparation: Reframing the education of school administrators.* Newbury Park, CA: Corwin.

Murphy, J. (1994, April). *The changing role of the superintendency in restructuring districts in Kentucky.* Paper presented at the annual meeting of the American Educational Research Association, New Orleans.

National Commission on Excellence in Education. (1983). *A nation at risk: The imperative for educational reform.* A report to the Nation and the Secretary of Education. Washington, DC: U.S. Department of Education.

Northrup, J. (1993). *Walking the rez road.* Stillwater, OK: Voageur.

Oakes, J. (1985). *Keeping track: How schools structure inequality.* New Haven, CT: Yale University Press.

Owens, M. (1994, February). *Administrative action research—Learning in the field: Visiting practitioners perceptions.* Paper presented at the meeting of the American Association of School Administrators, San Francisco.

Perrone, V. (Ed.). (1991). *Expanding student assessment.* Alexandria, VA: Association for Supervision and Curriculum Development.

Piaget, J. (1964). Development and learning. *Journal of Research in Science Teaching, 2*(3), 176–186.

Piaget, J. (1985). *The equilibration of cognitive structures: The central problem of intellectual development.* Chicago: University of Chicago Press.

Piaget, J., & Inhelder, B. (1971). *The psychology of the child.* New York: Basic Books.

Pirsig, R. M. (1974). *Zen and the art of motorcycle maintenance: An inquiry into values.* New York: Bantam.

Pirsig, R. M. (1991). *Lila.* New York: Bantam.

Poplin, M. (1994, November). *The restructuring movement and Voices from the Inside: Compatibilities and Incompatibilities.* Seminar conducted at the meeting of the Association of California School Administrators, Palm Springs.

Poplin, M., & Weeres, J. (1993, April). *Voices from the inside.* Claremont, CA: Institute for Education in Transformation at the Claremont Graduate School.

Prager, K. (1993, Spring). Collegial process versus curricular focus: Dilemma for principal leadership? *Brief to principals,* No. 5. Madison, WI: Center on Organization and Restructuring of Schools.

Reed, C., Mergendollar, J., & Horan, C. (undated). *Collaborative research: A strategy for school improvement.* Novato, CA: Beryl Buck Institute for Education.

Resnick, L. (1984). *Education and learning to think.* London: Falmer.

Rogers, C. (1959). A theory of therapy, personality, and interpersonal relationships as developed in the client centered framework. In S. Koch (Ed.), *Psychology: A study of a science: Vol. 3. Formulations of the person and the social context* (pp. 184–256). New York: McGraw-Hill.

Rosaldo, R. (1993). *Culture and imperialism.* New York: Knopf.

Rost, J. C. (1991). *Leadership for the twenty-first century.* New York: Praeger.

Roszak, T. (1992). *The voice of the earth.* New York: Simon & Schuster.

Sagor, R. (1992). *How to conduct collaborative action research.* Alexandria, VA: Association for Supervision and Curriculum Development.

Sarbin, T. (1986). The narrative root of metaphor for psychology. In T. R. Sarbin (Ed.), *Narrative psychology: The storied nature of human conduct* (pp. 3–21). New York: Praeger.

Satir, V. (1972). *Peoplemaking.* Palo Alto, CA: Science and Behavior Books.

Schaef, A. W. (1990). *Meditations for women who do too much.* San Francisco: Harper.

Schaefer, R. J. (1967). *The school as a center of inquiry.* New York: Harper & Row.

Scheiner, S., & Bell, D. (Eds.). (1990). *This is my story: Perspectives on the use of oral sources.* Deakin, Australia: Centre for Australian Studies, Deakin University.

Schlechty, P. C. (1990). *Schools for the 21st century.* San Francisco: Jossey-Bass.

Schön, D. (1983). *The reflective practitioner.* New York: Basic Books.

Schön, D. (1987). *Educating the reflective practitioner.* San Francisco: Jossey-Bass.

Schön, D. (1987, April). Educating the reflective practitioner. Invited address to the annual meeting of the American Educational Research Association, Washington, DC.

Senge, P. M. (1990). *The fifth discipline.* New York: Doubleday.

Sergiovanni, T. J. (1989). The leadership needed for quality schooling. In T. J. Sergiovanni & J. H. Moore (Eds.), *Schooling for tomorrow* (pp. 213–226). Boston: Allyn & Bacon.

Sharples, P. (1993). Kohanga Reo. *Mana Journal, 2,* 30–35.

Shawn, J. (1994). *Cycles of inquiry.* Unpublished manuscript, California Center for School Restructuring, San Mateo, CA.

Siegel, J., & Shaughnessy, M. (1994, March). An interview with Howard Gardner: Educating for understanding. *Phi Delta Kappan, 75*(7), 563–566.

Slavin, R. (1986). *Student team learning* (3rd ed.). Baltimore: Johns Hopkins Team Learning Project.

Spence, J. (1978). *The death of women Wang.* New York: Penguin.

Stacey, R. (1992). *Managing the unknowable.* San Francisco, CA: Jossey-Bass.

Stake, R. (1978). The case study method in a social inquiry. *Educational Researcher, 7,* 9.

Szabo, M. A. (1995). Rethinking restructuring: Building habits of effective inquiry. In A. Lieberman (Ed.), *Professional development in the reform era.* New York: Teachers College Press.

Taba, H. (1957). *Teachers' handbook for elementary social studies.* Reading, MA: Addison-Wesley.

Takaki, R. (1993). *A different mirror: A history of multicultural America.* Boston: Little, Brown.

Thompson, J. (1994). *Collaborative learning communities: A progress report.* San Anselmo, CA: Ross Valley School District.

Trask, H. (1993). *From a native daughter: Colonialism and sovereignty in Hawaii.* Monroe, ME: Common Courage Press.

Tyack, D. (1974). *The one best system.* Cambridge, MA: Harvard University Press.

Tyler, R. W. (1949). *Basic principles of curriculum and instruction.* Chicago: University of Chicago Press.

United States Department of Education. (1991). *America 2000: An education strategy.* Washington, DC: U.S. Department of Education.

Vaughn, L., Furtwengler, W., & Furtwengler, C. (1994, February). *Wichita State University's innovative Ed.D. program in educational administration: An overview.* Paper presented at the meeting of the American Association of School Administrators, San Francisco.

Vygotsky, L. S. (1962). *Thought and language.* Cambridge, MA: MIT Press.

Vygotsky, L. S. (1978). *Mind in society.* Cambridge, MA: Harvard University Press.

Waldrop, M. M. (1992). *Complexity.* New York: Simon & Schuster.

Walker, D. (1994). Reforming assessment in school leadership preparation programs. *The CAPEA Journal, 6*(2), 43–47.

Watkins, J. (1993). *Rationale, structure, and essential questions.* The Coalition of Essential Schools, San Mateo, CA.

Weatherford, J. (1991). *Native roots: How the Indians enriched America.* New York: Crown.

Weber, M. (1947). *The theory of economic and social organization* (A. M. Henderson & T. Parsons, Trans.). New York: Free Press.

Weber, M. (1968). *On charisma and institution building.* Chicago: University of Chicago Press.

Wheatley, M. J. (1992). *Leadership and the new science.* San Francisco: Berrett-Koehler.

Witherell, C., & Noddings, N. (1991). *Stories lives tell: Narrative and dialogue in education.* New York: Teachers College Press

Wood, M. P. (Narrator). (1991). China: The mandate of heaven. Program III. New York: Ambrose Video.

Zohar, D. (1990). *The quantum self.* New York: Morrow.

Zohar, D., & Marshall, I. (1994). *The quantum society.* New York: Morrow.

Index

About the Authors

The authors of this text have served in practically all educational roles: teacher, principal and assistant principal, district director, coordinator, assistant superintendent, superintendent, county office and leadership academy directors, international consultant, and professor. We have observed and worked directly in K–12 schools in seven states, as well as consulted with schools and educational organizations nationally and internationally. The reader will also come to understand that we share a common world view. We thoroughly enjoy our journeys together. Early in the process, Diane Zimmerman shared with us a quote from Mary Catherine Bateson that captures the spirit of our work:

> [the people] I worked with on this project share affirmations of unity, of natural beauty, of human interdependence, affirmations that the wholes to be guarded and the goals to be striven for cannot be specified in a fine positivistic mesh or accounted for as dollars and cents, but may be trapped in the vaguer mesh of poetry, like the moon in the boughs of the tree. (1989, p. 229)

Specifically, the authors bring both common and unique qualities to this project.

Linda Lambert is currently professor of education in the Department of Educational Leadership at California State University, Hayward (CSUH), a role that enables her to observe in and work with numerous Bay Area schools and districts each year. Before moving to CSUH, she worked as a teacher leader, change agent, and administrator in five middle schools and districts, two high schools, a district and county office, and regional academies. This work included the design and direction of three major restructuring projects from 1976 to 1985. From 1989–93, she worked in the establishment of a national curriculum center in Cairo, Egypt, and with leadership programs in Thailand and Mexico. Her writing interests include work with leadership, professional and international development, and school and district restructuring.

Deborah Walker is executive director of the Gheens Professional Development Academy, Jefferson County Public Schools, Louisville, Kentucky.

She is responsible for fostering innovation and assisting with the implementation of the Kentucky Education Reform Act for more than 150 schools in the district. She has experience as an assistant superintendent for instruction and a high school principal in California, and also as a faculty member at California State University, Hayward. While at Hayward, she led the development of the pilot of a master's degree program in educational leadership designed around constructivist approaches to learning and leading. She has served as a consultant to a number of school districts in the areas of leadership development, instructional improvement, and managing change; she has also written a number of articles on leadership development and preparation.

Diane P. Zimmerman is an elementary principal in Davis, California. After completing her master of arts from the University of the Pacific in communicative disorders with an emphasis in linguistic development, she worked as a speech and language specialist, a special education teacher, and an assistant director of special education. She is a consultant to the Institute for Intelligent Behavior and a staff developer for the Association of Supervision and Curriculum Development. Her writings are primarily in the area of educational administration. She is a doctoral student with the Fielding Institute in Santa Barbara, working in the field of organizational development.

Joanne E. Cooper is an assistant professor of educational administration at the University of Hawaii at Manoa. She holds a doctorate in educational policy and management from the University of Oregon. Her current research interests include the use of narrative and autobiography in professional life, organizational development, and qualitative research strategies. Her most recent publications include an article on the use of narrative in studying the school principalship in *The International Journal of Qualitative Studies in Education* and an article on the use of journal-keeping in the professional life of women administrators in *Initiatives* and in *Educational Considerations.*

Morgan Dale Lambert is a former high school teacher and counselor, principal and vice-principal in four schools, superintendent and assistant superintendent in three school districts. He has designed and implemented a broad array of innovative educational programs in schools and districts, all with a distinctly constructivist flavor. He is currently serving as consultant, facilitator, and coach in two California networks of restructuring schools, including suburban and urban districts such as Oakland and San Francisco.

Mary E. Gardner began her career as an English teacher in Rochester, New York, a large urban school district. In Rochester, she worked as a speech therapist and language development specialist in Project Follow-Through and had the opportunity to work with the committee reorganizing the district to achieve equal access and quality. In California she began her administrative career in Saratoga as coordinator of early childhood education and assistant superintendent of curriculum and instruction. After three intervening years as a visiting practitioner at the Harvard Principals' Center and teaching at California State University, Hayward, she returned to Saratoga as superintendent.

P. J. Ford Slack is an assistant professor in educational leadership at the University of St. Thomas. She first studied teaching in Sydney, Australia, when a career in medicine transformed into special education teaching of children and adults. Since 1972, she has taught or lectured in Australia, Papua New Guinea, China, Bali, and New Zealand. Stories from the "original people" of these countries guide her research and writing interests regarding international/intranational education, case stories, the work ethic's role in schools, innovative schools (tribal, charter, or New Zealand's correspondence school), and community.